As I Remember It

by Hugh Hamilton

*A feast of anecdotes
reflecting the joys and humour of life as I found it.*

Published by

GENERAL STORE
GSPH PUBLISHING HOUSE

499 O'Brien Road, Box 415
Renfrew, Ontario, Canada K7V 4A6
Telephone (613) 432-7697 or 1-800-465-6072

ISBN 1-897113-24-2
Printed and bound in Canada

Cover design, formatting and printing by Custom Printers of Renfrew Ltd.

General Store Publishing House
Renfrew, Ontario, Canada

No part of this book may be reproduced, stored in a retrieval system or transmitted in any form or by any means, without the prior written permission of the publisher or, in case of photocopying or other reprographic copying, a licence from Access Copyright (Canadian Copyright Licensing Agency), 1 Yonge Street, Suite 1900, Toronto, Ontario, M5C 1E6.

Library and Archives Canada Cataloguing in Publication

Hamilton, Hugh A. (Hugh Alexander), 1929-
    As I remember it : a collection of anecdotes reflecting the joy and
    humour of life as I found it / Hugh A. Hamilton.

ISBN 1-897113-24-2

    1. Hamilton, Hugh A. (Hugh Alexander), 1929-
    2. Businessman--Canada--Anecdotes. 3. Businessmen--Canada-
Biography. I. Title.

HC112.5.H35A3 2005   338.092   C2005-905103-5

"Happiness is determined
not by how much we have,
but by how much we enjoy."

Author unknown

Table of Contents

PREFACE ix

ACKNOWLEDGEMENTS xi

1 ALL THOSE STORIES 1

2 A SOJOURN IN ENGLAND 3
    OUR ENGLISH "RESIDENCE" 5
    OUR PROBLEM IN SOCIAL NICETIES 9
    THE IMPORTANCE OF GOING THROUGH CHANNELS 11
    THE PINNACLE OF MY CAREER 14
    JEAN-CLAUDE GETS SOME "HELP" WITH HIS ENGLISH 17

3 SCOTTISH ADVENTURES 19
    THE TROUBLE WITH BEING A SCOT 20
    THE SCOTTISH WAY 22
    GOLFING IN SCOTLAND, OR "MITHER'S WAITIN' FOR LUNCH" 24
    A GREGORY CLARK EXPERIENCE IN THE HIGHLANDS 27
    AUNT MEG VERSUS NEW YORK CITY 30

4 IRISH SOLUTIONS 32
    WE FIRST ENCOUNTER IRISH SOLUTIONS 34
    IRISH SOLUTIONS IN AN ECCLESIASTICAL SETTING 36
    OUR IRISH SOLUTION FOR SELECTING ANCESTORS 39
    LEPRECHAUNS AS AN IRISH SOLUTION. 42
    IRISH SOLUTIONS IN CRYSTAL 45

5 ADMIRING THE SWISS 46
    ACTUALLY THE SWISS DO HAVE A SENSE OF HUMOUR 48
    THE SWISS ARE VERY PRIVATE PEOPLE 50
    THE SWISS ARE BANKERS 52
    THE SWISS CO-OPERATE 55
    MOB CONTROL, SWISS STYLE 59
    WEATHER FORECASTING, ZURICH STYLE 62

6 JAPAN MAY NOT BE MYSTERIOUS	**66**
TWO'S COMPANY, TWO MILLION'S A CROWD	68
A SHOCK TO THE SYSTEM	70
LANGUAGE IS A BARRIER	75
AN ISHII-SAN IS ESSENTIAL	78
THOSE SHY JAPANESE LADIES	82
GOLF IS A PASSION	84
THE INEVITABLES	87
7 NORWEGIAN COLONELS	**90**
MY NORWEGIAN SKIING TRIP	92
A MEAL FIT FOR A KING	94
SHRIMP CAN INFLUENCE YOUR REPUTATION	96
8 WORKING AT BECOMING A GOURMET AND TO THINK I WAS ONCE A PICKY EATER	**99**
MEMBERSHIP HELPS	101
MAYBE BOB IS FATED TO BE FOREVER LOSING	104
I TAKE SALT ON MY MELON	107
MY PRIVATE CLUB IN BRUSSELS	109
I'LL NEVER BECOME A WINE EXPERT	114
PUB CRAWLS, HOWEVER INNOCUOUS, CAN CAUSE TROUBLE	117
A STROKE OF MARKETING GENIUS	121
9 THE WAY TO A MAN'S HEART	**126**
GRANDMA'S BUNS	127
MRS. TREMBLAY'S BOEUF BOURGIGNON	129
GOOD OLD-FASHIONED COUNTRY WISDOM	131
A DIFFERENT METHOD FOR MENU SELECTION	133
DO COOKBOOKS MULTIPLY?	134
THE MARTINI, KING OF COCKTAILS	135
10 GREAT MEN AT PLAY	**137**
A HANDSOME APOLOGY	138
A SURPRISING AURA	141
THE MAINTENANCE OF AN AURA	144
"AND THING"	146
THE STAMP	148
AN UNLIKELY IMP	150
A REMARKABLE PUT-DOWN	154

A QUIET WEEKEND IN NEW ZEALAND	157
MONSIEUR PAGET ACQUIRES MARCONI	161

11 IDIOSYNCRASIES IN BUSINESS 165
- LEVEL PLAYING FIELDS 166
- THE IMMUTABLE LAWS OF WAX AND WANE. 170
- ETIQUETTE IN ELEVATORS 173
- PLUS ÇA CHANGE 174
- THE GOOD OL' DAYS 178
- I WAS GODFATHER TO A BOAT 181

12 MANAGEMENT TRAINING 185
- THE MANAGEMENT GRID 186
- SOME TAKE THEMSELVES TOO SERIOUSLY 190

13 THE CARE AND FEEDING OF CUSTOMS OFFICERS 192
- HONEST, I'LL NEVER DO THAT AGAIN 194
- IT HELPS TO BE WELL KNOWN. 197
- BILL BUYS A CAMERA 199
- CONFUSION IN JAPANESE CUSTOMS 201
- GULLIBILITY ANYONE? 204
- A MOST CONSIDERATE CUSTOMS MAN. 207

14 MAINTAINING A REPUTATION 209

15 DUMB ANIMALS, EH? 213
- STUPID HUMANS 214
- PRICKLY PROBLEMS 217
- LIVE AND LET LIVE 220
- MIND GAMES 223

16 HOW I SAVED ROGER'S LIFE 226

17 BELIEVE IN SEA MONSTERS 230

18 I NEVER, EVER, ARGUE WITH A POLICEMAN 233
- ILLUSTRATING THE PRINCIPLE 234
- PATIENCE IS A VIRTUE! 236
- PUT YOURSELF IN THE POLICEMAN'S SHOES 238

19 A LEGEND 240

Preface

I believe I am amongst the most fortunate of people. It is difficult for me to imagine a career more diverse and satisfying than mine has been.

I started life with a very pleasant childhood, even if it was during the Great Depression. I grew up in the west end of Montreal, in an area where development had been halted by the Depression, leaving the district with a pleasant, semi-rural atmosphere. It was a time when everyone played sports and the neighbourhood park, with its pick-up games of hockey and baseball, occupied most of our energies.

I went to McGill University. I was a good student, and enjoyed school, so much so that I continued with graduate degrees in physics. I was fortunate that physics was in a period of rapid expansion, with many new technologies being developed. Physics in my time was still engaged, to some extent, with things that could be seen and physically manipulated. Today, it largely deals with minute particles that can only be addressed with computers and electronic instrumentation. We still had string and sealing wax in my day.

When, after a most enjoyable career as a student, I finally had to go to work, I found a position as a research physicist. As my physicist colleagues would say, I quickly "went bad." I moved into product development in a laboratory designing microwave radio relay equipment, one of the most challenging tasks in electronics at that time. That was my first contact with the telecommunications industry, the wonderful, far-flung and all-encompassing business where I spent my career.

I progressed to become manager of that lab, and then became engaged in the promotion and sale of the products we designed. I soon moved to management and for a time was manager of a very large division of the company.

But I finished my career in my real love, international marketing. I served in several posts overseas, travelling widely in Europe and the Far East. I lived overseas for extended periods in England, Switzerland, and Japan.

My career was full of variety, new experiences, interesting people and places, and offered unusual scope for independence of action. And, I am pleased to say, our teams achieved considerable success in developing new business and penetrating new markets, some of which had been considered impenetrable. It is certainly satisfying to look back and recognize that major businesses have now developed in many areas where our teams laid the initial foundations.

Most of my career was spent working for major corporations, first the Canadian Marconi Company, and latterly, Northern Telecom Limited, both very successful and reputable companies. Large companies may pay well, but they demand hard work and complete dedication. I expected to work hard, and did. However, I often felt that people in business took themselves far too seriously, and in so doing, they missed the opportunity for much enjoyment along the way.

I have always believed that in everyday life, and in business, there is a great deal of humour, much of which we overlook in our single-minded pursuit of success. I started to collect examples of humorous situations and tell them as stories, mostly of the shaggy dog variety. Those stories became a staple of my dinner table conversation.

I decided to write some of them down, hoping others would find them enjoyable. They'll never be uproariously funny, but might offer the occasional chuckle to my readers. It was with this in mind that I started to write this book.

As I progressed, I began to realize that I was not only telling amusing tales, I was making a kind of declaration of what I have learned about living a satisfying life. So, while this book was never intended to be a deep and revealing autobiography, I find I have assembled something like a collection of object lessons in stopping to smell the roses.

I have worked hard and made friends and always, somehow, seemed to find a way to thrive and enjoy life simultaneously. I hope these stories will entertain you, and if any of them move you to reflect on how you choose to meet the challenges and opportunities of life, I will have succeeded beyond my fondest hopes.

Hugh Hamilton

Acknowledgements

It would be impossible to name, or even remember accurately, all of the colleagues and friends who played a part in shaping my career, leading me to an understanding of the principles of management and business, and helping to build the successes I have enjoyed throughout my career. I happily acknowledge the great debts I owe to all these people.

There are several individuals who played key roles in the preparation of this book:

Roger Lawton, long-time friend and valued colleague. He first suggested that I write down some of my stories because he believed others might enjoy them.

Jack Pitt, Professor Emeritus at the University of Southern California, boyhood chum, and continuing close friend in spite of the geographical separation we now suffer. He encouraged me to finish this work at a time when I was discouraged and disillusioned about its outcome.

John Stevens, the editor of this manuscript. His special ability in selecting the exact word to achieve a desired meaning, and his questions subtly indicating places where a little extra effort on my part could provide significant improvement did much to provide a more professional polish to this book. Being edited by John is both an educational experience and an enjoyable event.

I must particularly salute the two main ladies in my life.

Jean, my first, very loving wife of twenty-nine years. Her wisdom and strength created the strong, stable, family situation, which made it possible for me to pursue my career so successfully. Her supportive attitude played a major part the development of my self-confidence and determination to succeed.

Barbara, my equally devoted and loving second wife. For twenty years now, she has undertaken the challenge of managing an aging and decaying autocrat, with ever so many set ideas and idiosyncrasies. Her energy and enthusiasm has kept me going over the years as my physical abilities gradually decline with age. She has consistently encouraged me in this work whenever I have become discouraged or disinterested. And she has patiently extricated me from every one of the myriad traps in which my computer has ensnared me as I worked on this manuscript.

My thanks to all of these major contributors to this work.

All Those Stories

When I was growing up in Montreal, our family attended Calvary United Church, even though that involved a considerable journey from our house in the western suburbs to the edge of the central core of the city. Although we certainly had many other options, we went there because my parents were attracted by the Reverend Doctor T.W. Jones, the minister of that church.

Dr. Jones was a Welshman who had immigrated to Canada as a young man, had managed, somehow, to earn his theological degrees, including his doctorate, and to become the minister of a major metropolitan church. He was a short, rotund, very energetic man, who seemed to be everyone's friend; he exuded a genuine liking for everyone around him, without, however, ignoring their manifest shortcomings. He was very down to earth and much preferred to be known as plain Tom Jones rather than by all his titles. However, I must say that, as a young man, I would never have dreamed of addressing him as other than Dr. Jones. I remember him as having very piercing eyes, which peered at me intensely from deep-set eye sockets under a shiny bald pate.

He was a marvellous minister. His was not a faith of fire and brimstone nor of deep, complex theological reasoning. Rather, he managed to preach about his faith very simply, in a manner that connected it with the problems of everyday living. For example, my mother suffered a fatal stroke while still relatively young. She lingered for a very long time, quite a few months, in a vegetative state. My father became increasingly concerned about the decision to put her into a nursing home, which was inevitably approaching. He was discouraged and worried about this probability, as it would signal the end of his hopes for her recovery. At the time, Dr. Jones was dying of cancer. But from his hospital bed, he found out about my father's dilemma, and, in spite of his own pain, wrote to him a long and effective letter of comfort and encouragement. He had a genuine love and care for his flock.

He had an endless fund of stories, on all possible subjects. He liked nothing better than to visit, and to sit with a plate of Mother's freshly baked muffins, a pot of strawberry jam, and a pot of tea, and tell stories far into the night, all the while attempting, or so he claimed, to arrive simultaneously at the conclusion of a story, a muffin, and a cup of tea.

He had a great reputation as an orator; his sermons were rightfully famous. In point of fact, he wasn't really an orator at all, and he really didn't "preach" sermons in the normal sense of the word. Instead, he drew upon that bottomless fund of stories; his sermons consisted of a series of those stories, strung together about some central theme. They were enormously entertaining, and at the same time illustrated very clearly the point he was trying to make. I believe they were what sermons were really intended to be.

Tom Jones served as the moderator of the United Church of Canada for two terms. That meant he was elected as the titular head of the Church, the largest Protestant denomination in Canada, for a total of four years. During that period, he went to Europe several times to represent the Church at international conferences. Each time he went, he arranged to visit the village in Wales where he had grown up, and to preach at the Sunday service in the village church. He obviously enjoyed these visits immensely.

I remember one occasion when he'd just returned from Europe. During that Sunday service, he told us how he'd again returned to the village of his boyhood, and how he'd again had the joy of preaching in the church he'd first attended. Then he told us of standing at the church door after the service and greeting all his old friends and acquaintances, in particular one old lady, who shook his hand enthusiastically, and said to him, "Dr. Jones, that was a marvellous sermon. I really enjoyed it, particularly all those stories . . ."

He told us how gratified he felt with this praise; gratified, that is, until she continued, ". . . but you'd think that a man who could remember the details of all those stories could remember where he'd told them before." Experience suggests this is a common failing among storytellers. I hope that if, in the following pages, I fall into this trap, or become too boring, my readers will remember Tom Jones's problem with all those stories and will excuse me.

Dr. Jones died in the early fifties. By that time the neighbourhood of Calvary Church had changed in character; there were far fewer residences. Such was the strength of his influence that, with his death, the church quickly withered away. The congregation joined another nearby congregation; the church building was sold to a union organization and subsequently torn down. Today there is no indication that a great church once stood on that site, and only a dwindling few, like me, who remember an outstanding minister.

A Sojourn In England

The first part of my career was spent working for the Canadian Marconi Company, which was a part of the Marconi group of companies. The leading company of the group was Marconi's Wireless Telegraph Company (MWT) in England. The great Guiglielmo Marconi himself founded that company, in the very early days of radio communication, when the name of Marconi was synonymous with the invention of radio.

In 1956, early in my career, I was sent to England for six months to act as a technical liaison between the microwave radio laboratories of MWT and a similar laboratory in our Canadian company. They allowed Jean to accompany me, possibly on the assumption she'd keep me out of trouble.

This was the first trip overseas for both of us, and was a great adventure for us. We were doubly pleased that "our trip" was to be to England, which had many close associations for us. In those days, we were all much more "British" in our ways and feelings. We had been brought up to feel the importance of the British Empire and of Canada's place in that great enterprise. And we had been educated in English literature and English history and had developed a strong feeling for our English roots. We had just finished fighting a major war on the British side, and were proud of Canada's part in that effort. This was the land of Shakespeare, Dickens, and Tennyson, Henry VIII, Queen Elizabeth, and Winston Churchill. All of these and many more were ingrained into our consciousness by our education and background.

Whenever I visit England, I always have a feeling of being in a never-never land, where all the things I read and learned about turn out, improbably, to be true. It was doubly so on that first adventure into England.

The England we found was still recovering from the war. It had spent all its energy in the effort and was just beginning to recover and enter into a new age. Indeed, they had just stopped meat rationing in the past few months and were broadcasting instructions on the radio to teach Englishwomen to cook a roast, since many of them had never seen such a thing. And while it certainly provided all of the historic places and things we expected, it was also something of a surprise for us. Comparing Canada, with its widely dispersed population and wide open spaces, with England, which had many more people compressed into a much smaller land area, we expected England to be a very crowded place. Instead we found that—notwithstanding the size and extent of London—England as a whole was surprisingly rural. There was much more "country space" than we expected. The countryside was beautiful, filled with quaint villages, ancient buildings, and famous sights. And such a wide variety. Each of the fifty or so counties seemed to have not only its own architecture and dialect but also its own distinct geographical identity and even its own weather system. We had a great time exploring as much of this grand country as possible in our limited available time.

MWT had its headquarters in Chelmsford, a county town about sixty miles north of London, and its laboratories were located in the nearby village of Great Baddow.

Chelmsford is quite an old city. Since the twelfth century, it had been the region's market town at the ford of the Chelmer River. It grew slowly through the centuries with very little change to its centre or its layout. But in the past half-century, several large industries, of which Marconi's was one, had established themselves in and around Chelmsford. Little if anything had been done to accommodate the consequent growth of the city. One might almost have thought that the town fathers were doubtful whether or not these "new" industries were there to stay. After all, they'd been there only about fifty years or so. In any event, there was an acute shortage of accommodation of all kinds.

Our English "Residence"

When Jean and I first arrived in Chelmsford, we found that arrangements had been made for us to stay at one of those peculiarly English institutions, an English residential hotel. We were to stay in The Vineyards, a large country house that had been turned into a residence for about twenty-five people. They were chiefly single people, middle-aged schoolteachers, London clerks, retired gentlewomen, and so on, with a sprinkling of people such as ourselves, young couples visiting the country temporarily. The house was a big, sprawling, decaying, brick building. It had a very nice "park," a grassy area surrounded by a brick wall, and containing some fine old trees, including, as I remember it, a magnificent copper beech. Residents each had their own room, but toilet and bath facilities were common, as were the dining facilities. "We serve breakfast and dinner, but not lunch," they told us quite firmly when we arrived. Even these meals were whatever the cook decided, and sometimes the cook's decision left much to be desired.

Our stay at The Vineyards could not be described as a great success. We had a big room on the second floor, but we soon noticed that the furniture was all carefully arranged around the outside edges, along the walls, and that the floor had a definite sag toward the middle. We became concerned that if we walked across the room we might fall through the floor. And being relatively newly married, the two narrow single beds on opposite sides of the room seemed less than adequate. The owner was not exactly the jolly host of literature. In fact, he was seldom in evidence, but never failed to turn up if there was some opportunity to charge you for some "extra."

But I think it was the eating arrangements and the meals that were the greatest drawback. Each individual or couple had an assigned table, and it was verboten for two couples to sit together at one table. We asked to join another couple that we had met and liked, and were sternly told that wouldn't be possible. The meals encompassed all the worst features of traditional English cooking: overcooked vegetables, unidentifiable meat, gooey and tasteless puddings—we had them all. But it was one exceptional dinner that finally drove us to the wall. The cook that night surpassed herself by producing a dish that can only be described as a "slurry"; we eventually identified it as finely ground-up liver. It was in the same class as boiled parsnip.

We left the table and immediately telephoned Mrs. Pryke. Mrs. Pryke's name had been given to us by my boss back in Canada. He had previously worked for Marconi's in England, and had lived in Great Baddow. Mrs. Pryke was a friend of his, and had a number of rental flats in and around Great Baddow. Unfortunately, when we first arrived, she had no vacancies. However, when we now called her, she said that she did indeed have one three-room, furnished flat available. Our response, strongly influenced by that ground liver dinner was, "We'll take it. Where is it?"

It turned out to be conveniently located just outside the gates of the MWT laboratories in Great Baddow, where I was working.

Mrs. Pryke had shrewdly taken advantage of the shortage of accommodation by simply buying up a number of large, unoccupied, country-style houses, giving them minimum renovation, and turning them into rental flats. Her process of turning them into flats was to put locks on the doors of all the rooms in the house and to give each tenant the keys to the appropriate number and type of rooms. Therefore, your "flat" wasn't necessarily all contiguous rooms. For all I know, some "flats" may not even have been all on the same floor. But she didn't charge too much, and I believe that, in the circumstances, most people were quite happy with the arrangements. Mrs. Pryke must have seemed a godsend to many of her tenants. She certainly did to us.

Our "flat" had a major advantage over the other flats in our house: it was self-contained. It had been the old kitchens, and had its own entrance and walled courtyard. One entered through a small, covered, wooden porch, just large enough to accommodate one person as he or she unlocked the door. You stepped down into a long, narrow kitchen and, if you were careful, you could avoid tumbling into the bathtub that stood just across from the door. There was a sink, a larder, and a proper three-burner electric stove with an oven. Even though we were told the house had been recently rewired, we soon learned you could only operate two burners at a time, or one burner and the oven. Otherwise you blew the fuse in that newly rewired electrical system. However, it was not too great a hardship if you did happen to do this. When we first blew a fuse, Jean went to the offices of the Electricity Board to obtain a replacement, as they had done the electrical work. She was told they'd used a new type of fuse and they had, as yet, no supply of replacements. However, the man at the desk very kindly instructed Jean on the finer points of "jumping" the fuse with a halfpenny coin.

The original kitchen had been a fairly large room, with a nice bow window. That room had been divided lengthwise into two rooms, each of which had been awarded half of the bow window. This resulted in two long, narrow rooms, which served as the sitting room and the bedroom. In the sitting room, you could sit in a chair with your back to one wall and, if you stretched, put your feet flat on the other wall. We could easily entertain up to two guests.

The original huge hearth and fireplace, which were in the sitting room, had been bricked up, but the outline could still be seen. It was replaced by a small, cast-iron "jacket heater" that was intended to provide some heat to the flat. I wouldn't have liked to try to survive a severe winter with just that stove, but as you may know, most English people seem to believe their country normally enjoys a semi-tropical climate, and is only going through a most unusual aberration of cold weather just now. The fact that this "aberration" has lasted for quite a number of centuries does not seem to have stimulated any action to alleviate the rigours of the frequent cold spells.

For this we paid the magnificent sum of one guinea a week. I believe there once existed a gold coin known as a guinea, but it has long since disappeared from use. However, certain people still quoted their charges in guineas as it was believed to add some mysterious panache. A guinea was one pound, one shilling, or twenty-one shillings, equivalent to about three dollars (Canadian) in those days. Remembering the ground liver dinner, we considered we'd found paradise.

We did make an effort to overcome the rigours of approaching winter. I called upon the local fuel merchant in hopes of purchasing a modest amount of wood for the jacket heater. The first problem was that the firebox in the stove was quite small. Accordingly, I asked the fuel merchant if he had any wood cut into six-inch lengths. To my surprise, he replied, "Certainly, Sir." But then when I asked the minimum quantity he would deliver, he said one ton. That created several problems. Firstly, I was used to buying wood by the cord, a measure of volume; I had never purchased firewood by the ton, and had little idea what a ton would look like. But I did know I didn't want a whole ton. I leaned heavily upon his sympathy, explaining we were visitors from Canada, and would only be in Great Baddow for a limited period. He relented enough to agree to deliver half a ton. But I still believed that would be too much for me. Finally, he proposed that if I could find someone else to take half (or a quarter of a ton), that would be acceptable to him. The logic of that escaped me, since he would be making two separate deliveries, but I happily accepted and persuaded one of our friends to purchase the requisite quarter-ton of firewood.

The great day arrived, and I came home to find a sizable heap of firewood in our front yard. And, true to his word, the wood was cut into six-inch lengths. The only problem was that it was in six-inch cubes, not sticks of wood as I had imagined. However, I was not discouraged; I thought it should be relatively simple to chop the wood into suitable sizes. After all, wasn't I a seasoned Canadian? I borrowed an ax from Mrs. Pryke, and set to. And then I found those six-inch cubes were cut from rock elm. If you've ever struck a block of rock elm in anger, or otherwise, you'll know the grain of the wood is all twisted, and it responds to any ax blow by just sitting there and sneering at you. It took me several weeks of chopping away, an hour a day, to transform the recalcitrant pile of blocks into useful firewood.

But they did provide many warm and cozy evenings, perhaps not by our fireside, but at least beside our jacket heater.

Our Problem With Social Niceties

One of the first things that struck us when we arrived in England were the drainpipes. Every building was festooned with vertical, cast-iron drainpipes, of great complexity. We asked why they were on the outside of the buildings, rather than hiding discreetly within the walls, as was normal in Canada. "That's so you can get at them when they freeze," we were informed, with some degree of superiority. But I'd never heard of a drainpipe freezing. Surely it's one of the most uncommon occurrences in our much harsher Canadian climate. "But if you put them inside the walls they wouldn't freeze," we said with what we thought was impeccable logic. Far from it. We were to find that the average house in England had only rudimentary heating at best. One of my bosses, who periodically found it necessary to visit an elderly maiden aunt in England, unfortunately sometimes in wintertime, called it "central warming." Many people didn't even have central warming and relied upon fireplaces and electrical heaters for some protection from the cold. Needless to say, drainpipes could quite easily freeze in a cold snap, whether within or without the walls, and the mess, and the problem, was certainly less if they were outside the walls.

All of that preamble was by way of explaining that there is usually a logical reason for the idiosyncrasies you observe when visiting a foreign country. However, there is one idiosyncrasy of the English plumbing of those days that I never did understand. It involved the English flush toilet.

Unlikely as it may seem, the English flush toilet was invented by a gentleman by the name of Thomas Crapper. You can still see his name on plumbing fixtures in public toilets in the city of London. And as you may realize, he gave his name to the act of using one of his fixtures, not the other way around. The English toilet works on a different principle from the North American toilet, which was presumably invented at a later date. The North American version works on the principle of filling the toilet bowl with water and having the contents of the bowl disappear as a result of adding additional water and activating a siphon action caused by a clever crook in the outlet drain pipe of the fixture. In the Thomas Crapper version, the siphoning action occurs in the tank above the toilet bowl, causing a great deluge of water to be released to rush through the toilet bowl, carrying all before it. Both systems work well, but the English one lends itself to a certain degree of complication, and it requires the development of certain necessary skills.

You see, the deluge of water is achieved by having a sizable tank of water placed several feet above the toilet itself. The deluge occurs when a chain is pulled, presumably opening a valve and allowing the water to escape. Sounds simple, eh? You'd think all you had to do would be to pull the chain, wouldn't you? Oh my, no.

In true British fashion, they managed to complicate this process. I don't know why and have never had a satisfactory answer. Every model of toilet seemed to have its own particular sequence of pulls on the chain. Some reacted well to a single, short pull; others demanded a long, sustained pull; still others required a short pull followed by a long, or vice versa; and so on. I never did get clear the reasons, either mechanical or cultural, for all this variety. But if you didn't know the particular toilet you were trying to operate, you could spend considerable time trying out the various sequences until you found the one that worked. However, I noticed my English friends never seemed to have any trouble with toilets, leading me to suspect that for people more experienced in the country's idiosyncrasies, it's possible to develop a sort of instinct about this.

Which leads me to the social problem we encountered. Our "flat," as I've explained, consisted of three rooms that had been the kitchens in a big country house. We had a small courtyard enclosed by a high stone wall. And while the flat had running water and even, occasionally, hot water, the "usual offices" were located outside the front door in the courtyard. Our social problem arose when a guest discreetly indicated he or she wished to use the toilet. It seemed to us the appropriate thing to do was to quietly say, "It's outside the front door, and around to the left." We also had no problem with telling guests the light switch was outside the door of the toilet on the right. But we never knew whether, in addition, the proper and polite procedure might be to call after them as they departed, "And it's a long pull followed by two short ones." Or did you assume they would exercise their own specialized instincts in the situation?

Should you, or shouldn't you? It's a difficult question.

The Importance of Going Through Channels

When Jean and I first arrived in England, we met quite a number of important people in MWT. We met the chairman, the managing director, the director of the microwave group, the director of the laboratories, and so on. But by far the most important person we met was Jean Threadgold. She was in charge of the Visitors Office, looking after all the foreign visitors who came from all over the world to visit Marconi's. And, God bless her, she took us under her very competent wing. Technically, we weren't really visitors, since I had been formally seconded to MWT, but I think she decided to practise on us and to use us to try out new places and locations.

During our first meeting with Miss Threadgold, she determined that a) we'd never visited England before, and b) we were anxious to see as much of the UK as possible during our six-month tour of duty. We could stay only six months less one day, lest Her Majesty's government start to levy punitive levels of income tax on me. Jean promptly arranged for us to have a car reserved each weekend at the local car hire. Then she proceeded to set up our first tour. She made hotel reservations, gave sightseeing recommendations, and provided detailed instructions. Thereafter, she would telephone me each Monday morning. Ostensibly her call was to inquire about the success of the previous weekend's travels, but in reality, it was to establish our instructions for the coming weekend.

"Where have you decided to go next weekend, Hugh?" she would ask.

Not having as yet given the matter a moment's thought, I would reply that we hadn't yet decided. At this point, Jean would reveal her already well-established plans for us. "I think you might like to go to Rye, on the south coast. There's a marvellous ancient inn there"; or, "I think you'd like to see the Norfolk Broads," and so on.

When I agreed, she would undertake to "make the arrangements." Soon thereafter, there would arrive in the company mail a package containing hotel reservations and AA maps and instructions. AA, or the Automobile Association, would, among its many services, provide individualized travel instructions giving, in great detail, routes to follow and things to see along the way. Also included in the package would be appropriate pamphlets and instructions. Jean-arranged trips were invariably successful and enjoyable, and crammed as much as possible into our limited travel periods.

Inevitably, my sense of independence needed to assert itself. I determined to forestall Jean's Monday morning call. There came the occasion when she asked, "Have you decided where you'd like to go this weekend?" and I said, "Yes, we think we'd like to go to Stratford-upon-Avon and see a play."

There was a moment of shocked silence, but then Jean reacted like the trouper she was. "Oh, that's a good idea, but it may be difficult at only a week's notice. Tickets are hard to get, you know."

I was surprised. This was the great Jean Threadgold. She could do anything in the way of making arrangements. And I said so. In the end, she agreed to try. She came back an hour later to say she'd managed to get a reservation in a good hotel (and she did subtly emphasize her point by saying it was only her second choice), but there were no tickets to the play available anywhere.

"Oh, dear," I said, "I guess there's no point in going, then."

But Jean had now become committed to the Stratford project, and she insisted we go anyway to see the very pretty town. "And there are nearly always tickets available at any theatre just at show time. You'll see," she assured me.

We were somewhat skeptical, but we set off early on Saturday morning and arrived at Stratford shortly after noon. It was a beautiful, sunny day, the trip was through wonderful countryside, and the town seemed full of beautiful and interesting things as we drove into it. Our spirits rose.

We found our hotel, an ancient, half-timbered building on the main street. We checked in and were shown to a very comfortable room by a diminutive bellboy. Having set down our luggage, he drew himself up to his full height of about four and a half feet and stated importantly, "Tea is served at four-thutty, dinner is served at six-thutty, theatah is at seven-thutty." And he looked at me with a hint of speculation in his eye. "You are going to the theatah, Sir?"

Mindful of Jean Threadgold's instructions, and perhaps sensing an opportunity, I replied, "Well, we had planned to go to the theatre, but we were unable to obtain tickets. We thought there might be some tickets available at curtain time. What do you think?"

"Well, Sir, that might work, but if I were you, I'd speak to the hall porter; he sometimes has tickets available."

But when I proposed to go down right away to see the hall porter, he told me the hall porter would only be in at about four o'clock. He did agree he'd have a word with this important personage on our behalf as soon as he came in. I saw fit to give the bellhop a half-crown tip, which was considerably more than the normal tip in those days (but still only amounted to something less than fifty cents Canadian).

We went out and walked around the town, visiting all the prescribed tourist places. There was Shakespeare's birthplace (or rather the house the town fathers had decided it would be best to tell visitors that Shakespeare had lived in as a boy). There was Ann Hathaway's cottage, the church with Shakespeare's tomb, and the very pretty riverfront, complete with a flotilla of swans, and so on. But we made certain to return to the hotel sharply at four o'clock in order not to miss the hall porter and the chance of obtaining those tickets.

As soon as we entered the hotel lobby, I spied the great man, ensconced behind his desk. He was a short, tubby, cheerful man, resplendent in his uniform.

"Good afternoon, Sir, my name is Hamilton. I had a word with the bellman earlier." I'd already spied the bellhop hovering in the background. "He suggested you might have some tickets for tonight's play."

"Ah yes, he did mention it to me. And as it happens, I do have a pair of tickets that a gentleman ordered some time ago, and unfortunately hasn't been able to take them up."

Just as I'd suspected, the hall porter and the bellboy had "an arrangement."

"But," the hall porter continued ominously, "there's a booking fee, and you wouldn't want to pay a booking fee, would you?"

With visions of New York scalpers doubling the price of already overpriced tickets, I said resignedly, "Well we've come a long way, and we may never come back, so how much would the tickets be?"

To my utter astonishment, he said, "Well, the tickets are twelve and six each (twelve shillings and sixpence, about two dollars), and with the booking fee they come to fourteen shillings. (His "fee" was about twenty-five cents). I gladly paid him two pounds, leaving him a substantial tip, and turned to walk away. The bellhop was discretely available so that I could also give him a further tip.

As I was conducting this negotiation at the porter's desk, I was vaguely aware of someone standing behind me. And as I walked away, a large gentleman in a bright red shirt said, in a booming Texas accent, "Now then, son, ah wants to get some tickets for tonight's show."

And that little hall porter looked him straight in the eye, blithely ignored the fact the Texan had to have seen him sell me the tickets, and said, "Oh, I'm very sorry, Sir, but we haven't had any tickets for tonight's performance for quite some time now."

Which only goes to show the importance of going through channels.

The tickets were front row centre in the first balcony. In my opinion, they were the best seats in the house. The play was *The Taming of the Shrew.* It was an excellent performance, and I can remember no play I've ever enjoyed more.

The Pinnacle Of My Career

It is perhaps some sort of a comment on our society in the English-speaking world that when we speak of licensing laws, nearly everybody understands that we're speaking of the hours and conditions under which we can purchase an alcoholic drink. Not even when shops and stores may stay open, much less the myriad other laws that govern our behaviour, and indeed are the very fabric of our civilization. No. We all understand it to mean simply the hours when we can legally purchase a drink of alcohol, or a bottle of similar preservative.

The British Isles brought the practice of licensing laws to a fine art, with laws as to when pubs may remain open, when they may not close, when and where you may purchase a bottle or a drink, and how. To make the study of such laws more complicated (everyone recognizes the absolute necessity of being able to determine the location and time of the next possible drink), the licensing laws are by no means uniform, even in a single district. The basic idea is that a pub is a working man's club, and therefore should be open whenever he has leisure time. Thus, if you're a porter in Covent Garden market, and you take your traditional break for "lunch" at three o'clock in the morning, then you should expect to find your pub open at that time. You can see how, to the very interested, a detailed study of pub licensing hours could become a lifelong occupation, since a really knowledgeable person may be able to find a drinking hole open for business at any hour of the day or night.

The situation I'm describing prevailed for the better part of half a century. It was initiated, so the tradition goes, to limit drunkenness among factory workers, who would "lift a few" on the way to work and then proceed to fall into the machinery, thereby damaging both the machines and themselves, in that order of importance. But in more recent years, I understand the English, in particular, have joined the rest of the world and allow much more leeway to individual pubs in the hours of opening. The Irish, I might note, are probably behaving as they always did. Licensing laws, in typical Irish philosophical manner, were more honoured in the abstract than in reality. And the Scots had a set of rules all their own. There was a general rule that a traveller, deemed to be in residence in his stopping place, was allowed to purchase a drink at any time. The Scots, being eminently practical people, simply defined a traveller as someone who was a relatively short distance from home, about ten miles, I believe, which resulted in pubs on the outskirts of cities doing a land office business on weekends.

I first experienced the idiosyncrasies of English licensing laws one fine August afternoon, shortly after our arrival in England. We had just moved into our "flat" and had invited a couple of people to visit us. We had been up in London for some reason on the previous day, and on the train back to Chelmsford, we decided we'd better buy some liquor if we were to entertain properly.

Our landlady, Mrs. Pryke, had given us a list of the shops we should patronize. We were to discover she had also informed the shops in question that they should "accept" us as patrons. For liquor, she had named the Victoria Wine Shop. Thus, as we came out of the station, we were alert for the location of this excellent establishment. And sure enough, there it was, just a few steps from the station.

It was a warm, sunny afternoon, and the door of the shop was standing open. We walked in and were politely greeted by the shop clerk. We introduced ourselves, and he said, "Ah, yes, I did understand you might be calling. What can I do for you?"

"Well, we'd like to purchase a stock of liquor. We'd like some of that Canadian rye whisky, some of that Beefeaters gin. And some Scotch. I don't see any Scotch."

"No, Sir, our shipment for this week will only arrive tomorrow, but I can save you a bottle then."

We had a short discussion of the probable brand of Scotch, and then we stood there looking at each other.

"Well, aren't you going to give me the other liquor?" I asked.

"Oh, no, Sir."

"Well, why not?"

"Because we're closed, Sir."

I looked around at the open door. I can still remember the dust dancing in the rays of the sun. And then I realized I had discovered yet another facet of the licensing laws. You couldn't circumvent the pub opening hours simply by going around to the off-license, as the liquor store is called, and purchase your drink there.

I asked, "So what were we just doing?"

"Oh, I was taking your order, Sir."

"And what happens now?"

"I'm going to deliver it, Sir," he said, with some suppressed amusement. (It's all quite logical. Really it is. Remember the traveller who is allowed to have a drink? Well, by the same token, you can have a drink in your own home. But I must admit, I thought at the time he'd wait until pub opening time to make the delivery.)

"Do you want any money?" I asked. And having been assured that they wished no payment at that time, we left.

We walked across the road to find our bus waiting for us. We got on, and went to a stop directly in front of our own door. We unlocked our door and were just hanging up our coats when there was a knock on the door. It was the deliveryman from the liquor store with our order. Do you suppose he was on the same bus?

He deposited the bottles and was about to leave. Just at that point, I reached a high point in my career. When I asked what we owed him, he looked somewhat affronted and informed us, "You'll receive your account at the end of the month."

I had achieved the, to me, very exalted status of having a charge account at the liquor store.

We continued to patronize the Victoria Wine Shop throughout our stay. Why not? I'd telephone our order, and the deliveryman would deliver it. Jean told me he always arrived about eleven in the morning and was always ready to sit down with a cup of tea. He turned out to be a mine of useless but fascinating information. "You're Canadians, aren't you? There's another Canadian couple over on the other side of town, and, drink! You never saw anything like it." Or, on another occasion, "The Wilkinsons just up the road are having a big party tonight. You should try to get an invitation. I can tell you there'll be lots to drink."

Unfortunately, my pinnacle of success was short lived. When we left England after about six months, I lost the privilege of a charge account at the liquor store and sadly have never achieved the same status again.

Jean-Claude Gets Some "Help" With His English

For the first few weeks of our stay in England, Jean and I lived at The Vineyards, a residential hotel in Great Baddow. Jean-Claude and his wife and baby daughter also stayed in the same hotel. My wife, Jean, came to know them because they spoke no English, and Jean used to go to the doctor with Jean-Claude's wife and baby and interpret for them.

Jean-Claude was a graduate engineer and a junior officer in the French navy. He was spending an exchange year in the Marconi laboratories in Great Baddow, where he was assigned to the microwave group where I was working. He was not particularly well liked, as he spoke no English and made little attempt to learn it, or to fit in. And his habit of smoking Gauloises, those particularly pungent—nay, foul-smelling—French cigarettes, was a bit difficult to live with. Nevertheless, the boys undertook to teach him a few phrases of English. I paid little attention, but I heard reports that there was some progress, if a bit slow.

One of the few redeeming features of living at The Vineyards, so I'm told, was that on Sundays, they served afternoon tea in the lounge, a large, comfortable room looking out over the garden. We had no direct experience of this event, as we were always off on one of our sightseeing trips on Sundays, but it sounded very nice for all the residents, disparate as they might be, to get together for a pleasant, genteel-seeming afternoon.

I'm told that on one of those occasions, when all were enjoying tea, polite conversation, and perhaps cucumber sandwiches, Jean-Claude was seated between two genteel, old-maid schoolteachers. As hard as the two ladies tried, conversation with Jean-Claude proved to be well-nigh impossible. They finally sat there in silence. Then, Jean-Claude decided to have a smoke. He lit up a Gauloise with apparent pleasure. In those days there weren't the strictures there are today about smoking in public places, but I'm not sure that smoking in a parlour, during afternoon tea, was exactly the "done" thing. And I'm certain the foul smell of the Turkish tobacco was not received with any degree of enthusiasm. In fact, one of the old-maid schoolteachers gave a genteel cough, and tried to cover her mouth and nose. The other lady said, meaningfully, "My, that's a strong cigarette, isn't it?"

Jean-Claude smiled and, trying his best to be sociable, dredged up one of the phrases the boys had taught him for use whenever there was any comment about his cigarettes. He gave a deprecating laugh, and said, loudly, "Yes, smells like horseshit, no?"

I'm told that finished afternoon tea for the day.

I never heard any other consequences of the "friendly" efforts of the boys to teach Jean-Claude English. Relations between the French and the English haven't been all that good ever since the days of the Black Prince, Crecy, and Agincourt.

Scottish Adventures

The Scots inhabit a portion of Britain that is far less hospitable in geography and climate than most of the rest of those "sceptered isles." I suppose that led to their warlike history. I remember as a small boy reading tales of the clans rising to fight the "Sassanac," as well as stories of the incessant inter-clan warfare. And there were the exploits of the "Ladies from Hell' as the Germans called the kilted Scottish regiments (including some Canadian Scottish regiments) during the world wars. They have a well-deserved reputation for warlike behaviour. And, one must say, that while the Scots always exhibited tremendous bravery, they were frequently led into hopeless and destructive situations by their leaders, from Wallace to Bruce to Bonnie Prince Charlie. However, to survive in those inhospitable hills and harsh climate, the Scots needed to rely upon each other for support and sustenance. Hence their very strong family ties and extended family connections from which, as you will see, I benefited.

The Scots developed an undeserved reputation for being very selfish with their money, a reputation I feel is belied by their warm hospitality and strong family relationships. However, they do have a well-deserved reputation as skillful businessmen and managers. Throughout Canada and elsewhere in the British dominions, more often than not you would find a Scot in charge of a remote station, a trading post, a factory, or a business. It would be true to say it was Scots who built the business of the British Empire.

While I bear a Scottish name, Hamilton, my family has always claimed to be Irish in origin. That is doubtless the result of Queen Elizabeth's decision to send large groups of Scots to Ireland in the sixteenth century to rule in Ireland rather than to continue to be unruly to the north of England. And while I am proud of my Irish heritage, I am pleased that, through the relations of my wife Jean, I also have some warm connections with Scotland. Her relatives have always included me in the extended family.

THE TROUBLE WITH BEING A SCOT

My wife, Jean, had an elderly great-aunt, who lived in Glasgow. She was one of those marvellous determined old ladies one occasionally meets—the kind who can wear you out just by taking you shopping. She was a tall, strong woman, with a stern countenance; not one with whom you would care to differ. You would not be surprised to be told she was invited to shoot the first round over the new golf course at Kerrie Muir, the town where her family originated. She offered us a warm family welcome, true Scottish hospitality, and, I'm proud to say, considered us full members of her extended family. We enjoyed her very much and loved her dearly.

Aunt Meg was a proper Scottish Presbyterian, by which I mean she was as frugal, thrifty, and careful as a Scot should be, while at the same time being warm and generous with her hospitality. And the Presbyterian portion meant, in part, that there would be no strong drink in her house.

In those days when travel was much less frequent than it is today, the intervening Atlantic Ocean meant that the Canadian branch of the family met Aunt Meg infrequently. Indeed, Jean had never met Aunt Meg, and knew her only through visits her various uncles had made to her during the war. When Jean and I first went to England, in the mid-fifties, one of our first adventures was to travel up to Scotland to meet Aunt Meg.

We travelled up on the overnight train from London. In that determined fashion we soon learned to recognize, Aunt Meg had not only met the train ("to save the taxi fare, ye ken"—all of a dollar), but she'd bullied the station-men into allowing her to drive her car right out onto the platform, where only the taxis were supposed to go.

When we arrived at her house, the first order of business was a hot cup of tea, for which we all repaired to the kitchen. It was a big, old-fashioned kitchen with ceilings at least twelve feet high. While we were waiting for the kettle to boil, Aunt Meg opened one of the high cupboard doors, and pointing to a number of neatly wrapped packages on the topmost shelf, she told Jean proudly that those packages contained all the tea Jean's mother had sent her in care packages during the war (ended, by that time, a good ten years).

"But what's it doing here now?" we asked. "Why didn't you drink it?"

"Well, ye ken, it's all in tea bags. Tea out of tea bags is not proper tea. I couldn't possibly drink tea made out of tea bags."

"Well, then, why didn't you give it away or throw it out?"

"Ah, well now, your mother had gone to all the trouble of sending it to me, so I couldn't just give it away, now could I?"

Which could help to illustrate some of the difficulties you might bring upon yourself just by being a Scot.

THE SCOTTISH WAY

As I've told you, Aunt Meg was very strict in her rule that there should be no strong drink in her house. And I was to find that most of the ladies in her circle followed the same rule. But I was also to find that the canny Scot has a solution to most problems.

First let me digress to explain that Aunt Meg seemed very pleased that her niece had seen fit to marry a Hamilton—"such a fine and well-known Scottish name!" (I thought it only good manners not to explain that most of my known ancestors had come from Ireland. My father used to explain the Scottish name by suggesting that in the distant past they'd probably been thrown out of Scotland for sheep stealing.) She even took us to the Scottish National Museum to see the portraits of the various Dukes of Hamilton to see if perhaps there was any family resemblance. I've always considered it fortunate there seemed little similarity. In fact that was one of the few occasions when being short and inclined to weight has been to my benefit. The ducal family all seem to have appeared to their portraitists as tall and elegantly slim. I thought it wise not to tell her that one of my cousins bore a strong resemblance to the portrait of the current duke. I hate to think what Aunt Meg might have done if she'd become convinced that a family connection did exist.

Nevertheless, she continued to feel some pride in me—indeed, on one occasion, she arranged a series of gatherings on a Saturday evening so that she could take me around and introduce me to her friends and relatives.

We set out early in the evening in her car to visit some distant relatives who lived a few blocks away. About a dozen people were gathered in the parlour to meet us. In my honour they'd built a roaring fire in the fireplace because it was well known in Glasgow that Canadians were used to central heating. The place was suffocating. And true to good Presbyterian standards, I was given a "good cup of tea" to drink. I struggled along politely to follow the conversation, which was mostly about local topics, carried on in a strong Scottish accent.

After a bit, I felt a hand on my shoulder and the man of the house asked me to come along with him, as he had something he wanted to show me. In some mystification I followed him out into the kitchen and partway down the cellar stairs, where he stopped, reached around a beam, and produced a bottle of whisky (I learned early on that to a Scot there's only one kind of whisky—what you and I know as Scotch whisky, but he calls merely whisky, maintaining that only lesser forms require a qualifying name to identify them.) My guide also produced two glasses and we enjoyed a quick drink standing on the stairs before returning to the parlour.

Shortly after our return, Aunt Meg announced that we had to be moving along, as we had other visits to make.

At the next stop, we again found a nice group of people collected to meet me in a stifling hot parlour. And again I was given the regulation cup of tea. And again after a decent interval, the host took me off to show me "something." This time I followed with more enthusiasm. And sure enough, we went out into a back shed where a bottle of the best was produced from on top of a rafter. After a quick drink, we rejoined the party.

And so it went; we visited five different groups, each assembled in overheated parlours, and I was treated by five different hosts to a drink from five different bottles of whisky secreted in various hidey-holes around the houses.

You'll see what I mean when I say that the Scots (particularly the menfolk) have developed ways of overcoming many of the little domestic impediments that may arise. But I should say that, for the visitor, all those hot parlours and the "good cups of tea," interspersed with chilly trips to the back shed (or wherever) for a hospitable dram, can get to be a bit difficult to handle when you get to the fourth or the fifth visit.

And I sometimes wonder just where those Scottish wives, otherwise so intelligent, thought their husbands were going when they made off with the guest of honour, particularly if, later in the evening, that guest should appear ever so slightly unsteady. You don't suppose they actually were a party to this Scottish solution, do you?

GOLFING IN SCOTLAND, or "MITHER'S WAITIN' FOR LUNCH"

Golf is a great game. Not only is it a great game to play, but you gain all sorts of insights and useful knowledge while doing so.

It was ten o'clock on a gray Sunday November morning. In a period when I was travelling frequently to Europe, during the early sixties, I had formed the habit of concluding my trips whenever possible, by passing through Scotland, with a visit to Great-Aunt Meg, She had two sons, fine strapping men, who were quite athletic, and, most important to me in those days, avid golfers. I was sitting somewhat impatiently in Great-Aunt Meg's parlour in Glasgow, making polite conversation with Lawson, one of my "cousins" (well, what do you call the son of your great-aunt by marriage, anyway?), when I had expected him to just pick me up at the door and take me off to play golf for the day. It would fulfill one of my great ambitions, to play golf in Scotland, the country that nurtured this great game through its infancy, and where golfing traditions are so deep it's like going to church to play on one of their courses. And here we were chatting away as if we had forever, as if there were no urgent matters to be settled between tee and green.

Finally, at ten-thirty, after discussing all the irrelevant subjects he could think of, or so it seemed to me in my impatience, Lawson stood up, saying, "Let's go and play some golf." I picked up my bag, which was waiting by the door, but just as we were leaving, was brought up short, as Aunt Meg said firmly, "Now ye'll be home in time for lunch!" What could she be thinking of? Why, golf is a serious business, which, in my experience, inevitably consumed the better part of a full day, four or five hours at least. How could we be expected home in time for lunch? But I did not want to display any ignorance of golfing customs as they might exist in this, the birthplace of the game, so I withheld my questions and awaited developments.

We drove off at speed through the streets of Glasgow, to Killairemont, a course in the centre of Glasgow that ranks immediately behind St. Andrews in age, making it the seventh oldest course in the world. (As I said, you learn all sorts of useful things playing golf. On this occasion I learned there are several courses in existence that claim to be older than

St. Andrews, but naturally none could lay claim to anything like the fame or tradition.)

I was hurried into the great, gray granite clubhouse, which has probably stood there for centuries, and hustled upstairs to change, with the admonition, "Hurry up, now, Mither's waitin' for lunch."

We came out on the first tee. There was a bit of rain (also a tradition, so I was told, for golf in Scotland), and the turf, as you would expect after centuries of mowing and rolling and being rained upon, was thick and soft. You could hardly get your spikes to the ground beneath the thick cushion of grass. The ball seemed to nestle down in the grass, but a few shots quickly showed the ball to be always nicely supported by that same cushion of grass. I noted from the scorecard that the course wasn't too long—about five thousand yards, if memory serves me, which might help in the objective to be home in time for lunch. But I remained puzzled.

However, not for long. My cousins had arranged a foursome and announced we'd play four ball match play, "because that'll be quickest, and Mither's waitin' for lunch." And it certainly was quick, for in that form of play, uncommon in North America, the foursome splits into two teams, and the best ball on each hole wins the hole. And as played "to get home in time for lunch," the minute you missed a shot you were told, "Come on, pick up your ball. You'll not catch up now, and besides, Mither's waitin' for lunch."

I never saw golf played with such efficiency. There was rarely more than one person putting out on any green, with the result that we played eighteen holes in just over an hour and a half. And we were in ample time to be home in time for lunch. Indeed, as we were walking up the front steps of that most imposing clubhouse, one of my cousins observed, "We have time for a wee one before lunch. D'you drink whusky, Hugh?" I've heard other silly questions in my life, and shortly found myself standing in the bar with a double whisky, neat, in my hand. I looked around and saw that everyone was simply "tossing theirs back," presumably because of the desire not to delay Mother's lunch. So I drank mine in one gulp, only to hear the other cousin say happily, "We've got time for one more." Well the second one took a little more time for me to work my way through, and I was constantly hurried, "C'mon now, drink up your whusky, Mither's waitin' for lunch."

Drinks finished, we hurried to the stairs to the locker room, and I was instructed, "Never mind washing, just get dressed. Mither's waiting for lunch." We quickly reassembled, in our street clothes, at the top of the stairs, where I once more heard the cheerful announcement, "We've got time for one more."

When we finally re-emerged onto the front steps of the clubhouse, my watch indicated we'd spent exactly one-half hour inside, during which time we'd each had four double whiskies, and a wee one for the road. At that point, one of my cousins, mindful no doubt of his mothers' Presbyterian strictures that there be no strong drink in her house, turned to me and said, "Ye'll no tell Mither we had onythin' ta drink!"

"Mither" would have had to be lacking the senses of sight, smell, and hearing not to have formed some deep suspicions on the subject, but perhaps long experience and good Scottish common sense intervened. In any event, no word of recrimination was spoken over lunch.

Later that evening, the whole family drove me out to Prestwick Airport to catch my flight back to Montreal, and we had a further demonstration that "Mither" had her full quota of Scottish common sense and frugality. For it seemed there had been some publicity in the papers that week that Glasgow Airport had finally opened a Duty-Free Store. The last thing I heard as I went through the gate was a familiar female voice calling, "Ye'll no furrget ta get your cheap bottle o' whusky!"

As I said, you can learn many things and perhaps gain important insights while playing golf.

A GREGORY CLARK EXPERIENCE IN THE HIGHLANDS

There are some experiences that just naturally seem to bring to mind certain people.

In his time, Gregory Clark became the best-known newspaper writer in Canada. He was a well-known war correspondent and a reporter of major events, but he really made his mark as a commentator on the Canadian scene, and as a teller of whimsical tales, usually based on homespun philosophy and a knowledge of Canadian ideas and traditions. Those of you who grew up as I did in the '30s and '40s will remember that for most of those years, he and his pal, cartoonist Jimmy Frise, filled the back page of one section of the Saturday edition of the *Toronto Star*. They told stories of their experiences and endeavours in their everyday lives. These tales were often based on their cottages, their adventures fishing, their gardens, or their likes and adventures in eating. Greg wrote the stories, and Jimmy provided a cartoon to illustrate. After the death of Jimmy Frise, Greg moved to the *Montreal Star*, where he continued to write for many years in the same whimsical style.

A typical Gregory Clark story would fill half a page of a newspaper, which gave him lots of space in which to explain his ideas and to philosophize about the subject. And it was typical that there would be a humorous twist at the end of the tale. For example, I remember one story based on puffballs or puff mushrooms, a form of that genre of fungus that is frequently found in pastures in Ontario (and elsewhere, for all I know). When dry, they look like gray balls, sometimes as big as footballs, but more often tennis-ball sized, which, when "stomped," emit a puff of brown powder (hence the name). But it is less well known that when they are fresh and still growing, and look like white balls, they are not only edible but quite delicious when sliced and cooked.

In the story, Greg and Jim had discovered a growing puffball in a farmer's field. They decided to let it grow to full size, which they calculated would be about the end of the week. This was a giant-sized puffball about the size of a soccer ball. They went on to rhapsodize about the wonderful, delicate flavour of such a prize, anticipating their enjoyment of this delicacy. They discussed at length the various ways of cooking the mushroom without finally settling on their recipe. And they expressed scorn and some sympathy for those people, the majority of folks, by their way of thinking, who were unaware of the delectable possibilities of puffballs. In particular, they expressed surprise that country folk were lamentably ignorant of the edibility of puffballs.

The appointed day of harvest finally came. Greg and Jim drove their car down a back road and parked it out of sight of the farmer's house. They could see the huge puffball, ripe and ready, gleaming white on the far side of the field. They crawled through the fence and scrambled across the field, trying to keep out of sight. They crept closer and reached out for their prize—only to find it had been replaced by a large white glass kitchen globe by some other admirer of puffballs. They were, of course, annoyed at the perfidy of the unknown pilferer who had made off with the prize they considered was rightfully theirs.

Jimmy Frise's cartoon showed the farmer sitting on his verandah, slapping his thigh and chortling over yet another pair of city slickers who'd been fooled by his glass globe.

Jean and I made our first visit to Great Britain, in 1956. On the occasion in question, we were travelling through the Highlands of Scotland, and in so doing, scandalizing our Scottish relatives. We only had an extra-long weekend, and they felt that trying to see the Highlands in only four days was almost an insult to the beauty and grandeur of this magnificent part of the world.

Our first day was blessed with magnificent, sunny weather, and we set out to enjoy ourselves and our adventure into the Highlands. We were doing our best with the limited time available to see as much as possible. I remember, driving north from Edinburgh, I even persuaded Jean to alter our route to enable us to pass over the famous Firth of Forth Bridge, which I knew as a great engineering marvel of the nineteenth century. I suppose I should have realized that in the nineteenth century, no one built magnificent bridges just for road traffic. It turned out, of course, to be a railway bridge. It took us some time to discover a small, precarious looking ferry to get across the Forth River. Nonetheless, we persevered and had a fine day sightseeing well into the foothills.

The second day started out with cloud and rapidly progressed to a steady downpour, which made sightseeing impossible. As a result, we arrived at our hotel, in Fort Augustus, deep in the Highlands, very early—indeed, shortly after lunchtime.

After settling into our room, we explored the hotel, which, in spite of its remote location, had considerable dignity and formality. We discovered a long, narrow room, with chairs lined up along each wall, and decided this must be the residents' lounge. On one of the side tables was a small collection of magazines, including, to my astonishment, four consecutive editions of the weekend magazine of the *Montreal Star*. I could only surmise that someone from Montreal had recently stayed at the hotel for a time.

Toward the end of the afternoon, the weather cleared, and we had a chance to sample the wild beauty of the remote Highlands, with a brief tour back into the hills in our rented car. We travelled miles along a single-lane road through wild, abandoned-seeming countryside, with several wandering mountain streams, all of which had a prehistoric appearance to us. I remember, the road had occasional wide spots where you were intended to stop and await oncoming traffic. But in two hours we met no one. That part of Scotland seemed completely abandoned.

Later that evening, back at the hotel, we had an excellent dinner, served with all due formality, but without the requirement that we dress for dinner, that custom of dinner jackets and black ties having been largely abandoned even then in all but the most demanding hotels. At the end of the meal, the headwaiter approached our table and announced, "Coffee is served in the lounge." We repaired to that long, narrow room with all the other guests.

There was a deathly silence, as each guest read or knitted and, above all, took care not to disturb anyone, least of all by speaking aloud. After all, none of us had been introduced. How could you possibly speak to someone without being introduced? So everyone took care to behave correctly, and not to act in any manner that could be construed as forward or familiar.

After a few minutes, the gentleman across from me picked up the top copy of the *Montreal Star* magazine that we'd noticed during our scouting trip earlier in the day. Thinking to help him, I leaned across and whispered, "Pardon me, but if you're going to read that, may I suggest Gregory Clark on the back page. He's one of my favourites."

He looked at the paper, stared at me, and exclaimed loudly, "But this is a Montreal paper. Are you from Montreal?"

The lady next to Jean piped up, "I lived in Montreal for four years!"

Another chimed in, "My son lives in Pointe Claire [a suburb of Montreal]."

A third was just about to leave on a trip to Canada. And so on. Everyone in the lounge seemed to have some connection to Montreal, and the conversation swelled and spread throughout the lounge, and lasted well past midnight.

No one in that silent room really craved silence or privacy; everyone welcomed the opportunity for the warmth of conversation and the chance of acquaintanceship. But nothing would have happened without the friendly hand of Gregory Clark reaching across the miles from Canada. Think how he would have philosophized about dignified and "correct" people just waiting for the chance to break out of their shells and act in a friendly fashion for once.

And the Gregory Clark twist in the tale? That gentleman across from me never got a chance to read the Gregory Clark story.

AUNT MEG versus NEW YORK CITY

Aunt Meg visited us in Montreal one summer. She stayed with us for about six weeks, and we took the opportunity to show her something of Canada. I remember her Scottish mind was quick to realize the value and potential of the huge forests we showed her on our trips through the countryside.

Jean took Aunt Meg down to New York City for a few days. It was one of the places Aunt Meg had always wanted to see. I guess, even in those days, the influence of American movies was worldwide.

One morning, they were sightseeing on Broadway, in the heart of the "Big City." At about eleven o'clock, Aunt Meg suggested they stop for a cup of tea. Knowing Aunt Meg's strictures about tea and tea bags, Jean somewhat dubiously selected a restaurant. It looked a typical New York coffee-shop-type of restaurant.

When they were seated at a clean marble-top table, a waitress came to take their order. Aunt Meg fixed her with her gimlet eye, and in her most imperious manner, said, "Young lady, I want a cup of tea. Now I mean a proper cup of tea, in a proper teapot. I don't want tea made with a tea bag, and I don't want simply a cup of hot water with some tea in it. I want a proper cup of tea."

Jean held her breath for the response she thought this was likely to bring. And the girl did look a bit startled by this determined instruction, but she said nothing, and went back to the kitchen.

It was noticeable that several heads appeared around the kitchen door, apparently inspecting this unusual personage who had the temerity to order "a proper cup of tea."

After quite a long pause, during which Jean continued to fear the worst, the door to the kitchen opened and the waitress reappeared. She was carrying a tray on which reposed a white china teapot, with steam issuing from its spout. And there were two china cups on saucers instead of the heavy mugs Jean had expected, together with a milk pitcher and sugar bowl. It was indeed a "proper cup of tea," every bit as good as if they'd been in a good restaurant in Glasgow. Aunt Meg received this miracle as if it was only to be expected.

Jean asked the waitress before they left how she had managed this extraordinary feat. The girl explained that the chef in the restaurant was a European who also liked his cup of tea, properly made in a china pot, and properly served in china cups. He kept all the necessary pieces of chinaware on the top shelf of the kitchen, to be touched or removed on pain of death. When he heard of the instructions given by this unusual customer, he'd agreed to lend his tea set for this special occasion.

Aunt Meg continued her sightseeing, blissfully unaware of the unlikely event she'd precipitated. I've always considered that the score stood at Aunt Meg, one, New York City, zero, although perhaps one should award some points to that considerate chef.

IRISH SOLUTIONS

The Isle of Erin, the Emerald Isle, Ol' Blarney; Ireland has many names, affectionately applied by millions of people all over the world. For Ireland has sent its immigrants in droves all over the world. It has been said, "There are only two kinds of people in the world, them that's Irish and them that wish they were." This affection for an Ireland that is part real and part imagined has grown up based on the memories of all those immigrants fondly remembering a land that had, in fact, been a harsh home for them. For Ireland, until the formation of the European Union, was a relatively backward country, more agrarian than modern. It was peopled by a race that had suffered much over the years, and who as a result had developed a distinctive character, part patient and long-suffering and part whimsical and self-deprecating, in order to avoid the harsh truth of their surroundings.

Ireland deserves the monicker "Emerald Isle" because of a climate that is very damp, where the rain seems to fall more or less continuously. It never rains very hard, mind you; it just drizzles damply much of the time. The Irish say the rain "falls soft upon them." That combined with the rich soil in the southern portion results in fields that do indeed achieve a special kind of green, which may indeed be the colour of emeralds.

Those green fields are really misleading because successive waves of invaders over the centuries have driven the original Irish people out of the rich southern areas and into the much less hospitable northwestern areas, which, while very picturesque, are much less suited to farming. It's no wonder that for centuries, and particularly the nineteenth century, millions of Irish people emigrated, mainly to North America. There, their ethics of hard work won them much greater comfort and success.

The Irish people developed a special view of the world and a special reputation. They adopted a whimsical, not quite real, view of the world, which often amuses the observer. For example, one of my managers in

Ireland explained Irish driving culture to me as we drove through a small town.

"D'you see that fellow in front signalling?"

And indeed, the driver in the car in front of us had his right arm stiffly extended out the window (right arm, since the driver's seat in Ireland, as in England, is on the right to facilitate driving on the left-hand side).

He went on, "You may think he's planning a right turn, but he isn't. That signal simply means he's about to do something. He probably hasn't yet decided exactly what!" And sure enough, after a pause, the car took a sudden turn to the left. But we had been warned he was about to do "something" and so were able to avoid a crash.

A little farther on, the car in front of us simply stopped in the middle of the street. Its dual flashers came on. "Ah," my informant said, "he fondly believes that by turning on his blinkers, he's effectively made the car disappear." And sure enough, the driver got out of the car and simply walked away.

Little habits like that serve to illustrate the sometimes irritating, often endearing, frequently convoluted, usually slightly vague and often whimsical, logic of the typical Irishman.

I've noticed over the years that the Irish typically avoid facing unpleasant facts head-on, but instead apply roundabout phrases, and whimsical ideas to address many problems. I have designated this habit as the use of "Irish Solutions." The following anecdotes may illustrate this habit.

> I should note that in the mid-sixties, the Irish government adopted very business- and investor-friendly policies. At about the same time, the formation of the European Union made Ireland eligible for significant subsidies from the EU. As a result of those policies, and heavy subsidies, Ireland has progressed considerably from the backward habits of the Ireland we all know from memories of the past. Ireland is now a very modern, progressive, industrialized country. Nevertheless, that whimsical nature has not disappeared and continues to contribute to the charm of the country and its inhabitants.

WE FIRST ENCOUNTER IRISH SOLUTIONS

I have always enjoyed Ireland, and my Irish friends are numerous. But I have noticed their tendency to develop and apply oblique solutions to problems, whether real or imagined.

All my life, I'd heard my father and my uncles talk about their Irish ancestry. (Did you ever notice that more people claim to have Irish ancestors than could possibly be accounted for if the population of Ireland were ten times as big?) However, it does appear that my grandfather and his brother were born near the town of Inniskillen in Ireland and emigrated from there to Canada when they were teen-aged boys. They came to seek their fortunes in the supposedly more promising and hospitable conditions in Canada. They ended up in the farming country around Peterborough, Ontario. It's worth noting that the country around Peterborough is very similar to that around Inniskillen in Ireland, with the same rolling hills and even with lakes similar to Loch Erne near Inniskillen. It would seem that these Irish immigrants wanted change, but not too much of it. Many of them ended up on very fertile lands near Peterborough. I'm told that the old Hamilton farm now forms part of the beautiful campus of Trent University.

Unfortunately, my grandfather and grandmother both died while their family was quite young. My great-uncle had moved elsewhere, and the family lost track of him. Therefore, all that was known of the "Irish connection" was that the two boys had lived in or near Inniskillen and had worshipped at the Church of Ireland, in Inniskillen itself.

In the mid-sixties, I was making frequent business trips to Europe in an effort to promote the sale of a tactical military radio system we'd developed at Canadian Marconi Company. I determined to try to help improve our knowledge of our ancestors by taking some time off and meeting my father and my Uncle Bill (his oldest brother) in Ireland. We planned to spend a fortnight touring around so that they could see the country of their origins. They were both more or less retired and looked forward to the trip. Indeed, my father wrote to all sorts of tourist boards and travel bureaus and spent weeks plotting and planning the trip.

I met them at their plane at Shannon airport in the west of Ireland. They'd had an all-night flight, so I was able to persuade them to rest and sleep one night in Limerick, the picturesquely named town near the airport. However, the next morning they were up bright and early and raring to go. But they proved totally impervious to the beautiful sights of Western Ireland. They were absolutely insistent that we make a beeline (or as close to a beeline as was possible on the somewhat chaotic Irish roads of that era) for Inniskillen to "find some relatives." (Irish roads, even today, are not noted for going directly from A to B. They tend to divert, sometimes rather sharply, to visit C, D, and E along the way, giving the route from A to B something of the nature of a random walk.)

We'd hired a car and we drove north as quickly as possible, with me doing the driving. After all, I was the only one who'd ever seen cars driven on the left-hand side of the road, let alone having any practical experience with this disconcerting habit.

But try as I might, it proved very difficult to make good time on those Irish roads. Late in the afternoon, still considerably short of our objective, we stopped for gas, or "petrol," as the natives would have it. We told the somewhat elderly station attendant that we were heading for Inniskillen, and he shook his head sadly. "Ye'll niver make it," he pronounced. We were astonished. We had a good, sound car and plenty of gas, so we could see no reason to doubt our ability to make it to our goal. But he explained that we had to cross the border into Northern Ireland, and seeing as this was a Saturday, the border post would close at five o'clock. And since it was now four-thirty ("half four," as he described it) and we still had about forty miles to go—well, as he'd said, we'd "niver make it." This was on a relatively major road, mind you, but I guess this was part of the rural charm of Ireland we'd heard so much about.

Seeing our consternation, he suggested tentatively that perhaps he could persuade the border guard at the post to hold it open and wait for us. It seemed the guard was a friend of his. (I've since learned that in Ireland everyone for thirty miles around is a friend, or nearly so.) But of course his friend would expect a modest tip for his trouble. If we'd agree to pay his friend, say, ten shillings, he thought it could be arranged. And so it was agreed. And when we finally arrived at the border post an hour later, the gate was still open and the guard cheerfully waiting to let us pass. But when I tried to pay him his tip, he refused it, with a broad smile, explaining that didn't apply to us. He only charged locals for keeping the gate open, lest they take advantage of him. He was only too eager to ensure we tourists enjoyed our stay.

IRISH SOLUTIONS IN AN ECCLESIASTICAL SETTING

Iniskillen is a sizeable town near the border between Northern Ireland and the Republic of Ireland. In those days, it was a pleasant and friendly provincial town. Unfortunately, since that time it has become a centre of incidents in the struggle between the Irish nationalists and the Protestants. One hopes that will soon disappear and it will return to its former peaceful and friendly nature.

We arrived on a Saturday night and felt we'd closed in on finding some Irish relatives. My grandfather and my great uncle were reputed to have worshipped at the Church of Ireland in Inniskillen. (For Church of Ireland, read Church of England or Anglican, but transported to Ireland.) Once we had checked into a hotel, nothing would do but that we immediately search out the church, "and see what we could find out." I protested that it was Saturday night and we'd be wasting our time because there'd be no one around the church. As with so many sure things in life, I was wrong. When we found the church on the main street, it was all lit up, the doors were open, and there was a lively party for the young people going on. And both the old priest in charge of the parish and his young curate were there.

We went and chatted with the elderly priest. When he learned our mission, he said, with the wonderful facility many Irish display in the English language, "Ah, I'd be loikin' ta help ye, ye do understand, but unfortunately, all of our records were destroyed in the unpleasantness." Now isn't that a marvellous expression to use to avoid referring to the civil war that raged in Ireland at the time of the liberation of Southern Ireland and the breakup with Northern Ireland? A fine Irish solution, I thought.

He did, however, give us the names of one or two very elderly people in town who could be relied upon to remember any Hamiltons still living in the neighbourhood, and we subsequently met with them. Unfortunately, they were unable to assist us in our quest.

We also had a chat with the young curate who'd been in that church for only a few years, starting directly after graduating from university. He pointed out that this church, whose name was St. Martin's Church, was directly across the road from the Roman Catholic Church, known as St. Marten's. This is a not unusual phenomenon, particularly in the northern part of Ireland. Centuries ago, when the English took over large stretches of the country, dispossessing the local people and settling people from Scotland and England on the land, they also took over many of the churches and transferred them to the control of the Church of England. The major change in those days was that the church answered to a king in England rather than to a potentate in Rome. As quickly as possible, the dispossessed Irish congregations set about building new churches, and they very often used the same name for their new church. Thus, you very often found this phenomenon of two churches in the same town, one Church of Ireland (Anglican) and one Roman Catholic, but with the same name.

The curate told us that in Inniskillen, with the two churches cheek by jowl, there was more than the usual amount of friction and acrimony between the two congregations. The two pastors had even arranged the times of worship services so that the two congregations wouldn't be coming in or out at the same times and thus would avoid meeting in the street. The young curate said he hoped that in his ministry he would be able to alleviate this situation, although he had difficulty seeing exactly how.

One thing he had noticed was that the two congregations differed over the spelling of St. Martin's name. His church spelled it St. Martin (with an i), while the Roman Catholics across the street insisted the correct spelling was St. Marten (with an e). This proved to be a wonderful controversy, providing endless opportunity for friction, debate, and argument, very intriguing to the people of this rural town. He thought to himself, "Now, there's something I should be able to get settled and thus remove at least one point of disagreement." So he wrote to the head of the Faculty of Divinity at his old university in Dublin, explaining the situation and asking him to advise on the correct spelling of the name.

He was surprised when he didn't receive an immediate answer. Indeed, he received no answer at all for such a long time that he'd given up expecting one. But finally, after about a year and a half, a letter came. At last, here would be the answer that would settle the controversy and prove one or the other church to be right.

His professor started by apologizing for the very long delay in responding. He explained that, in the circumstances, he wanted to be certain he gave the right answer. He had written to various church historians in Holland, Germany, Switzerland, Greece, and even in the Vatican. And some of those authorities had taken a long time to answer, presumably because they, too, wanted to be certain they gave the correct response. But he had now concluded that the best answer was that both parties were wrong. The correct spelling of the name should be St. Martan (with an a).

I laughed and told him I thought that was an excellent Irish solution to his problem. I believe that canny old professor knew better than to involve himself in judging between two parties in a centuries-old debate, and had delayed his answer until he found a neutral way of answering.

OUR IRISH SOLUTION FOR SELECTING ANCESTORS

We spent several days in Inniskillen, talking to people and following up leads to possible Hamilton relatives, but to no avail. It wasn't for lack of co-operation or trying on the part of the townspeople. They all seemed perfectly willing to stop and talk to us about our quest, to make suggestions, and even to drop whatever they were doing and accompany us to wherever we were going on our search. I suspect that given the opportunity, many of them would have volunteered to be our relatives.

Having had no success in our inquiries, we decided to take a day off and enjoy the scenery of the surrounding countryside. We set off to drive around Loch Erne, which was reputed to be very beautiful. My father never did gain any great confidence in my ability to drive on the wrong side of the road, and his confidence in my ability to navigate in Ireland was even less. However, even he agreed that driving around a lake seemed fairly safe, since all you had to do was follow the shoreline and sooner or later you'd come back to where you started.

And it was indeed a beautiful drive. But after some time, I spotted a small sign at the side of the road, which simply read, "CASTLE." It pointed to a side road leading uphill away from the lake. Without discussing it, indeed almost without thinking, I turned into this narrower road.

"What're you doing? Where're you going? We'll get lost," I was told in alarm.

"I'm going to the castle," I said. "We can't get lost. All we have to do is go back downhill and we'll find the lake again."

"Castle, what castle?"

"I don't know, but there was a sign at the side of the road."

At which point there was another CASTLE sign, pointing to an even smaller side road. I turned and was subjected to even more alarmed argument and had even more difficulty convincing my passengers that they weren't in danger of becoming hopelessly lost.

Along came another turning, and yet another, each time into narrower, more remote and, to my passengers, more frightening roads. Finally we were directed by the signs to turn through a gate into a field. The track ran across the sloping field to a stone fence at the top. And sure enough, there on the crest of the hill beyond, were the remains of an old ruined castle.

We bumped to a stop, right in front of one of those old cast-iron signs you often find at historic sites. It read:

**This castle was built
in 1626
by
Sir Malcolm Hamilton,
Governor of the District.**

Now I ask you, if you were looking for relatives, and had had little luck in finding any, and furthermore, had been guided to this place seemingly by the hand of fate, wouldn't you think that Sir Malcolm Hamilton was a good relative to select? Perhaps this was the Fates' version of an Irish solution. Without any discussion, we all gave up our search from that moment, and summarily adopted Sir Malcolm as our ancestor.

My father and my uncle had a great time scrambling over the ruins and getting me to take their pictures. That led to a further piece of evidence that Sir Malcolm was indeed an ancestor of our family.

You see, it was one of those picture-book summer days, with blue skies and a few big, fluffy clouds drifting by. But all of a sudden, without warning, those fluffy clouds ganged up on us. The wind suddenly started to blow fiercely, the rain came down in buckets, and almost instantly we were in the midst of one of those sudden, summer storms. We ducked underneath the archway of the wall to shelter from the rain. That archway was almost the only part of the castle left standing. (I never claimed my ancestors were great architects, now did I?) Just as my uncle was running in under the archway, the wind blew off his flat cloth cap and carried it away over the wall. I ran out the other side to see if I could catch it, but I couldn't see it. "I'm sorry, Uncle Bill, I'm afraid you've lost your hat," I told him.

He took it philosophically. Maybe he had visions of returning home with one of those distinctively Irish hats adorning his bald head.

We must have sheltered under that arch for twenty or twenty-five minutes. And then, just as suddenly as it had started, the storm stopped, and we walked back out into bright sunshine. And as we did, Uncle Bill's hat came fluttering down, to land right at his feet.

Now any Irishman will tell you about the wonderful little people they have in Ireland. Although you never see a leprechaun, they're supposed to be relatively thick on the ground, particularly around old historic places. I believe that the leprechauns of that castle, who had captured my uncle's hat, had spent all that time up on the top of the wall, examining it minutely. And they must have decided that he, being the oldest son of his generation, was the rightful heir to the castle. Therefore, as we walked back out into the sunshine, they threw back his hat as an indication that they recognized him as ruler of the castle.

For the record, it is an historical fact that the "Baron Hugh Alexander Hamilton" (my exact name) left the west coast of Ireland sometime early in the seventeenth century, to seek his fortune in the Scandinavian countries. And it is also a fact that today the premier duke in Sweden is a Hamilton. Now, I wouldn't think of suggesting any particular connection between all these facts, but I do think it only reasonable, in keeping with my now-established practice, to claim these distinguished gentlemen as relatives and ancestors, too.

LEPRECHAUNS AS AN IRISH SOLUTION

In an earlier story, I somewhat facetiously assigned the responsibility for the disappearance and reappearance of my uncle's hat to the leprechauns whom I imagined were inhabiting the ruins of the Hamilton castle. These legendary "little people" are supposed to be found in most parts of Ireland and in particular around any ancient or ruined buildings. Although they are supposed to be rarely seen, and even when seen, it is no more than the merest glimpse, they are thought to look like bearded old men, upwards of two feet tall, and dressed in distinctive elf-like costumes. Their presence is chiefly evidenced by the occurrence of myriad minor tricks, more benevolent than malevolent.

In modern-day, sophisticated Ireland, very few people would admit to believing in these mythical little people. However, their tricks provide a conveniently whimsical explanation of all the little things that may puzzle or go wrong over the course of a day. Thus, they fit well into the tradition of "Irish solutions." And besides, leprechauns provide an opportunity to subtly assert a kind of superiority over visiting strangers, as we shall see in the following story. Therefore, not many people in Ireland will be too adamant in maintaining the non-existence of these intriguing beings, either.

George was the closest thing to a tycoon I had ever met. When I first met him, he'd already retired from the chairmanship of a major corporation, he sat on innumerable boards, including that of Northern Telecom Limited, and he also sat on the board of our small Northern Telecom Company in Ireland. He'd been appointed to that post because he owned an "estate" in Ireland, which presumably, in somebody's eyes, made him an expert on all things Irish.

He was wealthy. He told us one day how he obtained his Irish "estate" (which he described as just a house with a garden and an acre or two), and that story illustrates how being a wealthy tycoon works. It seems he went to a party at a friend's house on St. Patrick's Day, and at the party he met an investment advisor who specialized in commodities. The advisor tried to interest George in making an investment. The next day he had a telephone call from this dealer who told him he should invest two or three hundred thousand in copper, "just to get the feel of it." And because it was such a "minor" sum, he agreed. He heard nothing more. No one ever called him to ask for the money and he simply forgot about it. I guess the investment house felt he would be well able to cover his investment at any time. However, a few months later, his advisor called again to say that copper had nearly doubled and he should sell. A few days later, he received a cheque in the mail for a quarter of a million dollars, all without any action on his part.

Reflecting on the whole caper, and the fact that it all started at a St. Patrick's day party, he determined to use the proceeds to buy a house in Ireland, a country he and his wife had liked very much when they had visited it. And so he acquired his "estate."

He told us he spent very little time there, but that his brother-in-law, a university professor, liked it very much and spent as much time there as possible. Indeed, he had spent one whole sabbatical year there writing a book.

It seems that when they acquired the estate, they also acquired old Sean (pronounced Shawn, the Irish equivalent of John). Sean was the groundskeeper and general odd-job man around the estate. George described him as cheerful, strong, and willing, but "just a bit simple, you know." Apparently, Sean came in for a lot of gentle teasing from the family.

George told us of one noon hour when Sean and the family were gathered in the kitchen for lunch. The brother-in-law, with a broad wink to the others, said to Sean, "You know that little arbour at the back of the garden where I've set up a table and where I often work on my book?"

Sean allowed as how he did.

"Well, I was working down there this morning when I heard a little rustling sound. I looked down and there was this funny little fellow, about eighteen inches high. He had a beard, and a tall, pointed, green hat. And he wore the funniest shoes with long, turned-up toes. As soon as he saw me looking at him, he scuttled away into the bushes and I never saw him again. Now what do you suppose that was, Sean?"

Sean had no intention of being bested by an outsider on the subject of leprechauns. Without batting an eye, he managed to look very pleased and replied, "Glory be, he's back!"

Simple, my foot!

Archeologists and historians tell us that in pre-history, Ireland was overrun by successive waves of invaders. First there came the Fir Borgs (pronounced in Gaelic, Fear Bullocks, meaning giants). They were followed by the Tuatha de Dannon (pronounced, in Gaelic, Tua de Dannon, meaning little people or pygmies). Finally, there came the Milesians, who were a Celtish race. It is not beyond the stretch of imagination to believe that small groups of

Tuatha de Dannon might have survived for a long time, even several centuries, hiding in the wilder parts of Ireland, which in those days would have been very wild indeed. Such survivors of a race that is described as being extremely small in stature would have had some contact with the subsequent settlers, and some of their interactions might have given rise to the legends of the "little people" who played tricks upon their neighbours. Such legends, in the normal course of events, would have been handed down to future generations, and could have become the basis of the leprechaun tradition.

IRISH SOLUTIONS IN CRYSTAL

Waterford crystal enjoys a well-deserved reputation among the fine crystals of the world. Perhaps it was in an attempt to emulate the success of Waterford that a number of other small crystal factories grew up in various parts of the country.

One of those factories was just down the road from our Northern Telecom factory in Galway. I judge it wasn't particularly successful, but it did have a large sign on the roadside attempting to lure passing tourists inside to purchase crystal glasses and tankards with "your own family crest engraved." They claimed to have a library of ten thousand family crests.

One day when passing, I thought it might be nice to have such a crystal tankard, and I went in to inquire. After a bit of a chat with the manager about his various styles, I asked, "Do you have the Hamilton family crest?"

He looked at me sharply and asked, with a shrewd look, "Do you know what it looks like?"

When I admitted I didn't, he replied promptly, with what might have been a relieved smile, "Then we've got it!"

An Irish solution of a different sort, I thought.

But to give him credit, a few days later I received a beautifully drawn design of "the Hamilton family crest." It featured an antelope and a human heart, both prominent elements of the Hamilton crests I have since seen. However, I don't remember any ermine pelts, which also feature in the Hamilton crest. I should admit that since that time, I've seen a sufficient number of differing "Hamilton Crests" that today, I'd probably agree that the one presented by that crystal maker could have as much legitimacy as the others. I must also admit that, in the end, I did not purchase the glasses, more because I found the styles too heavy and cumbersome, than because of doubts about the legitimacy of the crest.

ADMIRING THE SWISS

During the seventies, Jean and I formed the habit of travelling to Europe, hiring a car, and exploring some portion of the continent for a two-week period. We had some memorable vacations that way.

In June 1977, we fulfilled a lifelong ambition of Jean's by spending our two weeks for that year exploring Switzerland. That magnificent country, with its grand landscapes, its picturesque villages, and its ancient cities gave us a great vacation. I think Switzerland could have been invented by Kodak specifically to supply photographers with a never-ending range of gorgeous scenery to shoot.

I had hardly returned to work when I was called in and offered the post of managing director for Europe. With that exquisite timing typical of many corporate decisions, I would be based in Zurich, Switzerland. They could have saved me the cost of a fairly expensive vacation if they'd done all this a month earlier.

The problem the company faced in Europe was that, in those days, the telecommunications markets in each country were very tightly protected because the supply of telecommunications equipment represented one of the largest national investments in the country. Telephone companies were usually government monopolies, and suppliers limited to local nationals. This was accomplished in a number of ways, such as unique standards, specific designs, and outright closed markets. In most countries, Northern Telecom did not have approved products, and as a result was largely precluded from large portions of the markets. The idea was to establish a very limited presence and to try to identify specific opportunities while at the same time waiting for the markets to open up. In the interim, Northern Telecom might develop new or extended products better suited for these markets.

On the surface, it was not a very appealing prospect. It would be a long and difficult task, filled with frustration. And it would involve uprooting our family and moving them to Switzerland. While the country itself was not unappealing, the whole situation seemed less than ideal. I very nearly turned it down. If I had, I would have missed one of the greatest adventures of my life.

I spent seven years in Zurich, managing an organization that covered the whole of Europe, from Ireland in the west to Austria in the east. That meant there were ample opportunities to travel throughout Europe and to explore countries from Scandinavia in the north to Italy in the south.

Indeed, we started with a very small group of people, and it grew quite slowly. But we did manage to identify some opportunities, and the market gradually opened up to our products. Starting from almost nothing, the business grew to over seventy million dollars in my time. And today, even more gratifyingly, it has grown to be a multi-billion dollar business, through both growth and acquisitions. I'm proud of the achievements of that small team.

We enjoyed living in Switzerland. The pages following reflect some of the things we admired and enjoyed about our Swiss home.

ACTUALLY THE SWISS DO HAVE A SENSE OF HUMOUR

Life is a serious business for the Swiss, or at least that's the impression you get as you walk along the street. Our Scottish friends would probably describe them as dour. To be sure, they greet each other, and indeed, perfect strangers, with a courteous "*Greutzi*," but no smile. And if you observe two friends speaking in the street, it always appears that very serious matters are being discussed, even though, if you actually knew the subject, it might prove to be quite innocuous.

The climate probably contributes to this serious view of the world. In Zurich, the sun disappears behind a thick overcast about the middle of October, not to reappear in any strength until early April. If you lived in such a gloomy climate, you too might come to view life in a somewhat serious vein.

Switzerland has existed in relative isolation from the rest of Europe for most of its history. Indeed, the national policy has been to foster isolation. And that seems to have become a kind of national psyche. If you ask a Swiss for his opinion about any given subject, it appears as if he first thinks, "Is this good or bad for Switzerland?" If he decides it's good for the country, then, by definition, it's good for him as an individual.

The Swiss hold frequent national referenda, in which they vote on important issues. There are four such referenda each year, with four questions on each ballot. The results are binding and become law. In my few years there, the good citizens actually voted on two occasions to increase their taxes. Now, that's a serious approach to life. With all that serious thinking and voting going on, wouldn't you be inclined to think life is pretty serious?

However, I must assure you the Swiss were actually created with a sense of humour. It's just that they display it in a somewhat subtle manner.

The national pastime in Switzerland is walking. Everywhere you go, there are walking paths, well maintained, and fully equipped with direction signs, which identify not only the destination of the particular path, but also how long it will take the average walker to reach that destination. You can buy maps detailing all the walking paths in Switzerland. They're nothing if not organized. It is said that there are more miles of maintained walking paths in Switzerland than there are of roads. I don't doubt it. If you venture forth on a weekend, you will find all the parking places near the beginnings of such paths full of cars belonging to walkers. Nearly everyone goes walking. Once you venture onto the paths, you meet individuals, couples, and groups of all ages, all togged out in their walking clothes, their walking hats, often with a decorative feather, their walking boots designed for serious walking, and carrying their "*Alpenstocks*" (wooden walking canes with sharp steel tips). And while I'm sure most of these people firmly believe they are enjoying themselves, they still give the impression of being about some very serious business.

But it was in observing this walking phenomenon that I first recognized the very subtle Swiss humour.

Not too far from our house, there was a stream flowing down a steep valley through a wooded area. The Swiss have made this into a beautiful little park, complete with the obligatory walking path leading up the valley, along the stream. It is a very enjoyable walk. After about a mile along the path, you become aware of the sound of a waterfall. And, as you came around a bend, sure enough, there it is, about six feet high and very pretty, as you would expect in this country renowned for its beauty. But there, in the middle of the stream, with his behind stuck right into the falls, is a full-size, half-grown elephant, beautifully constructed of concrete. Furthermore, the beast is designed with its own hydraulics, so that water flows in at his tail, and out through his trunk, in a steady stream. I even imagine the expression on its face subtly expresses bliss.

Now, to me, that's a Swiss joke. That someone would take the trouble to build this pleasant though somewhat ludicrous surprise away back there in the woods has its own subtle humour. If you don't find it humorous right away, I suggest you think about it again tomorrow. I believe you'll find it begins to become comical. And the next day, it'll seem funnier still. It never quite gets to be hilarious, though. That would be un-Swiss.

THE SWISS ARE VERY PRIVATE PEOPLE
or
HOW TO "ONE-UP" YOUR FATHER, IN THE NICEST POSSIBLE WAY

Living in Switzerland has many advantages; the country is clean and outstandingly beautiful, the people have an extraordinary reputation for honesty, the services are efficient, and everything works. That everything works is a great advantage, particularly if you're a stranger learning to live in the country. It makes it so much easier if you're trying to get anything done, from a simple repair to making a train journey. And the Swiss have a great devotion to punctuality. If you invite someone to visit at five o'clock, or if a shop promises to deliver something at two o'clock, that is when it happens, not five minutes earlier or ten minutes later, but exactly on time. Even the tramcars run on a schedule. However, with all of these advantages, it must be admitted that the Swiss are difficult to get to know. Indeed, they might be considered standoffish. Oh, they'll all greet you, when they meet you in the street, with a "*Greutzi*" (similar to the Austrian "*Gruss Gott*"), but to progress beyond that simple greeting takes a long time. You must patiently demonstrate that you really are a civilized and sober individual who probably won't do anything to disrupt the even tenor of life in this quiet and peaceful place.

After we'd been living in Zurich for about five years, I finally achieved acceptance from our next-door neighbour, or so it seemed. I was working in our garden when, for the first time, he leaned across the fence and chatted with me. I was pleased to have reached this new level of acceptance. In the course of that conversation, he remarked, "Did you know that Roger Moore lived in your house when they were making the James Bond movies in Switzerland?"

You may remember that several of the famous (and outrageous) 007, or James Bond, movies were largely located in Switzerland, and that Roger Moore played the lead role in several of them. They were ideally suited to his style. He was a supremely handsome English actor, who often played the role of a completely unflappable character. In those stories, filled with action, and often involving unbelievable situations and mayhem, he seemed to stroll through scenes of violence and danger with complete indifference to all the possible threats and disasters surrounding him. I always enjoyed those kinds of pictures, and particularly Roger Moore.

When I returned indoors, I was not only very pleased that we finally appeared to have reached acceptance from at least one of our neighbours, but I was most intrigued with the information about Roger Moore. I thought this was an opportunity to impress our two teenaged daughters who were living with us in Zurich. As soon as I went into the house, I announced to them that Roger Moore had lived our house. Did I get a startled exclamation? No! Did I get any swooning or giggling as one might expect at the news this extremely handsome and charismatic star had inhabited our house? No! Did I get any reaction at all? Absolutely not! It was as if I hadn't spoken. I was most disappointed that my news seemed so unimportant to our daughters, but I tried to bear up.

Life went on. Our lives continued in their normal way. I went to work, Jean kept the house, and the girls went to school. I almost forgot my great discovery. And then a few days later, I ventured into the downstairs powder room, just inside the front door. There on the wall opposite the toilet was a large, neatly lettered poster, which read ROGER MOORE SAT THERE.

Who can predict the actions or reactions of teenagers? Who can even tell when they've heard you, much less registered what you said? I got more of a reaction than I could have hoped. I had a sneaking suspicion that, in the ongoing and seldom acknowledged contest between parents and children, I'd lost several "points," in the nicest possible way. Indeed nothing was ever said, but that poster was subsequently replaced, without any comment, with a most elaborate macramé banner, bearing the same wording together with many symbols of James Bond's adventures. I didn't know whether that cost any extra points, and I didn't ask.

THE SWISS ARE BANKERS

Switzerland is known worldwide as a banking nation. For a long time, the Swiss have been bankers to the world. I believe that, in large measure, this situation has arisen because of their determined neutrality, declared as a national policy about two centuries ago. At about that time, they realized that, as Swiss mercenary soldiers often went abroad to fight in other peoples' wars, they frequently found themselves fighting other Swiss mercenaries on the other side. Notwithstanding that the soldiers on whichever was the winning side often came home with considerable spoils of battle, they decided it wasn't very sensible for Swiss to be killing Swiss in quarrels that had little bearing on Switzerland itself. So they passed a law that no Swiss could fight as a soldier anywhere outside of Switzerland. The only exception to this rule is the Vatican guard, that famous corps of Swiss, dressed in those peculiar multicoloured uniforms, who act as the police force of the Vatican City. I believe those uniforms were originally designed by Leonardo da Vinci. If so, they're one of the few occasions when he missed his mark. In spite of the strange uniforms, they are a completely modern and very effective police force.

The Swiss accompanied this decision not to fight the wars of other people with a decision to maintain a very strong army to defend Switzerland itself. And given the very rugged terrain, Switzerland is very defensible. The result of that second decision is that to this day, every Swiss male must join the army, go through seventeen months of rigorous training, and thereafter, until he is about forty-five, spend six weeks every year in the army, maintaining his military skills. Every Swiss keeps his uniform and his weapons at home, and it is claimed the Swiss can mobilize nearly half a million men within four hours. Furthermore, it is a very modern army, with large numbers of battle tanks and modern aircraft.

A further requirement is that each individual must maintain his marksmanship to a certain level and he must pass a test of marksmanship each year. This has some disconcerting results. You may be travelling down a peaceful country lane and encounter a young man pedalling along on his bicycle, with his rifle or sub-machine gun slung over his shoulder. He's heading off to rifle practice. If you stop on a country road on a Saturday afternoon, and listen carefully, you can often hear the steady banging coming from the local rifle range, hidden somewhere in those peaceful hills. And for those who believe our high level of crime stems from the presence of firearms in the hands of private citizens, it's worth noting that there are almost no instances of those army guns being used in crime, and in particular, in murder. I have speculated that the penalty for showing up at army camp with fewer than the prescribed number of bullets in the clip you kept at home may be greater than the penalty for murder.

The Swiss are proud of their marksmanship. The story goes that during the Second World War, during which the Swiss remained neutral but maintained their army of a quarter of a million men on the alert along their borders with Germany, a German general met a Swiss general at a reception. The German general remarked that the Swiss were fortunate the Germans didn't simply take over Switzerland. The Swiss general bristled, and commented that it wouldn't be too easy, and that his army would be difficult to defeat. The German general pointed out that the Swiss had only a quarter of a million men under arms and suggested the Germans might invade them with half a million men. "What would you do then?" he asked. To which the Swiss replied, "Why, we'd each have to shoot twice!"

In all of this, the Swiss created, whether by design or by good luck, a situation whereby they replaced the rather perilous business of renting themselves out as soldiers by a much more lucrative business. For they established themselves as not only a determinedly neutral country but one that had the strength and determination to defend itself. Thus, in any war, they were very likely to be among the unharmed survivors.

Furthermore, they had a long-standing reputation for honesty and reliability. Now, when a war is looming (and in Europe that was an almost constant situation for centuries), it's wise to take precautions to protect your property. Wealthy people, in particular, are prone to such concerns. Switzerland appeared in such circumstances to be an ideal place to keep your money, and many people chose to deposit their wealth in Swiss banks. The Swiss were well aware of the opportunities this created, and concentrated on developing a very solid, reliable, trustworthy, and oh-so-discreet banking industry with worldwide connections. In particular, Zurich became a city of bankers, almost to the exclusion of anything else. The Swiss Gnomes, as the leading bankers became known, concentrated there, making it a very beautiful, wealthy, and most conservative city.

I can illustrate this almost exclusive concentration on banking. Whenever I was in town, I would attend the weekly luncheons of the Swiss-American Chamber of Commerce. However, opportunities were infrequent because of my extensive travelling. Whenever I did attend, I was given a tag that identified me by name and company. When I took my seat at a table, usually with seven or eight strangers, someone would invariably read my nametag, and comment, "Northern Telecom—that's a funny name for a bank!"

The Swiss simply couldn't imagine anyone indulging in any other business when there was all that lucrative banking to be done.

THE SWISS CO-OPERATE
or
HOW TO IMPRESS THE BOSS

Bill was a good friend, but, as president of Northern Telecom International, he was also my boss. He visited Zurich regularly to review our progress and discuss our problems. It was always wise to refer to problems as "opportunities," in Northern-speak, and, since the European business I was managing was in a start-up mode, there was always an ample supply of "opportunities" for us to discuss.

On this occasion, he was spending a weekend in Zurich and I had offered to show him some of the country. Thus it was that on a fine, sunny Saturday afternoon, we drove through the beautiful Swiss scenery, into the heart of the country, to the foothills of the majestic Alps. The Swiss countryside is always beautiful, with its fields of emerald green, and its farmhouses with great, overhanging roofs. The vast majority of houses in Switzerland have window boxes filled with bright red geraniums. Those red geraniums should be the national flower, rather than the edelweiss. I even knew people renting a house who found, as a condition of their lease, that they must maintain window boxes of red geraniums. The effect was truly outstanding. As I remember that day, the weather even co-operated, allowing us excellent views of the towering mountains along the way.

We went to Schwyz, a beautiful little town that, at one time, had functioned as the capital of the country. It is a very Swiss town in appearance, with a beautiful old town square, containing the obligatory, colourful statue of a Swiss soldier in medieval uniform. The square is surrounded by ancient, but extremely well maintained, buildings. All Swiss buildings are well maintained. They rarely demolish a building; rather, they remove the entire interior of any building deemed to be rundown, and rebuild it with modern rooms inside, maintaining the exterior with its original, ancient appearance. I do not know for certain that the buildings around that square have been subjected to this renewal process, but I know they do create the desirable, quaint, Swiss impression that you'd expect in this country that strives for visual perfection.

One of the buildings facing that square is a magnificent, baroque church, perhaps the finest example of baroque architecture I have ever seen. Some people find the baroque style excessively elaborate; they do not particularly like all the curlicues, carvings, colourful decorations, and general fussiness of the style. But you must certainly admire the enormous effort and extreme care that went into the creation of these buildings. In any event, after we'd admired the square, Bill and I went inside the church.

It was, indeed, a magnificent church, and we spent some time walking around admiring the decoration. Bill's eye fell on the huge pipe organ mounted in the choir loft at the back of the church. Bill is no mean musician himself; he plays the piano very well and acts as the reserve organist in his own church. He looked in awe at that magnificent organ filling most of the back of the church, and said to me, "My, I'd sure like to hear that organ!" At which point, almost as if on cue, a man entered the organ loft, sat down at the organ and started to play. I suppose it was the church organist practising for the morrow's services. In any event, for about half an hour, we had what amounted to a private concert, which we—Bill in particular—enjoyed immensely.

When we finally came out of the church, we decided to head back towards Zurich. However, we still had a bit of time to spare, so I suggested that, on our way back, we visit Einseideln. This is a small village somewhat off the beaten track that is the site of a very large ancient monastery, dating from the ninth century, together with a huge, baroque church built later, in the early part of the eighteenth century. This church contains an important "Black Madonna," a shrine to the Virgin Mary carved in a black material. That relatively tiny statue, only about three feet tall, has become a hallowed object of Roman Catholic pilgrimages, particularly from the villages in the surrounding area. As with most Marian shrines, pilgrims pray to Mary for her intercession in Heaven on behalf of the petitioner. As you would expect, the actual shrine where the Madonna is displayed in her finery is most elaborate and beautiful.

I understand this black Madonna is just one of several. I believe there are black Madonnas in a number of churches around the world. I know nothing of their history or origins. However, wherever they are, these Madonnas are revered and serve as the objective of pilgrimages for the worshippers of St Mary.

The village consists of a main street, perhaps eight blocks long, leading up to the enormous church. We explored the beautiful baroque interior of the church, and admired the Madonna, although surprised by her small size. Afterwards, we stood on the front steps, looking down that street. I thought the whole town made an ideal setting for a group of pilgrims to march up to the church. I explained to Bill that, although I'd never seen one, I understood such pilgrimages were often made by large groups of people from a single district or village. The participants often came dressed in their local costumes, and were frequently accompanied by the village brass band.

I should digress for a moment to explain that nearly every village has a brass marching band, which performs at any and all occasions: on holidays, summer outings, festivals, and, of course, pilgrimages to Einseideln. I imagine the brass bands occupy people in those villages that are isolated in the depths of the mountains. Of course, other villages, not so isolated, would not want to be seen to lag behind those more remote villages; hence, the ever-present brass bands. I do believe that ninety percent of all the bass drums in the world must be in Switzerland. Everyone seems to have one.

We stood there on the porch of the great church, trying to imagine the spectacle of a pilgrimage. Bill rose to the occasion again with the comment, "My, I'd like to see one of those pilgrimages." At that point, again as if on cue, we heard a brass band strike up in the distance. It came marching around the corner at the bottom end of the street, followed by a large parade of people bearing flags, banners, and other artifacts from their village church, and all dressed in traditional costumes. It was a magnificent sight, one you could only come upon by chance.

I've explained that Bill is a good friend, but at the same time he was my boss. I was operating a significant business, in quite difficult circumstances, where headquarters could easily become concerned with our handling of all those "opportunities" I described. Thus, I was pleased to find an occasion where I could demonstrate that I actually had the situation reasonably under control. I turned to Bill and asked, "Now, is there anything else I could arrange for you to see?"

I do think it was kind of the Swiss to be so co-operative that day.

In the fifth and sixth century, there was a great religious upheaval in Ireland, led by Saint Columba. Ireland was one of the centres of the Christian Church in that period. However, in the eighth and ninth century, Ireland was ravaged by Viking raiders, who concentrated their expeditions on the rich Irish monasteries. This resulted in groups of Irish monks fleeing to safer locations. Several such groups settled in Switzerland; hence the growth of great monasteries in St Gallen and Einseideln that started in the ninth century. I imagine those groups of fleeing monks brought with them some of their treasures. Certainly the libraries of those great monasteries hold some amazing artifacts. The monks did leave behind in Ireland the famous *Book of Kells*, generally recognized to be the outstanding example of a surviving book of the sixth century, particularly because of its outstanding decoration and illumination. But the libraries of Einseideln and St. Gallen each contain a number of books of the same age, albeit without the same degree of elaborate illumination, and hundreds of books dating from the ninth and tenth centuries. You can visit these libraries on guided tours and view some of these treasures, a few of which are usually laid out on display.

It's a commentary on the conservative nature of the Swiss that the treasures of the monastery at Einseideln are not widely publicized. I knew nothing of them at the time so we missed the opportunity to visit them. But we did see that pilgrimage.

MOB CONTROL, SWISS STYLE

The Swiss are very good farmers, even though their country is largely vertical, which severely limits the amount of available farmland. There is a certain amount of fruit farming, and some mixed farming, but they really shine as dairy farmers. They utilize every available inch of space, even going so far as to rent the verges of roads and highways to grow hay. They make good use of the rolling land of the foothills. The best land is, of course, the rich valley land, at the foot of the Alps. This valley land is surprising when you first see it; it's usually perfectly flat, right up to the mountains, which then rise precipitously almost at the edges of the fields.

There isn't nearly enough land in the lower fields to support all the cattle in Switzerland. The solution is to utilize the high pastures, away up in the mountains. These pastures, which are also relatively level, are accessible only in the summer, but provide good pasture for a period of five or six months of the year. During that period, the farmer works furiously to grow and harvest hay from the lower fields. That hay must sustain the cattle during the cold winter months when they are brought down from the high pastures and sheltered in the barns at the farm. The cattle seem to thrive on this treatment; they look sleek, well fed, and extremely contented.

The Swiss appear to harvest as many as six crops of hay each summer. In this, the farmers are assisted by a special technique. Every farm has a huge, sunken, concrete pit, into which all the cattle manure is dumped every day. Some water is added, according to a recipe known to all farmers, and the whole is allowed to ferment for some time. Just as in the fermentation of whisky, when this liquor is deemed to be sufficiently aged, it is drawn off. However, this liquor is then sprayed on the fields as fertilizer. It must be extremely effective, judging by the lush fields, which are almost emerald green. But, on the day when any farmer within five miles decides to spray his fields with this mixture, you are left in no doubt as to what is going on. The smell is intense and all pervading, although fortunately it does not seem to persist for longer than a day or so. That stuff would easily outdo a whole herd of terminally irritated skunks for intensity and repulsiveness of smell. If it weren't for that, I think they could bottle it and sell it to lawn maintenance companies around the world. But I don't think the neighbours would put up with that smell.

As you may imagine, the transport of the herds of cattle to and from the high pastures represents something of a problem, as the distances involved may be as much as thirty or forty miles. The cattle are driven on foot, and the whole community turns out in national costume for the event. Even the cattle are dressed up with garlands and ribbons. The drive becomes a carnival as the herd is driven along country roads, and is quite a sight if you're lucky enough to see it. .

Every Swiss cow has a bell hung around its neck, even the young calves. A herd on the move, or even grazing, presents a constant chorus of bells. The bells are all different sizes, from tiny calf bells to huge bells weighing more than a hundred pounds and measuring more than two feet across. The reason for the difference is quite ingenious; the strongest cattle are given the biggest bells in order to slow them down to the pace of the slower ones during those long marches. It's much the same principle as handicapping horses in a horse race. But the Swiss have a better way of determining the handicap; they hold cow fights while the cattle are up in the high pastures. I don't know exactly how a cow fights, but I'm assured the battles can become quite intense. The winner is given the largest bell, and I'm also told the cows know they have won, and seem quite proud to be the champion and to wear the championship bell. I guess they never figure out they've been duped into extra work by this stratagem. But then, I never thought the cows I've met were any great intellects.

Many things in Swiss life reflect this background of dairy farming. For example, our house in Zurich had a huge pear tree on the front lawn, with all the appearance of having been there for a century or more. It was gnarled and twisted, and was over four stories tall. The fruit were abundant but quite small; I thought, initially, they could probably be used for pickling. However, they began to drop off the tree while still extremely hard, much too hard to use. And yet, when you cut them open, they had already begun to rot at the core.

Puzzled, I asked some Swiss friends about this strange tree. They explained that I had a "*muscht*" tree and that the pears could be gathered, pulped, and fermented into a liquid that was decidedly alcoholic and was known as *muscht*. It was further explained that I wasn't allowed to make *muscht*, that privilege being reserved for farmers with cows. Some time in the distant past, the farmers had persuaded the authorities that *muscht* is useful as a medicine for cows, and thereafter, a farmer was allowed to collect pears and make *muscht*, the quantity being determined by the number of cows he owned. To this day, many farmers make *muscht*, and I was told I could have given my pears to any local farmer with the requisite supply of cows, and could then have expected to find a bottle or two of delicious *muscht* on my doorstep one morning. I'm sure the farmers had excellent uses for *muscht*, and equally sure that no cow in Switzerland had tasted this delicacy for many, many years.

The Swiss are a very law-abiding people; indeed, their honesty is legendary. If you accidentally leave something in a tram, or even on a chairlift in the mountains, as I did one time, you can absolutely count on its being turned in by whoever finds it, and it will be returned to you. There isn't even any expectation of any reward for the finder. Nevertheless, the Swiss do have their quota of protesters and troublemakers; and at times, they have unique methods of dealing with them.

A few miles outside Zurich, in a pleasant village, there is a federal prison. Most of the time, it attracts little attention, to the extent that the village boasts only a single policeman to keep the traditional Swiss peace. However, as will happen anywhere in the world, a group protesting some real or imagined problem relating to the prison or one of its guests chose to gather on a Saturday afternoon in the village square. The crowd grew and became quite unruly, definitely disturbing the customary afternoon quiet. The crowd was far beyond the ability of the single policeman to control, much less disperse. The situation could have turned ugly at any moment. However, the villagers had their own solution: Two of the farmers resident in the village (many farmhouses are located within the borders of villages) got out their tractors, loaded up their spray tanks with well-aged manure liquor, and drove through the crowd, spraying happily as they went. I was told of this incident by a Swiss friend, who said, "When you get that stuff on you, there's nothing to do but go home and burn your clothes." In any event, the crowd lost all interest in close association, and dispersed before the villagers could think up any more crowd-control measures.

I think our police forces might consider importing a few tanks of vintage cow liquor (the manure sort, not the *muscht* sort) for use in riot control.

WEATHER FORECASTING, ZURICH STYLE

In the preceding sections, I believe I may have given the impression that the Swiss are a very dull, serious people with no sense of fun or inclination to enjoy a party. That is far from the truth. Indeed, they do have their times for complete enjoyment. It's just that they are designated times, identified as festivals or carnivals. When they switch into festival mode, they enjoy themselves with energy and vigour. They have many festivals where the whole population joins in the fun. They enjoy themselves uproariously. And, equally, at the conclusion of the festival or event, they almost instantly switch back to their familiar serious demeanour.

A good example is *Fasching*, their version of Mardi Gras. This festival revolves around Ash Wednesday, and most towns of any significance hold a *Fasching* parade. In true Swiss fashion, they make the most of their time by holding the *Fasching* parades in Catholic towns before *Fasnächt* or Ash-Wednesday evening, while the Protestant towns hold their parades in the week after *Fasnächt*. One suspects this is to allow the same people to march in several parades. The whole populace usually turns out for the parade in the town, and children often dress up and demand contributions from passers-by, much like Halloween in North America.

There are a few floats and wandering clowns and performers, but the parades depend largely upon the brass marching bands coming from the surrounding villages. There is no shortage of such groups. Nearly every village has a brass band, in the same way that most have a very good choir; the villagers seem to be willing to work together to provide entertainment for all. Many of the villages are isolated in the mountains throughout the winter months, and there isn't much to do but to attend band and choir practices, I guess. Each band in the parade is accompanied by most of the inhabitants of their village, all in costume and each sporting a huge papier-mâché mask perhaps four or five feet tall, painted in garish colours and very ferocious in appearance. The masks and indeed the costumes of each village will have strong similarities as if from the same family or theme, but each costume and mask will be unique. It appears that a village acquires a supply of cloth and paint and each individual makes use of these materials to make his or her own costume. It must take considerable organization. The overall effect of a parade of these groups, all different, is very entertaining. The noise level from the bands, many of whose instruments seem very battered and worn, but played with great gusto, is almost overwhelming. All those bass drums beaten together have a very pervasive beat; you almost think the city is jumping off its foundations with each thump. When there's a *Fasching* parade going on you have little choice but to join in.

Perhaps an even better example of a typical Swiss festival is *Sechseläuten*, which takes place early in February. This is a festival maintained by the Zurich *Zunfts*, which are the modern embodiments of the ancient trade guilds in Zurich. There are twenty-five such *Zunfts*, eleven of which, the "historic *Zunfts*," trace their history back to the year 1336. The remaining fourteen Zunfts, the so-called younger line, were founded in the years between 1867 to the present day. They were originally the representatives of the various trades and as such exerted enormous influence on the government and commerce of the town. In medieval times, the *Zunfts* would have been enormously wealthy, and accordingly they each built impressive *Zunft* halls or houses. However, as time passed, they lost their influence and gradually declined. Today, they are very exclusive private men's clubs, and membership in no way implies any association with the particular trade represented by the *Zunft*. There are *Zunfts* of the goldsmiths and bakers, fishmongers and blacksmiths, and so on, but membership simply indicates you have either acquired your place either through inheritance or through a very difficult process of application and election. I doubt there are any goldsmiths in the *Zunft* of the goldsmiths, and there are certainly no fishmongers in the fishmonger's *Zunft*. Membership is a mark of distinction.

The great guildhalls, built in medieval times, gradually fell into disrepair, even as they continued to be used by the declining *Zunft* societies. In the mid-twenties, the city of Zurich took over all those ancient guild houses, gave them extensive reconstruction externally, and renovated them internally, making them into delightful medieval-style showplaces. Most of them are now leased to restaurant owners, and house upscale restaurants. But the restaurateur is required to maintain the guildhall, usually the top floor of the building, as a magnificent hall for the monthly meetings of the *Zunft* in that building. I suspect this renewal of the buildings led to a renewal of the *Zunft* societies as well.

In our northern regions, most people get tired of winter long before spring. The coming of spring becomes a subject of much conjecture and desire. In Canada, in an effort to answer the vexing question of when spring will arrive, we reserve the second of February for "Groundhog Day." On that day, the groundhog is supposed to awaken from his winter's sleep, climb tentatively out of his burrow, and survey his surroundings. A groundhog is a very nervous and careful critter, and if, on that first tentative venture out into the new year, he sees his shadow, tradition has it that he will be frightened and retire into his burrow in dismay. That calamitous event will signal that winter will continue for a further forty-five days. As you may imagine, people watch the antics of groundhogs on that day very carefully. Of course, there are lots of groundhogs, so we can't watch them all. We give the honour of this prophesying activity to selected, or designated, groundhogs in specific small villages. For example, in our neighbourhood we have Wiarton Willie. Elsewhere they have Puxatawney Pete, and Penetanguishine Phil, among others. These animals live in relative luxury and are fed and protected, and observed constantly by their local keepers. Otherwise they might fall victim of the local farmers, who look upon groundhogs as vermin and kill them if they can.

I'm not aware of any study having been done to evaluate the accuracy of this method of forecasting. However, it may well be as accurate as any other we have available, judging by the forecasts I hear regularly on my TV. Nevertheless, apart from a little comment in the newspapers, it's difficult to work up any great festival atmosphere around Groundhog Day. The sport of groundhog watching is, by necessity, a very quiet occupation. There's no hint of a festival involved. After all, the slightest disturbance, much less a resounding cheer, would send Wiarton Willie, or any of his chums, instantly back into his burrow, thereby defeating the purpose of the exercise. The Swiss, however, in Sechseläuten, have corrected that aspect of long-range forecasting by adding a major festival to the proceedings, and have even added an aspect of greater accuracy.

The festival starts with a grand parade of all the members of the *Zunfts*, in medieval costume, representing their trades. As you may imagine, some of those costumes are quite spectacular, with colourful materials and much gold braid. Many guilds have a float depicting their trade and. sometimes they distribute to the crowds tokens of their guild; the fishmongers, for example, may throw small fish to the crowd, while the bakers may pass out small bread rolls. Unfortunately, this custom of distributing souvenirs of the craft does not extend to the goldsmith's *Zunft*. And most have troops of mounted horsemen, also in costume. Of course, there are the obligatory marching brass bands. It's a very grand and noisy parade through the town, ending at the main square.

In the main square, a huge bonfire has been built, more than thirty feet high, I would estimate. On top of the carefully piled stack of wood is a large snowman, representing winter. He is called the *Böögg* and is the central figure in the ceremony. I suppose he's made of papier mâché. (The öö stands for a sound we don't have in English, resembling the sound of the latter end of the bleat of a sheep.) Once the parade has finished, the fire is lit. And while the fire gets started, the troops of horsemen take turns galloping around the fire, no mean feat, given a horse's instinctive fear of fire. Eventually, the fire reaches the top of the heap and the *Böögg* takes fire. The head of the *Böögg* has been loaded with gunpowder, and it eventually explodes, marking the end of this phase of the celebrations.

Now, the point of this whole exercise is that the number of minutes it took for the fire to reach the zenith and explode the head of the *Böögg* is supposed to represent the number of days of winter yet to pass before the arrival of spring. No wonder the crowd cheers the progress of the fire lustily. While the accuracy of this method may be as suspect as the North American version, I submit that it is a much better way of resolving the question. Holding a festival, a parade, and a bonfire with an exploding snowman seems much superior to the rodent-based technology used in North America.

The festival having gone through these elaborate and uproarious preliminaries, it now moves to the real objective of the exercise, a mammoth party. The *Zunfts* open their doors to all the members of other *Zunfts*. The members visit each other back and forth far into the night. I'm told the hospitality is grand and freely flowing. But the following morning, in true Swiss style, the whole town is very, very quiet—perhaps even quieter than usual, in deference to numerous sore heads.

JAPAN MAY NOT BE MYSTERIOUS BUT IT'S CERTAINLY DIFFERENT

In October 1983, while we were still living in Zurich, my beloved wife, Jean, died after a long and courageous battle with cancer. She had been my helper, supporter, and partner in my adventures for twenty-eight years. Her ashes still lie in a pleasant Swiss cemetery, near Zurich.

That seemed to mark the end of an era for me. Our great adventure in Europe seemed to be over; I no longer had anyone to share my adventure with. It seemed that my task, to prepare for a further major expansion into the market, was nearly complete. I felt at loose ends in many ways. Early in 1984, I was given a challenging solution to this problem. I was invited to take my perceived patience and persistence to attack a supposed impenetrable target. I was offered the new position of President of Northern Telecom Japan. The company wanted to try to penetrate this hitherto completely closed market, and I was fortunate to be chosen for the task. It was just the kind of new adventure I needed to renew my life and energies.

At the same time, I felt that marriage had been a very successful condition for me. I decided I would like to try it again. Moving to Japan might complicate that ambition. However, I was extremely lucky that Barbara decided I "would do" and agreed to marry me. She's an Irish girl who was employed in the International group at Northern as the director of Information Systems. I'd met her earlier when she visited Europe in her capacity as a systems expert. Her enthusiasm, energy, skill with people, and love, have contributed enormously to my well being and our mutual enjoyment of life for some twenty years now. Barbara moved to the Singapore office at about the time I moved to Japan, which made for some very long-distance wooing. (It usually comes as a surprise to learn that Singapore is six hours by plane from Japan.) We were married in late 1985. Perhaps it was one of the most widespread weddings in history, as we were married in Montreal, but included all our friends in the international world by holding receptions in Zurich, London, Dublin, Montreal, Toronto, and Tokyo. Our friends must have seen us as well and truly married.

In a subsequent reorganization of the company, the scope of the post in Japan was enlarged and I became the president of Asia Pacific operations. That meant I was responsible for activities from New Zealand and Australia in the east, to China in the west, and included offices in Singapore, Hong Kong, Manila, and Seoul, as well as Tokyo.

Moving to Japan was a much different proposition than moving to Europe. European culture has many similarities to our Canadian pattern, whereas Japanese culture is radically different. We had to adapt to many differences in custom and lifestyle. Fortunately, the company took account of those problems and supplied us not only with a house that was relatively North American in style, though somewhat smaller than our norm, but a maid and a car and driver as well. These were all essential, as we were both working in a complex and difficult situation.

A comprehensive analysis of the Japanese economy and government of the time is beyond the scope of this little book. The pages following contain some observations of Japan and its culture. I will include such comments on the economic situation as are necessary to explain some of the idiosyncrasies.

The initial task in Japan was to penetrate the hitherto impenetrable market with Northern's products. The Japanese economy was a completely managed one, and was notorious at the time as being closed to any outside suppliers, in any field, not just telecommunications. And, as I've said previously, telecommunications equipment tends to be one of the largest capital investments in any country, and thus this segment of the market tends to attract a lot of attention. We found ourselves in the midst of an ongoing argument at government levels about so-called "levelling the playing field," and thus opening the market, with particular attention to the telecommunications segment. The situation was complicated by the fact that the Japanese are extremely nationalistic and consider any Japanese product to be, by definition, superior to the product of any other country. It was a matter of great satisfaction to me that we managed, by patient application of basic marketing principles and by avoiding the ongoing strife at government levels, to win a major contract from the NTT (Nippon Telephone and Telegraph company), the largest telephone company by capitalization in the world. That contract still ranks as the largest contract ever awarded by that company to a foreign supplier.

Living in Japan wasn't nearly as satisfying, however. The following pages contain observations about life and customs in Japan that may illustrate some of our frustrations and discomforts.

TWO'S COMPANY, TWO MILLION'S A CROWD

One of the first things that strikes you about Japan is just how crowded things seem. It's no wonder. There are one hundred and thirty million people living in a country about the size of the state of California, but having only about ten percent of its area suitable for habitation. If you start in Tokyo in the north and travel south to Osaka and Kyoto by train, a distance of about three hundred miles, you see very little rural scenery. It seems like one continuous suburb of a major city. The whole area is very heavily populated.

This has the immediate effect that land becomes extremely valuable, and people are forced to live in very cramped circumstances. The average Japanese family lives in an apartment of about six hundred square feet, about the size of a large sitting room in a North American house. Those that are fortunate to have houses may have as much as twelve hundred square feet, with the house perched on a parcel of lane just large enough to accommodate it. And that house is most probably about two hours' commuting distance from their place of work. Such a house would cost the equivalent of two to three million dollars and thus would be very difficult for the average person to acquire.

Our house was located in Seijo Gakumai, the Beverly Hills of Tokyo, where film stars used to live. Even that house had only a few feet of land around it and sat cheek by jowl with surrounding houses. Our house was considered to be very large by Japanese standards; it had about fifteen hundred square feet, and consisted of a fairly large living room, a minimal-sized dining room, a tiny kitchen, and a garage on the ground floor. On the second floor, we had a master bedroom about twelve by twelve, with attached bathroom, and three other tiny bedrooms, one of which became our office, together with a Japanese-style bathroom. (When we returned to Canada, we copied that bathroom's facilities with an open shower space and separate bathtub, together with toilet and hand basins in separate cubicles. We found that to be a very convenient arrangement.) But that house, convenient as it was, was over an hour's commuting distance from our offices, even if we attempted to travel in off-peak hours.

I deliberately chose that house in preference to living closer to downtown in an American-style apartment where we would be surrounded by other expatriates. I felt that, by living in Seijo, I would have a greater chance of experiencing Japanese life and neighbours. In that, I was correct, and we had some interesting experiences with intriguing and caring neighbours. We enjoyed that house.

The lack of living space influences much of Japanese life. For example, while Japanese wages are high, there's not a great deal one can buy for the home. Where would you put a giant-sized TV or a North American-sized refrigerator? The consumer in Japan is severely limited in his choices, even taking into account the extremely high prices of most things in the market. Similarly, he is very limited in buying a car; he must have a parking space for the car both at home and at work before he's even allowed to buy.

Of necessity, the Japanese have become experts in public transportation. It's essential for them to move millions of people around every day. Our village, Seijo, was on one of very many commuter rail lines. With the exception of three hours in the middle of the night, there was a commuter train passing through that station every three minutes, all day long. While I used that train only about twice a week, nevertheless, it's a measure of the crowding that in all the time I used it, I never had a seat.

The commuter trains were connected to a tremendous subway system in inner Tokyo. They covered an area I'd estimate at about twenty miles in diameter. Those subway trains are the object of amazement for many visitors. A downtown subway station will be about four city blocks long. They have to be to accommodate trains up to eighteen cars in length. The train enters the station still at full speed, and the engineer only reduces power and applies the brakes when he's about halfway down the platform. He then brings the train to a stop with the doors within an inch of marks on the platform indicating where the doors should be. People line up on those marks and rush into the trains as soon as the doors open. And it is really true that, in downtown stations, there are attendants on the platform, with white gloves, to push people onto the trains. In thirteen seconds, the doors close and the train moves off. It has to because there's another train due in less than a minute.

This system moves enormous numbers of people. There's one station in the system where a number of commuter lines and subway lines intersect, where more than two million people a day move through the station. Try to imagine walking through one of the pedestrian hallways of that station, leading to the trains, when a rush-hour crowd is intent on moving through it in the opposite direction. It's a lost cause.

Living in Japan gives a whole new meaning to the word "horde."

A SHOCK TO THE SYSTEM

One of the greater shocks your system can sustain is your first venture at shopping in Japan. No matter that your company has given you an allowance to cover the differences in the cost of living, the prices you are faced with seem unbelievable, and to many people, emotionally unacceptable. You might be in a major department store, or in one of the tens of thousands of tiny mom-and-pop shops selling any and all varieties of goods, or in their version of a supermarket. The prices of clothes, groceries, and everything else seem astronomical. This is mostly the product of the government control of the economy, and their policies of protecting Japanese suppliers from competition from outside the country. To supply the vast number of tiny shops, an enormous, complicated and extremely inefficient distribution system is maintained. An outsider attempting to save money by bypassing this system is doomed to failure, as all Japanese conspire to maintain it. One of the results of this system is a very high level of employment, with many people having meaningless and superfluous jobs. An example is the elevator girls, who wait outside the elevators in any big hotel. Their sole purpose seems to be to learn which floor you intend to go to, and to push the button for that floor.

It takes some time for anyone to get used to paying those high prices. You really only become even moderately comfortable with those high prices when you begin to think in terms of the local currency, instead of translating back to your original currency.

Some of the most elegant department stores I have ever seen are in Tokyo. Entering one of these stores, you will be immediately greeted by uniformed assistants who will direct you to the floor you require for whatever you may be seeking. When you go to that floor on an escalator, you find standing at the exit to the escalator, a whole row of uniformed sales clerks. The one on the nearest end of the line greets you with the obligatory little bow, and becomes your personal attendant while you are on that floor, with the capability of showing and describing any item for sale. She will consummate any transaction you make, and if you happen to be the first customer of the day, which happened to us on one occasion, she will present you with a gift, which is not an insignificant item. In our case, it was a nice piece of costume jewellery. It's a level of service you could easily become used to.

However, the prices of the merchandise would astound you. That day, we saw wedding gowns, admittedly handwoven with magnificent patterns and much gold thread, for the equivalent of $25,000 and up, and the accompanying obis, the elaborate hand-woven girdles worn with a formal Japanese gown, priced from $35,000 and up. You might think such prices would make any weddings in Japan very rare events. The solution, however, is to hold your wedding in a "wedding factory," an institution dedicated to weddings. Such an organization may be found in almost any major hotel, or perhaps in an independent building dedicated solely to the wedding business. These businesses supply all the services for a wedding, including conducting the ceremony in a dedicated "chapel," a magnificent reception meal, rental of the necessary garments, and the services of a professional wardrobe mistress. This is all for a fee which, while still exorbitant, may be manageable to a determined couple (or their parents). I'm told the minimum charge would be in the vicinity of $25,000. I guess one hopes those traditional red envelopes each guest gives to the happy couple will together contain enough cash to offset this expense. At such a wedding, managed by these experts, the bride might wear several different gowns at various times during the ceremony and festivities, including a very chic Western-style going away outfit, all supplied by the organization. I imagine that after such an event, the lucky couple must consider themselves well and truly married.

Those obis, which look so elegant when worn by diminutive Japanese girls, are, in themselves, a source of income. One of the girls in our office told me that, in order to get the obi properly tied in that elaborate bow, she goes to an expert in her neighbourhood, who will do the job for about $100. Even services are expensive! I wonder what you call yourself if your trade is the tying of obis?

Our village of Seijo boasted a modern supermarket not far from our home. (Seijo was called a village although the suburb contained about one hundred thousand people.) In true Japanese fashion, it was the smallest supermarket I've ever seen, consisting of just two aisles in a long, narrow space. However, they managed to cram into that space almost every item of groceries, meat, and fish, both occidental and Japanese, that you'd care to purchase. But the prices would certainly astound. Simple apples ranged from the equivalent of two dollars to five dollars apiece. To be sure, they were magnificent apples, huge and juicy and without a blemish, produced by pruning all but the very best fruit from the tree. I don't know what they did with inferior apples; they were never offered for sale anywhere I ever found.

Similarly, melons, at one hundred dollars apiece, were on offer. Mind you, they were magnificent melons, perfectly round and without a blemish of any kind. They are produced by someone turning the individual melons on the vine every day, by hand, in order to make certain they develop in a perfectly symmetrical fashion, without the slightest blemish. But those melons weren't intended for eating. They were intended for use as prestigious gifts. The Japanese were forever exchanging "gift-os." You would send a melon, in a neat little wooden box, carefully wrapped to protect the precious fruit, to someone to whom you felt you owed a gift. Of course, the recipient wouldn't consider eating a hundred-dollar melon, either. They'd immediately think of someone to whom they owed a gift and send the peripatetic fruit on its way. Now, this process had its limits. At some point, the melon would be approaching its demise, and one of the recipients would be faced with the sad duty of actually consuming the expensive symbol.

One of the delicacies we were told about were pine mushrooms, which were prized for their delicate flavour when they became available in season. Having been forewarned, Barbara and I pounced upon the packages of pine mushrooms, each mushroom in its individual little box, when they were finally offered in our store. But, to our chagrin, they were priced at a minimum of one hundred dollars for even the smallest specimen. We forbore experiencing the thrill. Subsequently, in a restaurant, we were offered this delicacy. I regret they didn't live up to their hundred-dollar reputation, as far as we were concerned.

Our supermarket had a full butcher's counter, with a wide variety of meat. Again, it was buyer beware of the prices. Japanese housewives do not offer much meat in their menus, and the reason seemed obvious to us. Meat is just too expensive. On one occasion, we held a dinner party for about a dozen people. Barbara decided to serve a beef Wellington and to that end approached the butcher in our shop. To be sure, he had a whole beef tenderloin, which looked very nice and would serve admirably. After considerable discussion, the purchase was made. I hope the guests enjoyed it. The meat for that meal cost over one thousand dollars. Of course, it was Kobe beef, the renowned Japanese beef that is so tender you can cut it with a fork. On the farm, there is an attendant for every two cows. Each cow is massaged every day to force the fat into the meat, and each cow receives a bucket of beer every day. It's no wonder it's tender—and expensive.

I have identified a few of the most outrageously priced items. Not everything was so extremely expensive, but most things were much more costly than we had ever experienced. Imported items were expensive because of tariffs and quotas, while local produce was heavily protected, and accordingly the prices were much elevated.

I remember the first time I went to our local supermarket. It was before Barbara and I were married, and I went alone to buy supplies for my bachelor existence. I took the car and managed to navigate myself the few blocks to the parking lot near the store, which I'd observed earlier. It was a tiny lot, located about two blocks from the store. After waiting patiently for a while, I was awarded a parking spot by the uniformed attendant.

Once in the store, I remember my astonishment at the range and variety of the goods offered. I was given a cart about a quarter the size of the monsters they give you in the average North American market, presumably because of space limitations. When I finally pushed my fully loaded cart to the exit where there were a couple of cash registers, I was surprised at the number of girls, all in uniform, who were available at the cash out. One of them fell upon my cart and began to unload it onto the counter, the cashier worked feverishly to record the sales, and a third girl reloaded my goods into another waiting cart. I paid the cashier, and when I turned around, my cart full of groceries had disappeared. With only minimal Japanese, I was at a loss to ask where it was. However, the cashier recognized my plight, and offered, helpfully, "*Ikimashita*." My rudimentary Japanese translated that into, "It went." Not a particularly informative statement. Went where? Went how? In puzzlement, I went out the door, to see if they'd merely moved it outside to save space in the crowded store. I couldn't see it. Further questioning of the cashier, in English perforce, elicited no further useful information. In spite of the apparent disappearance of a cart full of extremely expensive groceries, I don't remember feeling particularly alarmed. In my short time in Japan, I'd learned that the Japanese have a way of preventing visitors from coming to any harm. However, I was puzzled about how they'd make my groceries reappear. Confused, I headed back to the parking lot. And there, I found one of those cheerful, smiling uniformed girls from the store with my cart of groceries, patiently waiting for me to arrive so that she could unload the cart into my car. I have no idea how those cheerful smiling girls decided I had a car in the parking lot. The service was excellent, if a bit worrisome during the process.

By a combination of high tariffs, import quotas, industry control, and careful isolation of their consumers from the outside world, the government managed to maintain a regime of extremely high prices and consequent full employment. By this means, a Japanese company that was planning to export its products could recoup all its development and initial overhead from the domestic market, leaving it free to offer its goods on the export market at very attractive prices. It also meant that one would be very ill-advised to purchase a Japanese camera, electronics item, or automobile in Japan. The same item would be available at very much lower prices back home in Canada, or even a few thousand miles down the coast, in Hong Kong.

Shopping was always a mixture of pleasure, because of the excellent service, and anguish, because of the prices.

I have described in this note conditions as they existed in Japan in the mid- eighties. Since that time, a number of things may have influenced the situation I have described. These include extensive travel outside Japan by a large portion of the population, demonstrating to them how the rest of the world lives, and leading to demands for more competitive pricing. As well, there have been several severe recessions in Japan in the intervening period. And maybe melons, as gift-os, have fallen out of favour. Nevertheless, I believe Japanese prices are still astonishing to visitors.

LANGUAGE IS A BARRIER

When one arrives in Tokyo, a major problem is immediately evident. You are immersed in a sea of kanji. There are billboards, fluorescent signs, banners, painted signs, signs on the fronts of shops, all manner of communications on the walls and buildings. All in kanji. These are the complex and incomprehensible pictographs, mostly square in format, that make up most of the written Japanese language. The display is colourful and exciting, but there is no sign of the familiar western Roman lettering to help the stranger.

Kanji characters are made up of a series of lines, straight and curved, interspersed with a few small circles and other shapes. They are an advanced form of picture writing, with each complete kanji standing for some idea or thing. It is difficult to realize that they do not, in themselves, stand for words, but for specific things, and as such they represent a form of universal writing. For example, if one presented the kanji for a house to a group of Europeans, the English would read it as house, the French as *maison*, the Spanish as *casa*, and the Germans as *haus*. Each group would translate the kanji into a different word, albeit with the same meaning. Since the kanji are an Asian form of writing, their use spreads far beyond Japan. The Chinese, in particular, use the same writing form and indeed are able to read Japanese texts, but in Chinese words, of course. Incidentally, thus universality is of considerable utility to the Chinese, since they have a number of mutually exclusive dialects. Using kanji, they are able to communicate throughout China with a single form of written communication.

There are tens of thousands of individual kanji. I found it almost impossible to identify even the simplest of them. I'm told you should be fluent in about twenty thousand kanji in order to read a daily newspaper. I also understand an educated Japanese learns two new kanji every day of his life. The scope of the problem for the visitor in deciphering the written language is almost insurmountable.

But you find out that they also have two different phonetic alphabets, each with one hundred and twenty relatively simple symbols, each symbol standing for a two-letter sound in Japanese; ka, ki, ko, ku, ke, for example. The two alphabets are known as *hiragana* and *katakana*. They are used for proper names, and "new words" such as anglicisms that might have slipped into the language in the past two centuries. One could become quite encouraged by learning these alphabets. After all, to memorize two sets of one hundred and twenty symbols should be manageable if one considers the alternative of thousands of much more complex kanji. But then you realize that they are used not independently of the main kanji, but interspersed in the whole general mess.

One quickly despairs of learning anything of the written language. However, one ought to be able to learn the spoken language. And indeed, I took language lessons all the time I was in Japan. In the end, I came to believe the major advantage that gave me was the realization that anyone who used that convoluted and confusing language must have thought processes very different than my own. It is a language with severe limitations, having, for example, only the present tense and one past tense. There is no future tense, nor any conditional tenses of any sort. Such ideas must be conveyed in the context of the sentence. "I go to Tokyo tomorrow," for example, conveys the idea of the future tense. This lack of flexibility in the language means it is difficult to convey exact meanings.

This lack of precision in the language has the curious, and, some would say, beneficial, effect of reducing significantly the number of lawyers. Lawyers spend much of their time drawing up documents that are intended to clarify and make the meanings of agreements very precise. With no such precision possible in the language, and also the propensity to do business on the basis of personal commitments and a handshake, there is much less for lawyers to do, and lawyers are thus not nearly so plentiful in Japan as in the West.

There are other barriers to using the spoken language. Japan has been an isolated island nation for millennia. Its people have been completely isolated from the outside world. They are thus intuitively opposed to the idea of other languages. That means that, unlike a European, who will try to understand what a stranger is trying to say, the Japanese has no instinct to attempt to decipher anything he doesn't immediately understand. Japanese imperfectly spoken becomes unintelligible to him. This problem is exacerbated by his ingrown belief that all *gaijin* (foreigners) are somehow inferior and are thus incapable of speaking a complex language like Japanese. They will literally not listen for Japanese from a *gaijin*. I have had the experience, at a large reception, of trying to speak Japanese to several Japanese, only to be greeted by a blank look. When the interpreter assigned to me repeated what I had said, word for word, there was instant understanding. I found it useful to start any attempt to speak Japanese with the word "*sumimasen*," literally, "excuse me." That seems to have the effect of saying, "Pay attention! I am about to speak Japanese." Sometimes that will gain your audience's attention.

Fortunately, many Japanese speak some English. In the engineering field, English is a common language, perhaps enhanced by the fact that computers commonly "speak" English. Japanese does not lend itself easily to a keyboard. In any event, I often found myself conducting conversations in English. Indeed, while I found it useful for my Japanese contacts to know that I was energetically trying to learn Japanese, I came to understand they were just as happy to learn I was having a difficult time with the task. I believe they liked the idea that Japanese is too difficult for a *gaijin*.

In speaking English, the Japanese have a major problem. There are no "l" or "r" sounds in the Japanese language. In speaking English, they conjure up a sound somewhat like someone gargling and use it interchangeably for both r and l. When it comes to writing English, they very frequently choose the wrong letter, using an r where an l should be and vice-versa. One frequently sees things like the popular tee shirt with the words "I ruv New York" emblazoned on it. Indeed, there is a story from the time of the American occupation. General MacArthur became very popular with the Japanese. At one time when he was considering running for the presidency, and his name was entered into the electoral primaries back home, Japanese well-wishers made a huge banner and placed it across the front of his residence. Of course, they managed to interchange the letters in the usual manner. Accordingly, it read, "We play for General MacArthur's erection."

Enough said about language barriers.

AN ISHII-SAN IS ESSENTIAL

Finding one's way around in Japan, and particularly in Tokyo, is extremely difficult. Firstly, there is the language barrier. There are no direction signs in English or any western language. Any location information is likely to be in kanji. Only the major thoroughfares have a name. Smaller streets have no name. And Tokyo is a rabbit's warren of tiny streets and laneways. Addresses are determined by a quite different process, although quite logical in its own Japanese way. Each city block is assigned a number. Then each house is numbered sequentially according to its position on that block. For example, our street address in Seijo was 3-19-13 Seijo, meaning we were the third house in the nineteenth block in the thirteenth section of Seijo. The numbers of the houses directly across the street bore no relation to ours, since they were in a different block and their numbers had started in a different spot in the block. Not surprisingly, it was said that the postman was the only person who knew where everybody lived.

Clearly, this system made finding any address very difficult. And one couldn't simply fall back on taking a taxi and relying on the taxi driver to find the address. If you gave a taxi driver the address of your destination, he would simply sit there and wait for you to direct him to your destination. Often, you even had to select the route. The driver couldn't find the address any more than you could. Most people took the precaution of having a map printed on the back of their business card, showing the location of their home or business. Taxi drivers were adept at utilizing such card-maps.

In spite of these difficulties, I never felt completely lost in Japan. The Japanese seem to have an inbred belief that *gaijins* are somewhat inferior beings, and need careful tending. They take great care to ensure you're never too lost. If you stood on a corner in Tokyo, or anywhere else for that matter, and pulled out a road map, you would soon be surrounded by Japanese, all peering over your shoulder and trying to figure out where you wanted to go. If they can determine that, then some one of them will take you by the hand and lead you there. Which is all very well, but sometimes you get to some startling places.

The thought process might go something like this. "He's a *gaijin*. Where would a *gaijin* standing here want to go? He probably wants a subway station. But which one? Where would he want to go on the subway?

Perhaps to his hotel. There's a big hotel near here on the Omoto Sando line. We'll take him to that station." Which they proceed to do, even though it may be several blocks away. And, all the while, you may be looking for an entirely different station that happened to be just around the corner. However, the intention is good, and most often it works out for the best.

One major headache in Japan is the perpetual traffic jams on virtually every major throughway. They have vastly too many automobiles for the available road system. In Tokyo, the major expressways are elevated four-lane highways. Because they have no shoulders, and thus no possibility of finding your way around any impediment, the slightest accident tends to cause a complete stoppage. And there does not seem to be any off-peak time. We encountered traffic jams at three o'clock in the morning. Indeed, for an extended period, I visited Australia for a week at a time every fifth week. I would fly home on Friday evening, arriving in Tokyo's Narita airport at six o'clock in the morning. Barbara and our driver, Ishii-san, would leave our house at three a.m. for the sixty-kilometre drive to the airport to meet me. Fully half the time, they failed to make it in time because of traffic jams, at that hour of the day. One wonders where all those people were going at that time of day. And this also meant that you couldn't get up on a fine Saturday morning and, on the spur of the moment, decide to get in the car and go somewhere. All you'd succeed in doing would be to get parking space on a long thin parking lot masquerading as a superhighway.

Our solution for easing many of these problems was Ishii-san. With more than my usual foresight, I had persuaded the company that I would need a driver if I were to survive in Tokyo. Ishii-san was the professional chauffeur who acquired us and carefully managed us throughout our stay in Tokyo. I choose those words carefully, because it often appeared that Ishii-san believed we belonged to him and it was up to him to maintain us properly.

Ishii-san would appear at our house about six-thirty in the morning. He looked upon our car as "his" and often seemed to chide Barbara if, on a weekend, she drove the car on an errand. "You've been driving my car," he'd say somewhat accusingly. And he'd be able, from the reading on the odometer, to work out exactly where she'd driven. Only on occasions when the car was in for servicing would he concede some portion of the ownership to me. "Our car is broken," he'd explain.

The first order of the day, before we set out for work, was to wash "his" car. Ishii-san was meticulous about that. I don't know whether there was a law that everyone's car should be clean, but you very seldom saw a dirty car in Japan. It was certainly a matter of pride with Ishii-san that the car was always sparkling clean.

Ishii-san was not an aggressive driver—far from it. But he drove with a certain assurance, as if he were saying, "I'm the driver for Dr. Hamilton. He's the boss. Therefore he's important. This is his car. Therefore this car is important. Other people will know this and will automatically allow this important car first place." It was astonishing to me to see how well this worked. We did seem to be ceded the right of way more often than not.

In the crowded circumstances in which we frequently found ourselves, I was often surprised at the patience of drivers who were constantly battling traffic jams. For example, Ishii-san would take me to a meeting someplace downtown. Most of the downtown streets were just three lanes wide. As they allowed parking on both sides of the street, that left just one lane for traffic. The streets were all one-way as a consequence. Ishii-san would drive down the street until he found the address we were seeking. There would, of course, be no convenient parking space. So he would simply stop in the middle of the street. He'd leisurely get out of the car, and walk around it to open the door for me, first pausing to open his umbrella if it was raining (as it frequently was). He'd then escort me into the building and have a discussion with the concierge, making certain that I was delivered to the person I'd come to see. He'd then return to the car, still parked in the middle of the street. By this time there must have been traffic backed up as far as Yokohama, but there was no angry chorus of honking horns, and no apparent angst from the waiting drivers. There was no sign of road rage as we often find it in North America. Indeed, there seemed to be a stoic, almost cheerful acceptance of the immutable fact that no one, anywhere in Japan, was ever going to get anywhere on the roads in a hurry.

The most amazing thing of all was that when I returned from my meeting an hour later (all meetings seemed to last one hour), Ishii-san, by some magic I never understood, would have our car parked directly in front of the door of the building. He must have used dynamite to selectively clear away the car that had already been parked there.

Ishii-san displayed the same uncanny ability to get the car parked in the ideal position in the chaos at Narita airport when he came to meet me returning from one of my many trips. The parking lot would be completely full when I walked out to the car, but there it would be, as if by magic, in the first row, as close as it could get to the exit gate from the terminal.

There was one occasion when Ishii-san took Barbara and me to the ministry to renew our residence permits, which we had to do once a year. The ministry had a substantial parking lot, but all the spaces nearest the door were inevitably full. Unperturbed, Ishii-san drove steadily towards the door. The last row of parked cars had a sign that must have meant the row was full. Undeterred, Ishii-san turned into the row. There was a policeman guarding the entrance; he held up his hand for us to stop. Ishii-san just kept right on driving steadily towards the door. The policeman leapt out of the way, shaking his fist. Ishii-san simply turned into the walkway leading to the front door of the building, stopped, and helped us out. I left him to somehow placate that policeman. He must have succeeded royally, because when we returned, about an hour later, he had the car parked in the minister's parking slot, right next to the door.

For anyone contemplating living in Tokyo for any period of time, my advice would certainly be to get an Ishii-san. It makes things so much simpler, and provides a certain amount of associated humour as well.

Note that I have described the situation as I knew it in the mid-eighties. Since that time, I understand the Japanese authorities have put up many new signs in English to assist the foreign traveller.

THOSE SHY JAPANESE LADIES

Traditionally, in Japan, the ladies remain at home, and are seldom seen at public events. Japanese men spend a considerable portion of their time enjoying themselves in clubs, bars, and steam baths, and Japanese businessmen are notorious for the time they spend entertaining customers and acquaintances in the evenings. If they can manage it, they spend their weekends playing golf with their friends on exorbitantly expensive golf courses. But they would never think of including their wives in any such activities. Indeed, no. The traditional place of any woman is in the home. There she manages the house, raises the children, does the shopping, and prepares the meals. She may occasionally meet with other ladies in the neighbourhood, but rarely ventures far from her home. The result is that, while she may rule supreme at home, she is very likely to seem very shy and retiring when you meet her. Indeed, even the "modern" girls working in offices all seem to have the habit of shyly holding their hand in front of their face when speaking to you, and of tittering inexplicably behind their hands.

However, the good Japanese wife does make certain that, no matter what time or in what condition her husband returns home at night, he departs for work the next morning in good order. It is even whispered that many wives confiscate their husband's paycheque, and from that they give their husband only a limited allowance for his lunch. (These males must bless the invention of the credit card.) Thus, while they may be shy and retiring, the ladies appear to rule at home.

When I first arrived in Japan, and had taken possession of my modest (I thought) house in the suburbs, I asked one of my Japanese friends in the office what the custom was for meeting my neighbours. Should I wait for them to call and introduce themselves, or should I call on them? I was told that the Japanese custom would be to take a small gift and call at the doors of my neighbours to introduce myself. I later learned that there is a specific type of rice that is traditionally given as an introductory gift, but I wasn't told that. Instead, I procured some picture books of Canada, wrapped them neatly, and set out to meet my neighbours. My *giftos* seemed to be quite acceptable, even if not edible. (The Japanese often make Japanese words out of English words simply by adding "o.") I was a little concerned that my Japanese was pretty rudimentary, but hoped to get by on good luck and the fact that Japanese are particularly polite to foreigners, treating them as guests in their country.

I need not have worried. Most of the people who answered the doors in my neighbourhood spoke quite acceptable English, and seemed to accept my small gift in the spirit I intended.

But it was the shy and retiring Japanese ladies that surprised me when I met them at their own front doors. Typically the conversation ran something like this.

"Oh, you're Mr. Hamilton!" (They all seemed to know my name and who I was.) "And you live in that big house down the road?"

Once I had replied to that first sally, the lady would continue, "Are you married?" I would explain that my wife had died the year previously.

"Oh, that's too bad. Are you here all alone? That's too big a house for one person. Have you any children?"

When I answered that I had four daughters, there was the immediate question, "Why isn't one of them here looking after you?"

I guess the idea of a man looking after himself seemed outlandish and perhaps even dangerous to them. I'd explain that all of my daughters had careers of their own, also an idea that, in retrospect, I suppose they had difficulty in understanding.

Then, "Where do you work?" I'd explain my position as president of Northern Telecom in Japan. That seemed to reassure them somewhat. Perhaps it was an acceptable position for one of their neighbours.

"Will you get married again?" When I said that, yes, I planned to remarry, that seemed to please them. It apparently made me fit better into their ideas of what is right and proper.

But it was the last series of questions that really surprised me. "Do you have a maid?" And indeed I had a daily maid who kept the house for me. I said, "Yes, I do."

Then came the final question. I never did figure out what answer was expected. They all asked, "What does she do for you?"

I leave their thoughts on that subject to your imagination.

So there you have it. A Japanese housewife, on meeting a stranger at her door, proceeds, in the course of a five-minute conversation, to develop a complete dossier on her new neighbour, gathering information it would take even the most forward and progressive Canadian housewife at least five years to amass. Don't give me shy and retiring.

GOLF IS A PASSION

I have already described how the proper Japanese man spends his days in business and his evenings with his friends. He has his wife sequestered in their home, where she manages the house without thought of joining him in any of his activities.

When you first meet Japanese men, you notice their obvious priorities. The conversation is usually a series of questions, in a very significant order.

"Do you play golf?"

If your answer is in the affirmative, the next question is, "Do you drink whisky?"

Finally, "What's your name?" I don't know whether they even asked the third question if you didn't give an affirmative answer to the first two.

Nearly every Japanese man will tell you he plays golf. It's said that eighty-five percent of all Japanese men claim to play golf. But there is a great shortage of land in Japan. Very little of it can be dedicated to golf courses. The land that is made into golf courses comes from an exorbitantly expensive real estate market. Consequently, membership in a golf course is monumentally expensive. A corollary to that is that, of the eighty-five percent who state they play golf, only fifteen percent ever get to actually play on a golf course in Japan.

But do rest play golf? They certainly do. They play golf at driving ranges. Frequently, a driving range is constructed on one city block, not infrequently on a roof. The entire area, including the top, is enclosed by high fences or nets. Such a driving range may have several tiers of tees, one above the other, which leads me to wonder what happens when the occasional "player" over-swings and loses his balance while hitting from one of the upper tees.

Many of those driving ranges are private clubs, some having all the amenities of a full-sized golf course, with locker rooms, bars, and restaurants. Thus, the Japanese man who "plays golf" in all probability belongs to a driving range club. And a distinct culture has developed around those clubs. There was one near our house. On a Saturday or Sunday morning, I would see the "members" walking by on their way to the club. They would be all dressed up in their golfing clothes, every bit as garish as some of the outfits worn at our country clubs, and each would carry his "golf bag," a slimmed-down version of a golf bag designed to hold a single club. Because, you see, that's all you'd need to play golf at that club.

But the stories we've all heard about the astronomical cost of golf in Japan are quite true. I was invited by a friend to play golf at his club. He was one of the fifteen percent. I was delighted by the invitation, even though it meant leaving home at six in the morning in order to reach the golf course in time for a 9:30 starting time. Of course, the club was located on land that was outside the district of extremely expensive land around Tokyo. That meant it was in the foothills of the central mountain chain, and, in Japanese driving conditions, a good three hours' drive from the city. I noticed that the arrangements to play were made well in advance, as much as six weeks ahead of time.

But, setting aside the distance to be travelled, and the long lead time of the invitation, the club itself, when I reached it, had every possible amenity. A lady caddie met my car at the curb, addressed me by name, instructed me to proceed "that way" to the men's locker room, and made off with my clubs. When I reached the locker room, it was to find my name on a plaque on a most luxurious locker. When our party emerged, ready to play, the lady caddie was waiting with all four sets of clubs mounted on a small, electric cart. It turned out that we would walk the course, and the cart would follow us around, guided by a cable buried just beneath the grass at one side of the fairway and that apparently emitted some sort of radio signal that guided the cart around the course. The cart was started and stopped by a remote control operated by the caddie. She herself worked very hard, running from the cart to wherever your ball came to rest, bringing you the necessary club with which to continue your assault on par (or in my case, the somewhat higher numbers). It took her very little time to assess her players and to accurately predict the club you would expect. Note I do not say "need"; in my case, I usually "needed" a small cannon.

The course itself was spectacular, set as it was in the foothills and thus presenting challenging rolling fairways. It was in excellent condition, and furthermore was lavishly provided with gardens and flower beds, rivalling the floral displays we see at the Augusta National course when the Masters' tournament is played. After all, that's what a golf course is supposed to look like, isn't it?

When we finished (or perhaps I should say, when the course was finished with us), we repaired to the immense clubhouse for a soak in a steaming communal tub in typical Japanese fashion. We then had a fine lunch, during which I gathered some of the financial aspects of membership. The Japanese are quite proud of their memberships in prestigious clubs and not at all backward about discussing the costs. It was explained that a prerequisite of membership was to own a share in the club. The shares of that club are traded on the Tokyo stock exchange, and at that time were trading at about the equivalent of one and a half million US dollars each. My friend noted casually that he owned seven shares as an investment. Golf club developers in North America should be so lucky.

However, it turned out that once the first hurdle of share ownership was passed, the annual dues were only about $2,500 US; not at all extravagant, I thought. But then I learned that having paid the fee, one was entitled to little more than to come through the clubhouse door. Members were charged green fees of about $100 US per round for themselves and considerably more for their guests. All in all, my delightful and memorable day of golf cost my host something quite a bit in excess of a thousand US dollars.

It's no wonder that whole planeloads of Japanese golfers regularly descend on Hawaii and the west coast of North America to play golf. A round trip such as that, including the airfare and several rounds of golf, would be much more economical than the costs of a similar outing in Japan. And it is easy to see why so many Japanese business trips to North America include a day or two of golf, often at a cost that would seem extravagant to us. You must remember the frame of reference they have for what passes for "expensive" in the world of golf.

Some years ago, a golfing friend of mine made arrangements to play at a prestigious club in Georgia. When his foursome was assembled and ready to play, they paid a visit to the pro shop, probably to register for play. My friend asked the attendant for a box of balls. The assistant apologized that he had no balls available. When told that was a most peculiar way to run a railroad, not to have golf balls for sale at a golf club, he explained that the club was normally well stocked with all forms of golf equipment. But earlier that day, they had received a request to allow a group of distinguished Japanese businessmen to play. And since it was a slow day, they had agreed, contrary to their normal practice which would have involved, at the very least, negotiations concluded well in advance.

In due course, a large bus appeared and disgorged about fifty enthusiastic Japanese businessmen, all in their "uniform" of dark blue business suits. It seemed the golfing excursion had been hurriedly planned when a long-scheduled meeting was cancelled. Such was their enthusiasm for this round of golf, that each one of those Japanese businessmen then purchased a full set of clubs, golf slacks and shirt, golf cap, gloves, at least one pair of golf shoes, and of course, a more than adequate supply of balls. I'm sure that golf pro was delighted at this unexpected boost to his cash flow; maybe he even thought he'd died and gone to Heaven. But it had left his shop absolutely denuded of essentials such as golf clothes, clubs, balls, and tees.

Isn't it a pity we don't all run businesses that can attract the occasional visit of a busload of enthusiastic Japanese businessmen.

THE INEVITABLES

Historically, the Japanese were an isolated island race who rarely ventured beyond the shores of Japan. Indeed, for much of their history, they were forbidden by their rulers to travel outside the country. I believe there was some idea of preventing Japanese culture from becoming contaminated by outside influences. (I know of some Canadian politicians who claim to be exercised today by similar concerns about preserving cultures.) Even after the country was opened up by the USA in the latter part of the nineteenth century, travel abroad for Japanese was most unusual.

And then, along came a great war, which brought about the destruction of much of Japan, and was a severe shock to the culture.

Out of that catastrophe grew a renewed Japan, much stronger in its industry, and with a burgeoning economy. This was achieved at the price of enormous effort and sacrifice by all Japanese. The Japanese economy became one of the largest and wealthiest in the world. However, this isn't reflected in the standard of living of the average Japanese, even though wages and salaries were among the highest in the world. As I've noted earlier, prices for everything from real estate to groceries are extremely high. The result is that the average Japanese wasn't living as well as might be expected, and, because of space limitations, there was little he could purchase to improve his well being.

But they soon discovered one thing they could do: they could travel. Travel anywhere else in the world appears to them to be a bargain because prices are so much lower than in Japan. And there were no longer any restrictions on travel outside Japan. Soon, a flood of Japanese tourists appeared, almost as if by magic, in nearly every country of the world. Within a few years, you met them everywhere you went. One of my friends dubbed them "the Inevitables," since you inevitably encountered them anywhere you went. In recent years over ten percent of the population of Japan has, each year, joined the flood of Inevitables around the world.

The Inevitables have some key characteristics. They rarely travel alone; indeed, the genus Tourist-Japanese generally appears in flocks of up to fifty people, led by a flag- bearing guide. The group nearly always has some distinguishing mark or sign; frequently they even have a uniform, or jackets or hats supplied by the tour agency. At the very least, each carries a carryall with the symbol of the group emblazoned on it. All Inevitables invariably carry a camera, which they use enthusiastically to record their adventures and their presence in familiar tourist spots. Often, you can't get a clear view of some key site, a statue or a building, because of the crowd of Inevitables snapping pictures. Indeed, they'll sometimes line up for their turn to stand in a selected spot, in order to each take the identical photo of a specific scene.

I once observed their passion for uniformity gone seriously awry. We were staying in a large, modern hotel in Zurich, Switzerland. It was a hotel that catered to guided tours. We've all seen these groups being shepherded into or out of hotels, often at what seems to me to be ungodly hours. But such trips are efficient, economical, and often very enjoyable. The roads in Europe in summer are full of tour buses.

Our hotel accommodated such tours, and often had a dozen or more buses arrive at the peak hours between five and six o'clock in the evening. That obviously posed some serious organizational problems. But the Swiss are nothing if not efficient. The technique adopted was to have the tour operator provide, in advance, a list of all the tourists on the bus. When the bus arrived, the hotel had all the room keys laid out on a table in the lobby, each assigned to an individual or couple. The tourists collected their keys and went directly to their rooms. In the meantime, the luggage was unloaded from the bus by a team of bellboys. Each bag had a nametag, and the luggage was delivered to the rooms based on those nametags and the prearranged list of room occupants. This system worked extremely well and efficiently, although it does explain why the poor tourists, when leaving, are often coerced into having their bags outside their room doors for collection before six-thirty in the morning.

I happened to be standing near the door one evening when a busload of Japanese Inevitables arrived. I suppose this bus came directly from the airport and this was the first stop for that particular tour. Fifty-two Japanese gentlemen, all about five feet two inches tall, and each wearing a brightly coloured jacket provided by the tour, disembarked from the bus and went into the hotel. So far, so good. But when the boys came to unload the luggage, the luggage compartment was found to contain fifty-two identical, aluminum suitcases, each with a nametag—written in kanji. They were, of course, completely indecipherable to the bellhops. When last seen, the team was standing there completely baffled.

One of my friends has since suggested that, in the face of such uniformity, the best solution would be to assume even further uniformity. One could assume that the contents of each suitcase would also be identical, thereby allowing the luggage to be distributed without any worry about the identity of the recipient.

Because prices abroad seem to him to be so low, the Japanese tourist will patronize the most expensive boutiques and purchase the most expensive items. He insists on paying top dollar in order to be able to display his purchases from abroad as authentic trophies. And, in addition, there is no tradition of bargaining in Japan. This is completely contrary to the usual practices in cities with a basically Chinese culture, such as Hong Kong and Singapore. In those cities, each and every transaction is the subject of extensive negotiation and haggling. Indeed, any shopkeeper in those cities would be very disappointed if he didn't have the entertainment of a stiff negotiation. He has added respect for a customer who is a good haggler.

When the secretaries from our Tokyo office took a vacation in Hong Kong or Singapore, we would always have them visit our offices in those places. And the Chinese secretaries would try to entertain their Japanese visitors. As girls will, their thoughts turned immediately to shopping. But the Chinese hosts rapidly became confused. They would offer to take their visitors to local outlets where they could purchase items bearing the labels of prestigious Parisian and Roman couturiers. Most of the goods sold by such firms were actually made in factories in the Far East. Naturally, Chinese entrepreneurs quickly found ways of obtaining merchandise from the same factories, and even from the same production lots, but at vastly reduced prices. The goods were in all respects identical. But the Japanese girls could not be convinced. They insisted on going to the boutiques operated by the couturiers themselves, where they paid at least double the price. However, when they got home, they could always talk about the time they visited Chanel or Gucci.

Talk about cultural differences.

> I believe these "Inevitables" played a major role in the breakdown of the Japanese economy, which has occurred in the past decade. I understand that major Western retailers have broken into the Japanese market, and, in so doing, are well on the way to breaking down the expensive and inefficient internal distribution system. That, in turn, has had a major effect on the traditional full employment in Japan. And I believe that has happened because the Inevitables have demanded access to bargains and pricing similar to what they encountered abroad.

NORWEGIAN COLONELS MAKE GREAT CUSTOMERS

By the beginning of the sixties, I had become the head of the telecommunications laboratories of Canadian Marconi Company. That laboratory was devoted to the development of microwave radio relay equipment. Initially, it concentrated on high-performance, long haul commercial equipment, but by the sixties, it had changed its focus to the development of a battlefield radio relay system, which carried the US army designation of AN/GRC 103. It represented one of the earliest applications of digital technology, more than a decade before that technology became viable for commercial application. The equipment became the standard of the US army, which purchased tens of thousands of units, and deployed it throughout the world.

We believed the GRC 103 could find application in the armies of most countries, and to that end, my friend Bill, who was a vice-president of Canadian Marconi, and I, undertook to introduce it to as many countries as possible. For some years, we travelled, together and separately, several times a year, to Europe. We visited most of the military authorities and government offices of all the countries in Europe. In those travels, I visited the Scandinavian countries many times. I came to like the citizens of these rocky northern countries very much, and particularly the Norwegians. Of course, I could have been influenced by the fact that the Norwegians gave me the first orders of my international business career.

My favourite customer was the Colonel. At that time, he was the head of the Signal Corps of the Norwegian Army, and I counted him as both a good friend and a good customer.

I should explain that the Norwegian Army, in my experience, was somewhat different from most armies of the day. For one thing, it had no generals. The highest rank was colonel, and my friend was one of the higher-ranking colonels. And the army was unionized; all the enlisted men and, I believe, most of the officers belonged to a union, which had surprising powers. For example, contrary to normal military practice as I've encountered it elsewhere, anyone could refuse an assignment that he didn't fancy. This resulted in some of the key northern observation bases being under the command of non-commissioned officers, because no one in the officer's corps would agree to accept the assignment. And yet, I was told that discipline in the army was excellent. They were particularly proud of their ability to operate in the cold, bitter climate of the interior and north of the country and the deep snow they often encountered. Perhaps this was the result of a Viking heritage. Maybe we could learn something here.

The Colonel was a dapper man, always well dressed. He was perhaps fifteen years older than me, and slightly shorter in stature. But he could easily tire me out simply by walking down the street at his normal walking pace, which seemed designed to keep any fleeing enemy in sight. And while walking at this extraordinary pace, he could carry on extended conversations, just as if this was the norm for everyone. I would be completely exhausted after such a walk with him. Somehow he kept himself in excellent physical condition. And I must note that, while he displayed (as often as possible) a very hard Viking head for alcohol, I never saw him the worse for wear in the slightest.

As the Colonel was a good customer, we often had occasion to have dinner together, frequently with some of our colleagues. Before dinner, we always had several drinks. That would be followed by a more than adequate supply of wine at dinner. After dessert was served, and we were all feeling mellow, the Colonel would lean back, survey the assembled company, and say, "Now I think we should have some of those light French wines." By that he meant the derivatives of wines, as distilled by cognac-makers such as Courvoisier, Martell, or Remy Martin. He seemed able to consume them as freely as the more normal varieties of wines. Perhaps this was a taste passed down by his Viking forbears. Maybe they never distinguished between the various products of the French liquor industry of their day. Certainly the Colonel's taste for "light French wines" was highly developed.

MY NORWEGIAN SKIING TRIP

The Norwegian army placed a substantial order with us, and in the course of negotiating that order I visited Oslo a number of times. In those days, Norway was the acknowledged leader in the supply of "proper" cross-country skiing equipment. Indeed, they may well have been the only source of good cross-country skis and boots. Certainly in Canada, while cross-country skiing was very popular, with many devotees, we normally used ordinary hickory skis and heavy, only slightly flexible, boots, with little to distinguish them from the equipment used in those days in downhill skiing. The modern craze for specialized and highly developed equipment for each form of skiing had not yet become apparent to any but the most sophisticated skiers. However, I had somehow become aware that the Norwegians had much superior equipment, and decided to buy some of their cross-country boots for my wife and myself. And they certainly were superior, being much lighter and more flexible. We enjoyed skiing with them very much.

At some time during one of our dinners together, I must have mentioned to the Colonel that I had purchased these boots and how much we enjoyed them. That may have been a polite thing to do, but it was to prove most unwise. For the Colonel, like most Norwegians I know, was a most avid and, I would guess, accomplished lang laufer or cross-country skier, and he apparently filed my remarks away in his formidable memory.

The contract with the Norwegians called for regular meetings of the Project Steering Committee, of which both the Colonel and I were members. Frequently, when the subject matter was not too important, neither the Colonel nor I would attend, leaving the meetings to the other members. However, there came an occasion when, for some reason long forgotten now, I needed to attend. As the meeting was to be held in Norway on that occasion, I sent a message to the Colonel that I would be coming to Norway. He promptly replied that we would hold the meeting in the Signal Corps headquarters, in Lillehamer (which, some years later, became familiar to the whole world as a small village deep in the interior of Norway, where they held the Winter Olympics). I believed the Colonel wanted to hold the meetings on "his own ground," so to speak, where he could entertain me and act the host with the support of his own organization.

Shortly thereafter, there came a message from our company agent in Oslo that I should bring my ski boots, as the Colonel wanted to take me skiing. With considerable misgivings, and remembering the Colonel's undoubted prowess in this sport, I included in my bag my boots (those lovely, lightweight boots that now seemed likely to be my undoing) and some heavier, outdoor clothes.

When I arrived in Oslo, I was not encouraged to be told that the Colonel thought we should jointly inspect the microwave test link over which our equipment was being tested. He planned to ski the length of the route and back, a total distance of some fifty miles. I was horrified at the prospect.

We set off to drive to Lillehamer, in a car equipped, so I was told, with studded tires. These were a novelty for me, but I was glad we had them, as the road seemed narrow and extremely slippery and the surrounding snow very deep. We drove through the blackest of black nights, for while Scandinavia has very long days in summer, it also has correspondingly short days in winter. As we drove, it became colder and colder; they told me the temperature was dropping and might get to forty below zero. (Fahrenheit or Centigrade, it doesn't matter; at that temperature, it's the same, and cold enough to freeze the private parts off a brass monkey, as they say.) I remember our agent made a hero of himself by producing a bottle of cognac, "for purposes of frost prevention" while we travelled.

When we arrived in Lillehamer, it was indeed forty below zero, and we were grateful to get indoors into the well-heated buildings of the base.

Those meetings went on for three days, and throughout that time the temperature stayed determinedly (and mercifully, from my point of view) at forty degrees below zero. For I soon discovered it was quite safe, when we had some free time, to say brightly, "Wouldn't this be a good time to go skiing?"

Someone was sure to say, "Oh, don't be silly. You'd freeze out there in five minutes. Sit down and have another drink."

Towards the end of the meetings, the Colonel did take us for a drive around the district, and we did step out of the cars briefly to view a ski resort. However, I managed to escape the necessity of gasping my way in the Colonel's wake as we had our "little ski around."

A MEAL FIT FOR A KING

The Colonel and I shared many good dinners together. One of the most memorable was during my visit to the Signal Corps headquarters, in Lillehamer. During that visit, he even gave me some indication that he respected my knowledge of food, beverages, and places to eat.

The Colonel announced that we would have a dinner in the officers' club. He also explained that since the army had a union, we would see enlisted men in the "officers' Club," as all ranks were allowed the use of the club. While that may have seemed a bit quaint to me, it certainly didn't interfere with the Colonel's dinner arrangements, nor his ability to give us an excellent meal.

As I remember it, we were shown into a dining room with the table set with fine linen, crystal, china, and elaborate silver. And the food matched this display. We started with *gravlax*, a special Norwegian dish consisting of salmon cured by burying it in the ashes of a wood fire, and served in thin slices with a fine mustard sauce. This was followed by reindeer steaks. Needless to say, the Colonel provided excellent liquid accompaniments. And the meal finished with a dish containing "cloudberries," berries that are similar to blueberries, but which grow on the inhospitable, rocky hillsides of the interior of Norway. Often, cloudberries are quite bitter, but these were as sweet as strawberries. It was explained that they had been picked especially for the Colonel by the club staff the previous summer and carefully preserved. It seemed that at least one officer had retained some privileges in that unionized army.

When the meal was finished, the Colonel turned to me with a very serious expression, and asked my opinion of the meal. I was somewhat surprised at his question but assured him I had greatly enjoyed the dinner and the company.

"But aren't there any suggestions you could make to improve it the next time?"

I denied any ideas for any improvements. He persisted with his questions yet another time, until I asked him why he was asking all these questions. He then explained that they would be holding the Norwegian National Biathalon championships at the base the next week, and the King of Norway would be coming to act as a referee. Biathalon is a combination of cross-country skiing and rifle shooting invented by Scandinavian military men—not as strange a combination as you might at first think, given the military role likely to be required of Scandinavian armies. The biathalon became familiar to Canadians only recently with the outstanding success of Canadian Miriam Bedard in this sport at the 1994 Olympics.

And the point of all the questions was that the meal I had had was the same meal they intended to give the king. I was part of a "practice run."

I was most flattered that they should choose me as their trial horse, and I have always remembered that I was given a meal "fit for a king."

SHRIMP CAN INFLUENCE YOUR REPUTATION

The Scandinavians are, historically, a seafaring race. The sea surrounds them. It's hardly surprising, then, that their diet leans heavily on fish and sea products. Indeed, one might say they're specialists in seafood. They've invented countless ways to prepare and eat seafood.

Fairly early in my travels, I learned about the astonishing number of delicious ways they've invented to prepare the lowly herring. Someone once told me there are over seventy standard ways to prepare herring, starting, of course with raw herring, and proceeding on from there. And every one is delicious; yes, even raw herring. Mind you, it helps to have a glass of ice-cold aquavit on hand before you start. Aquavit is the Scandinavian response to the German schnapps, or the Russian vodka, except it more closely resembles unreconstructed rocket fuel than the others. Nevertheless, a shot of aquavit beforehand certainly helps you get started when faced, for the first time, with raw herring.

I have a theory, which I attempt to verify at any and all opportunities, that the national drink of any country is designed specifically to match the particular atmosphere and conditions of the home country. For example, I maintain that when in the damp, gloomy atmosphere of Holland, there's nothing tastes as good as a Geneva gin, a common drink in the Netherlands. But don't offer me one when I'm anywhere else. Then it tastes like crankcase oil. And so with aquavit—it tastes best when facing a plate of herring, and the herring are the better for it.

But to return to the number and variety of herring, not to mention other seafood. I remember being taken to a country inn in Sweden, where they had a famous *smorresbrod*, which translates to "butter and bread," but is anything but. It is often a most elaborate buffet table, consisting entirely of delicious snacks, which I suppose, if you really wanted to, you could consume along with bread and butter. We were taken into a large dining room. And the *maître d'hôtel* was at great pains to apologize profusely for the paucity of the spread on that particular day. It seemed they had neither smoked salmon nor gravlax, which deeply pained him. We would just have to content ourselves with herring. This proved to be no serious drawback, since there were, by actual count, fifty-two varieties of herring dishes on the table. It would have taken a strong man and a real trencherman to eat his way through that display.

When I was young, growing up in Montreal, you rarely saw any of the more exotic seafood. As a boy, I can only remember white sea fish such as cod, halibut, and sole fillets. Once or twice in later life, I'd had a shrimp cocktail, made in the North American fashion, with a few large shrimp perched around the edge of a glass similar to a sundae glass, and filled with seafood sauce. I don't think I ever thought about it, but I might have imagined shrimp came from the sea already prepared in that form. Thus, I was fascinated, one day in Stockholm, to see tiny North Sea shrimp served in their shells. I had to try that right away. I soon had a bowl filled with pretty, pink shellfish, which I then had to learn to remove from their shells. I must say those shells are not designed for optimum ease of removal. But then, I don't suppose that is, in any way, a priority requirement for the shrimp in their natural habitat, which explains this oversight in their natural evolution. The shrimp, eaten thus at a table at a sidewalk café, proved delicious.

Later that afternoon, we flew over to Oslo as we had planned, arriving at our hotel fairly late in the evening. So late, in fact, that we decided we'd better have dinner in the very elegant main dining room of the hotel. When the waiter came to learn our choices from the most elaborate menu, I noted they didn't list any shrimp, but I asked him if perhaps they could offer some. He regarded me doubtfully, but, after some consultation with the kitchen, he agreed they had enough shrimp to make me a meal. And the shrimp came in a huge mound, all carefully arranged in tiers. I don't know how many there were, but there must have been hundreds. I set out to devour them, in a perfect orgy of peeling and eating. The mound of shells removed from the delectable morsels grew and grew. As I remember it, I enjoyed the shrimp immensely, but was quite unable to consume them all.

The next evening, we were to entertain the Colonel, which we considered a signal honour, since Norwegian officers at home in Norway rarely accept invitations from suppliers. We decided the occasion demanded that we take him to the same elegant dining room. We were seated almost directly across the great dining room from the table we had had the night before. And we had a different waiter. I was still fascinated with shrimp, and again I asked if I could have fresh shrimp, even though they weren't on the menu.

"Oh, I'm sorry, Sir," replied the waiter with a look of some distaste on his face. "There was a gentleman last evening—he sat right over there—who ate all we had!" I gained the distinct impression that he did not approve of anyone shelling shrimp in his most elegant dining room. Perhaps it was my technique in shelling, or perhaps I shouldn't have dropped quite so many shells on the floor.

I later learned that in Scandinavia, the shrimp are boiled immediately they are caught, right on board the shrimp boat. That undoubtedly contributes to their excellent flavour. Further, I found that in Oslo, you could go down to the harbourfront, to the sparkling clean seafront steps in behind the town hall. There you can buy a lunch of fresh-caught boiled shrimp, right from the fisherman. If you have a lovely, sunny day in Oslo, that's one of the nicest lunches I know of anywhere.

WORKING AT BECOMING A GOURMET
AND TO THINK, I WAS ONCE A PICKY EATER

I was a picky eater—my mother said so. Frequently. Some of it was her fault. She was always trying to persuade me to eat a lot of things that were "good for me," including such delicacies as boiled parsnip and overcooked liver. And, like President George Bush Sr., I never developed much of a love affair with broccoli. But I must admit that I wasted the first twenty years of my life being very particular and finicky about what I ate. Why, I graduated from university weighing less than 140 pounds! Then, one evening, I was introduced to a Chinese restaurant by a group of my colleagues in graduate school. I never looked back. I hadn't realized the great variety, the wonderful tastes, and the different ambiences that were out there to be sampled. And in Montreal, which had a well-deserved reputation as a gourmet's paradise, there was ample scope for me to explore the delights of eating and drinking.

When I reached a position where I was required to entertain customers, I was delighted, and eagerly extended my knowledge of restaurants, developing a list of establishments suitable for any type of occasion. I didn't become this shape for nothing.

Then I started to travel extensively in Europe, in an effort to market the military, tactical, radio relay equipment we had developed. The opportunities to explore new restaurants, new pubs, and new cuisines multiplied greatly. I could always use the excuse that this was "research" I needed to do, in case I ever needed to entertain a customer. I used to keep a list of my favourite restaurants and pubs in Europe, for the use of my friends and colleagues. I had it made up into a small, mimeographed booklet, complete with codes indicating the types of food, price levels, ambiance, and so on. It turned out to be a very useful sales aid.

For example, a friend who was familiar with the booklet would call to say his boss was going to Europe and was asking advice about restaurants. Often, these senior people were relatively inaccessible in the normal course of events, but I could always gain access on the pretext of delivering one of my booklets. I found that most people welcome reliable information on the care and feeding of their tummies, particularly when they are in strange places. And they often remember favourably the provider of such information. Many lifelong friendships grew out of that little book.

The day I started work at Northern Telecom (Northern Electric in those days), in 1972, I was visited in my new office by one of the senior vice-presidents. I was very flattered. They certainly made sure a newcomer was made to feel wanted. I thought it an excellent omen for my new career. But then I found out he just wanted a new, updated copy of my booklet to replace the one he'd obtained years before.

In the following pages, I will describe some of my experiences and adventures in restaurants and pubs all over the world. I've had many such happy occasions, more than most people, I dare say. I've received surprisingly good service so consistently that I've come to believe I'm charmed in restaurant circles. Perhaps it's because of the enthusiasm and anticipated enjoyment with which I habitually approach a restaurant. And perhaps it's because I respect the crafts of the restauranteur and the waiters. I believe that you receive better treatment if you're visibly enjoying the experience. People like their efforts to be appreciated and reciprocate in kind when their efforts are clearly enjoyed. Perhaps you can determine more reasons for my consistent success as you read of my adventures.

MEMBERSHIP HELPS

Sometimes it's because you go there frequently, sometimes it's by accident, and sometimes it's because of some incident, that you become well known in a particular watering place. But one way or another, you gain what I call "membership" in certain restaurants and pubs. This brings with it a higher level of enjoyment, a special sense of well being or belonging. You have a sense of familiarity, as if you are among friends. You're often treated by the staff as one of the family.

For example, Jean and I were travelling through Provence, in France, by car. It was early in the '70s and we were on one of our regular European vacations. We had no particular itinerary, and were just following our instincts and stopping wherever we pleased. We reached Aix-en-Provence in late afternoon and decided to treat ourselves to the town's three-star hotel, the George IV. Once installed in a nice, spacious room, we started to think about dinner. My practice has always been to consult the available experts, and in this case there was one. The hotel boasted a jolly looking and certainly well-fed *concierge*. After some discussion, during which he loyally proposed the hotel's own restaurant, he was persuaded to recommend a small restaurant within easy walking distance. He warned that this was a new restaurant, just being started by two students of the legendary Père Bocuse, recognized as the father of the famous *La Nouvelle Cuisine Francaise*. This revolutionary change called for much more moderate portions, healthier foods, lighter sauces, and more attention to the presentation of the dishes, in order to enhance the attraction to both the taste buds and to the eye. The concierge stated he hadn't actually tried the restaurant himself but had heard very good reports.

We took his advice and enjoyed an excellent meal of the best lamb I've ever tasted.

When we returned to the hotel, the concierge was off duty, but in the morning, before we left, I made a point of reporting to him that this was an excellent restaurant. We fell into conversation, and he recommended several places to visit in Provence. Then, when he discovered we came from Montreal, he reached behind him into a pigeonhole and produced a business card, telling me this was for a restaurant in Montreal, operated by an old friend. It seemed his own son had worked there for a while before moving on to Toronto. We would be certain to get a good meal there when we returned to Montreal. I looked at the card, read "Chez Pierre," and said, "You're not going to believe this, but we had dinner at Chez Pierre the night before we left Montreal on this trip!" And indeed we had, on the recommendation of a friend.

He snatched back the card and wrote a few words on the back, telling me to give that to Pierre along with his regards when next we visited that restaurant.

And we did, with the result that Pierre spent most of that evening sitting and chatting at our table. Needless to say, the food was outstanding, and the service was excellent. And any time we returned after that, we were treated as long-lost friends.

Pierre has since retired several times, and subsequently reopened another restaurant somewhere else in Montreal. I think the last time I looked he was up to Chez Pierre IV. I haven't had the chance to visit him for some time, but I'm sure I'd still be welcomed as a good friend, although I doubt Pierre remembers that connection with his friend in Aix, and the reason he remembers me as a friend. You see, I've become a member of his restaurant.

On another occasion, on a snowy Sunday evening, in the mid-sixties, I had taken a guest to old Montreal, only to be embarrassed that the restaurant I had chosen was closed for that night. What to do? Then we walked past Le Saint Amable, a restaurant I'd seen reviewed in the newspaper. It looked very nice, in an old stone house that had been renovated and seemed to glow as a result of its refurbishing. We decided to try it, and when we went in were given the last available table. We were glad we went in, because we had an excellent meal and good service. We enjoyed the warm, friendly ambiance they'd created.

When the bill came, it seemed too little, and I was able to point out that they'd forgotten to charge for a bottle of wine. Of course they were duly appreciative, but I soon forgot the incident. However, they did not, and the next time I went to that restaurant, the wine was "on the house." And thereafter, I was always treated as a special customer in that restaurant, although I doubt that, with the passage of time, they remembered the reason. Again, I had become a member.

It's nice to enter a restaurant and be greeted as a friend rather than just a customer. However, there are occasions when it's very helpful just to be recognized.

I had a good friend who was an executive in the New York offices of a major American cable supplier. Whenever he visited Montreal, or I visited New York, we would meet over lunch or dinner. On this occasion, I was visiting New York to attend the IRE convention (The Institute of Radio Engineers, whose week-long convention was the largest and most important in our industry in those days). When I called Ken, he immediately invited me to lunch, and named "his restaurant," La Saleil, near Forty-sixth Street and Sixth Avenue.

Ken had asked me to arrive at noon, but when I arrived, the lunchtime crowd was only beginning to come in, and there was no sign of Ken. However, as soon as I walked in the door, the headwaiter came forward, and said, "Dr. Hamilton, Mr. Wyatt just called and he has been delayed. He asked if you would take a seat, and have a drink while you wait."

He showed me to a table and brought me a drink. I was very impressed that he had recognized me, particularly when customers were arriving in increasing numbers; this was a very busy restaurant. The headwaiter was kept very busy greeting his clients. I noticed he addressed most of them by name.

After about twenty minutes, when there was a pause, the headwaiter returned to my table to ask if I needed anything. I asked him how he could possibly pick me out of such a crowd of customers and greet me by name when he'd never seen me before. He replied, "Oh, that was easy. You see, I know pretty nearly everyone who comes in here regularly. All I had to do was look for someone alone, that I didn't know. That had to be you."

In due course, Ken showed up and we enjoyed an excellent meal together.

Several days later, at the convention, I invited several clients and friends to lunch. A couple of them wanted to go to a restaurant in the Time-Life building, which featured Mexican food. This restaurant was enjoying a wave of popularity at the time, and we decided to try it. However, there was the drawback that they would not accept reservations and you had to line up to be seated, on a first-come, first-served basis. By the time I had marshalled all of my guests and got them to the restaurant, the lineup waiting for tables stretched to New Jersey; well, at least well past the front door. We decided it would take too long, and we'd have to go somewhere else. But where? That was the question.

I thought of the friendly reception and good meal I'd had at La Saleil, and said, "I know a good restaurant within walking distance."

And so it was that I led our group up to the front door of that pleasant restaurant, hoping they'd have room for us at this busy hour. I needn't have worried. As we went through the front door, the headwaiter came forward, took my hand, and said, "Dr. Hamilton. It's so good to see you again."

With those few words, that friendly waiter with the knack of remembering faces and names enormously increased my reputation as an experienced and knowledgeable host, who was obviously well-known in restaurant circles in important cities.

MAYBE BOB IS FATED TO BE FOREVER LOSING

Bob came to our division in the mid-seventies as an assistant group vice-president. I didn't know exactly what the duties and responsibilities of an assistant group vice-president were supposed to be, and I sometimes suspected that Bob didn't, either. Bob certainly didn't think they included interfering in the management of the division in any way, and he was scrupulous about avoiding any interference in my responsibilities in that regard. But we had a spare executive office in our building, which he occupied, and we included him in our activities whenever possible. He was a warm, friendly guy, and we made a point of having him join the party whenever we were entertaining someone to lunch or dinner, or were going out of the office on any other occasion.

The division was located in a brand-new building, in one of the western suburbs of Montreal, far from the location of the original Northern Electric factory downtown on Shearer Street. In my normal fashion, I had consciously tried to extend my knowledge of Montreal restaurants to cover all those in the vicinity of this new plant, as I had many occasions to entertain visitors. And it was therefore quite natural for someone in the group to ask, "Where are we going today?" and for me to make the choice of a restaurant.

A year or two later, in the cyclical pattern of reorganization that any big corporation seems convinced is necessary to success (perhaps they believe it confuses the enemy; it certainly confuses the employees), the senior management involved in our division was scattered throughout the corporation. I found myself as the managing director for Europe, based in Zurich, Switzerland, and Bob became the managing director of the major joint venture in Turkey, based in Istanbul. A third friend, Brian, became managing director for the Middle East, based in London, England.

We had hardly moved into those new positions when we were all called back to Montreal for a week of meetings. I've observed that in big corporations, top management becomes very nervous unless they see your face fairly frequently, preferably at a long, dull meeting, where someone can criticize your results and exhort you to greater effort. It doesn't matter how well or poorly your group is performing, the form is always the same—criticize, then exhort. Our little group formed the habit, after a hard day of "meeting survival," of gathering in the bar at the hotel we had chosen, directly across the road from headquarters. There were others in the overseas management group that favoured more prestigious hotels, but I think our group had a lot more fun. After a bit of restorative elixir, Brian would ask me, "Where are we eating tonight?" I would name a spot, and off we'd go. And I thought we ate pretty well, not least because there was a plethora of good restaurants in Montreal from which to choose.

But one night, when Brian asked his question, Bob responded before I had a chance. "I know a place!" he almost shouted. And right then I realized we had never involved Bob in any of those important decisions about where to go to eat or be entertained, and that he probably felt a bit slighted. So we immediately agreed to go to his restaurant. Although he couldn't remember its name, he insisted he remembered its location, down in old Montreal. I was always ready to explore new restaurants, and besides, Bob announced he would pay the bill. Since he had the honour of choosing the restaurant, Brian and I thought this only fair. So we set off.

As we approached Old Montreal, I became increasingly suspicious that Bob had inadvertently chosen one of my old haunts. Sure enough, Bob led us to the familiar Le Saint Amable. As we entered, I hung back a little, and Bob, in his role as the host, walked up to the headwaiter, holding up three fingers and saying, "We'd like—"

But the headwaiter brushed him out of the way and rushed to embrace me, exclaiming, "Monsieur Hamilton, Where have you been?"

We had an excellent meal, and even if he didn't have the satisfaction of finally introducing me to a new restaurant, Bob was true to his word and gamely paid the bill.

I guess Bob retained the suspicion he'd never get the recognition due to him as an expert on restaurants and a bon vivant.

Shortly after I moved to Zurich, I travelled to England to renew old business acquaintances from my previous employment—contacts I hoped would prove useful in my new role. Of course, I told Brian I was coming. He met me at the plane and took me to my hotel in the West End of London, where we repaired to the bar for some revitalizing liquid. After a bit, Brian proposed we go out to dinner, but I suggested that, instead, we go to a pub (those marvellous English institutions where you can drink, socialize, sometimes sing, and often eat a good simple meal). But Brian replied that, while he'd like to go to a pub, he hadn't yet located any good ones in the neighbourhood, since he'd only been in England for a short time. However, I said that, while I hadn't been in London for over five years, I thought I could still remember one or two.

So we set off. It was now dark, but we had no difficulty in hailing a taxi. "Take us to the Admiral Codrington in Mossop Street," I directed.

"I don't know where that is," said the taxi driver, somewhat surprisingly, since London taxi drivers are renowned for their detailed knowledge of that great city.

"Well, do you know where the Australians is?" I asked.

He did, so I had him take us to that pub, which was located in a major street, and thus better known. I then directed him through the darkened streets to the Admiral Codrington. Brian was duly impressed at my ability to find this obscure pub in the tangle of little streets we'd traversed.

The next night he asked me if I knew any more good pubs. So I introduced him to some of my old favourites in and around Belgrave Square. Now the pubs in that neighbourhood are not on the main streets. You have to go into the back alleys or "mews" to find the wonderful little local pubs. At one time, when I was visiting London regularly, I had made it my business to locate as many of these watering holes as possible. I found that my instinct for relocating dimly remembered pubs didn't fail me. Brian and I had a good evening of visiting tiny pubs hidden in the back streets.

A few weeks later, Bob visited London from his post in Istanbul. And of course, Brian met him and the two set off for an evening together. Bob, being of UK origin, was looking forward to visiting some pubs. Brian took him on a tour of those same pubs in Belgravia. Bob was delighted. "These pubs are wonderful. I'll bet Hughie would enjoy them. I must tell him about them."

Brian looked at him in some sorrow. "How do you think I found them?" he asked gently.

Poor Bob, he seemed forever fated never to be able to introduce me to a new eating- or drinking-place. But I must say that, in the ensuing years, he bore up bravely, and never complained when he was taken along to some restaurant or pub chosen by his friend.

I TAKE SALT ON MY MELON

Our parents knew many things that have been largely forgotten in these more modern times. For example, my mother always put sugar on her sliced tomatoes, and salt on her piece of melon, particularly if it was a cantaloupe. And I have an elderly friend, with a reputation as a gourmet, who puts a tiny dab of hot English mustard on his strawberries. Try these some time. The sugar reduces the acidity of tomatoes, although modern breeds of tomatoes seem to be less acid than those of my mother's time. And the salt and the mustard, used appropriately, are flavour enhancers, and serve to emphasize the delicate flavours involved.

In these days of dieting, I've long since given up sugar on my tomatoes in favour of domestic peace, and I'm seldom in a position to have mustard on my strawberries. But I do like salt on my melon.

When one travels a lot, and revisits the same cities regularly, one tends to establish in one's mind favourite sights or restaurants, as symbolic of that city. So it is for me with Simpson's in the Strand, in London. I do not feel I've properly visited London unless I've had dinner in this fine old restaurant. Simpson's is Edwardian in style, with a large, brightly lit dining room that has a high ceiling, linen tablecloths, and good old-fashioned waiters in proper waiters' uniforms. They have a long menu, based on good, plain English cooking. Most people would say the thing to have is the roast of beef, which is wheeled up to your table on a huge silver trolley. The roast, done to a turn, seems to be larger than any single cow could be expected to produce. And the carver is acknowledged as the single most important person in the restaurant. At Simpson's, you do not tip the waiter, you tip the carver. The custom is to tip the carver a certain amount for each person at the table, and the host at the table is expected to stack up the appropriate number of coins beside his plate as the carver approaches. It used to be two shillings per head, but in these days of new coinage and inflation, it may well be that the appropriate tip folds. I still prefer the old-fashioned stack of coins. Once the carver sees that the niceties are being properly observed, he will start to carve wonderful, thin slices of succulent beef, and will not stop until assured that everyone at the table has sufficient.

On the occasion in question, I was alone in London and had an evening free. What more natural than I should dine at Simpson's? I arrived with the peak of the theatre crowd and found I'd been assigned a table in a smaller dining room that was already nearly full. I ordered my regular Simpson's meal—smoked salmon followed by roast beef (and I didn't forget to tip the carver). By the time I was finished, well satisfied with my meal, the rest of the diners in the room had left, the waiters had cleared their tables, and I was alone. But my waiter politely asked if I would have a sweet (dessert, for you uninitiated). He suggested treacle pudding, a favourite of many of the patrons. I find that concoction of a bread-like pudding laced with heavy treacle syrup much too heavy, to say nothing of the danger that it will pull all your fillings loose. I asked for a slice of the delicious-looking melon I'd seen being served earlier as a starter. Only after the waiter had gone off to fetch the melon did I realize he'd already cleared my table of cutlery and dishes, including the salt and pepper shakers. However, when he returned with a giant slice of melon, together with a large silver cellar of ginger, which is often served with melon in England, I asked him if he could bring me a saltcellar. He replied, in extremely doubtful tones, "Well, I can see, Sir." And he went off to wherever waiters go.

I waited patiently, if somewhat mystified, for his return. He seemed to be gone a long, long time. I began to be concerned that my unusual request might have offended the sensibilities of this tradition-bound place. But, after what seemed like fifteen minutes, but was more likely about seven, the waiter reappeared. He was carrying a large silver tray, with the largest salt cellar I've ever seen, an ornate silver affair at least fourteen inches high. This he placed on the table with as much ceremony as any waiter could muster in the circumstances (how many ways are there to put a salt cellar on a table anyway?). He then waited and watched carefully while I sprinkled salt on my melon. Perhaps he thought it was a hoax, and wanted to call my bluff.

As I started to eat, I realized he had been followed into the room by none other than the *maître d'hôtel* himself. He had stood in the corner and watched the proceedings. When I caught his eye, he approached my table, drew himself up, bowed slightly, offered his hand, and said deferentially, "I wanted to shake the hand of a man who knows enough to put salt on his melon."

I felt considerably encouraged and vindicated.

Of course, there is the possibility he had only come over to see if there actually was an idiot who would put salt on a melon. When he was caught in the act, so to speak, he might have tried to get out of an awkward situation by flattering the customer. However, I much prefer the original explanation, and have continued ever since to claim his support for my use of salt on my melon.

I continue to take salt on my melon, and I frequently feel called upon to explain my eccentric action by repeating this story. And my table companions not infrequently complain they've have heard it all before. That headwaiter has a lot to answer for.

MY PRIVATE CLUB IN BRUSSELS

When I first knew Brussels, it was a wonderful old city, which had somehow avoided damage and destruction down through the centuries. It contained some marvellous medieval architecture. It was peopled by cheerful, friendly people, who spoke a brand of French that, wonder of wonders, I could easily understand, in spite of the fact that they occasionally threw in a few words of Dutch. Unlike some other major cities, it did not seem to put on airs, and the prices were quite reasonable. I understand that, today, with the advent of the EEC, much of whose government is centred in Brussels, progress has afflicted this beautiful city, with resultant high prices, and probably, less friendly people. I'm not always certain progress is a good thing.

I have always had a soft spot for Brussels, ever since I first visited it by accident.

It was 1955. Jean and I had travelled from England, where I was posted at the time, to Cologne, in Germany. I went to represent Canadian Marconi in initial discussions with a major German cable maker about a possible project in Canada. At that time, much of Germany was still recovering from the devastation of the war. In particular, we had found that, while our tickets clearly stated we were going to Cologne, our flight actually went to Bonn, located about twenty miles away. The airport at Cologne was still closed to civilian traffic. That posed little problem, as our hosts sent a car to meet us at the Bonn airport.

We spent ten days meeting with our German hosts, discussing the project and their products, being royally entertained, and doing as much sightseeing on the side as possible. When it came time to leave, we asked our hosts to have their car drop us at the airport in Bonn, at the appropriate time. I remember they sent us off a bit early in order to give us time to explore the main shopping street of Bonn, which, even in those days, boasted some superb specialty shops, and some of the finest pastry shops in the world. Their pastries looked, and were, absolutely fantastic. Fortunately, they were equipped with tables so that you could sample the goodies right there.

In due course, we arrived at the airport, somewhat the heavier for our visit to the pastry shops. We walked up to the British European Airways desk, and presented our tickets for the four o'clock flight to London. The airline staff were somewhat surprised to see us, as that particular flight really did leave from the Cologne airport, some twenty miles away. It seemed that just that week, they'd started flying civilian flights out of Cologne Airport again, but of course we had never checked. Now we had a problem. We were too far away to catch that flight. However, the problem didn't turn out to be insurmountable. There was a Sabena (Belgian) Airlines flight leaving soon for Brussels, and going on from there to London. There was space on it, certainly as far as Brussels. They couldn't be certain there was space on the next leg, to London, but if there wasn't, then there was a British European Airways flight, about five hours later, where there certainly was space. We were relieved to accept this solution.

However, when we arrived in Brussels, two agents from Sabena, both looking very sad, met us at the door of the aircraft. They explained, very apologetically, that the onward flight to London was fully booked, and they would be unable to accommodate us. We'd have to wait for the British flight five hours later. They were very "*désolés.*"

"In that case," I asked, "would it be possible for us to visit Brussels?"

They brightened instantly. "You'd like to stay?" our greeters chorused. They appeared relieved, delighted, and more than a little bit surprised, that this problem couple they'd inherited would actually want to visit their city. "Quickly, the bus is just leaving! Give us your passports." And one seized our passports and ran off ahead of us, while the other hustled us along.

When we arrived at the immigration desk, the first agent was dancing in front of the officer, almost shouting, "Here they are. They're staying." He was holding the open passports up, at least six feet away from the immigration officer, where he couldn't possibly have read them, but he seemed satisfied. The passports were thrust back at us, and we were bundled into the bus amid assurances they'd look after our luggage. Those were two happy agents. I wish I could make everyone's day that way.

Everyone else—the bus driver, the bus agent in Brussels, and even a policeman we stopped to ask directions of—seemed to share in the delight that we would visit their city.

The bus deposited us in the middle of Brussels, and we had a couple of hours to explore a delightful city, with medieval squares, wonderful-smelling restaurants, and a general air of joie de vivre. Our visit was much too brief.

When we arrived back at the airport on the bus, the same two Sabena agents met us, escorted us past immigration, explaining cheerfully, "They're back!" and took us to the British European Airways desk, where our ticket formalities had already been completed, and our luggage awaited us.

Now, with an introduction like that to any city, how could you help but like it?

It was quite a number of years after our first brief visit that I again had occasion to go to Brussels. This time, I had business in the city. Bill and I were travelling around Europe, visiting military authorities in an effort to sell Canadian Marconi's tactical radio relay equipment. This was an excellent product, and with time and persistence, we eventually managed to make a few sales. Fortunately for our personal enjoyment, our efforts took a number of years to achieve success, involving repeated visits to each of the capitals of Europe. This time, we were visiting Brussels.

Bill was familiar with Brussels, having visited it in the marketing of some of Marconi's avionics products. Thus, we had hardly checked into our hotel when he was at my door volunteering to show me some of the sights before our scheduled meetings.

It was only a short walk from our hotel to the "Grand Place," a magnificent medieval square that is one of the finest and best-preserved examples of medieval architecture in all of Europe. The Grand Place is the size of about three city blocks, and is completely surrounded by ancient gothic buildings, many with tall spires and towers, and all festooned with gingerbread carvings. I understand all of the buildings were built within a space of about fifteen years, in about 1485. The square is dominated by the city hall, which occupies about half of one side of the square. It is about five stories high, with arcaded windows, and is topped by the tallest of the magnificently carved spires. When you look at it you realize that it isn't quite balanced; there is one more set of windows on the left-hand side of the spire than there is on the right. Local legend claims that the architect never realized he was building an unbalanced building until it was finished. He took one look of horror at his finished masterpiece, then climbed to the top of the spire and threw himself off. I wouldn't vouch for the truth of that story, but I can assure you that I found the whole square enchanting.

It was a warm day, and we soon found need of liquid sustenance. I should digress here to explain that, while the Belgians loved their food and drink, their drinking establishments were governed by restrictive laws that greatly favoured the brewing industry. While there were many bars and taverns where you could buy almost any amount of beer, it was illegal to sell anyone any stronger alcoholic drink in any quantity less than three litres. That's an almighty large drink of Scotch.

Several things resulted from that rule. Firstly, and to my surprise, the Belgians were far and away the world champion consumers of beer, consuming nearly twice as much per capita as their nearest rivals, the Germans. This involved some serious beer drinking, as the quantities were up in the hundreds of litres per year for every man, woman, and child. The second thing was that the Belgians had, of course, developed ways to circumvent the rule. They established private clubs where it was legal to serve drinks in civilized sizes. In those days, when you checked into a hotel in Brussels, you were handed a card, which made you a member of the drinking club (the bar, that is) in the hotel. I would assume that with the advent of the EEC, progress dictated that these rules should change. That bit of progress I guess I'd approve of. However, you will realize that, at the time, these rules mitigated against our finding suitable liquid sustenance in the middle of the Grand Place on a hot day.

Bill had a solution. Leading me over to one corner of the square, he announced he would take me to a private club, the Aviation Club. It was so called, I guess, because most of its members had some association with aviation, either as pilots or as members of the industry. "I've been in here before with my friends from the aviation industry, and I think it will be all right," he said, "but if anyone says anything, just say we were introduced by Rene Bayense. He's a member here, and he's the marketing manager for Aviation du Nord, a major Belgian aircraft company."

And so we passed through a low, arched doorway in the extreme corner of the square, and entered a beautiful old barroom. I imagine it has been there since the square was first built. It certainly looks the part, with its ancient woodwork that gleams with the patina of old age, and its plasterwork that has faded to that mellow brown shade sometimes found in buildings of great age. We sat at a worn table, ordered drinks, and sipped and soaked up the atmosphere. Nothing was said, and we eventually paid our bill and left without incident.

It was several months before I was again in Brussels, this time without Bill. Indeed, I don't believe Bill ever came with me to Brussels again, although I visited it many times. I arrived in late afternoon, in preparation for meetings the following day. I had the evening to myself, and decided a good start would be to have a drink in the Aviation Club. I went in, and since I was alone, sat up at the bar. The barman served me a drink, and a few minutes later, even brought over a tray of canapés. I spent a pleasant hour, and then went off in search of dinner.

I enjoyed visiting that ancient barroom, and fell into the habit of visiting it every time I went to Brussels. The barman and I worked up a nodding acquaintance. I even took a small party of visiting Canadian government officials in there for a drink one evening, thereby greatly enhancing my reputation as an experienced man of the world.

Nothing was ever said to question my right to be in that clubroom until, one evening, when I walked in, there was an official-looking *maître d'*, complete with black tie and tails, who was walking about, greeting the members. I'd never seen him before. However, I'd never been questioned, so I sat down at the bar, ordered my usual drink, had it served to me, and indeed, sampled the usual tray of canapés. I saw the *maître d's* eye fall on me, and I saw him question the barman about who I was. The barman shrugged, and, I suppose, said I was a harmless Canadian who came in from time to time, but no, he didn't know who I was.

When the *maître d'* was next in my end of the room, he came over to me in a purposeful fashion, and said, "Pardon me *M'sieu*, but I don't believe we've met."

From the moment I'd first seen the threat of authority, I'd been desperately trying to drag up from memory the name of the member Bill had first given me, so many years before. At the last instant, it popped into my head, and I was able to reply to the *maître d'*, "I'm Hugh Hamilton, visiting from Canada. I was introduced here by *M'sieu* Bayense." Well, it was worth a try.

The *maître d'* replied, "Ah yes, *M'sieu* Bayense. We haven't seen him in here for some time. The next time you come in, you must bring him with you." And he walked away. I thought, what an elegant way to warn me off without harsh words or recrimination. But I had no doubt I'd been told to leave quietly, and not come back unless I could produce M. Bayense in the flesh, to corroborate my story. I finished my drink, somewhat sadly, hadn't the nerve to order another, and looked around for a last look.

I went to my meetings the next day, and flew on to another city.

It was several months before I had to visit Brussels again. I was sitting in the bar of my hotel (where I was indeed a member) not far from the Grand Place. It wasn't a bad bar as hotel bars go; indeed it was quite nice. But it wasn't as warm and friendly seeming as the Aviation Club. But then, I'd been warned off at the Aviation Club. They might throw me out if I went in there, and would it be worth the hassle? On the other hand, I'd been there many times and only encountered the *maître d'* on that one occasion. He might not be there tonight. I turned the matter over in my mind for some time, and finally concluded it was worth the risk. I got up and walked out of the hotel and over to the Grand Place. I'd hardly gotten inside the door of the Aviation Club when I saw him. The *maître d'* was there, and furthermore he was walking over to me very purposefully. I braced myself. He held out his hand, shook mine, and said, "*M'sieu* Hamilton. We haven't seen you for too long. Welcome back."

I concluded then and there, that I'd somehow mysteriously achieved membership in that club, and have considered myself a member ever since. I've even sent others to visit the club, telling them to tell the headwaiter, if asked, that Hugh Hamilton sent them.

I'LL NEVER BECOME A WINE EXPERT

I first met Herr Hans Von Koenen in 1955, when Jean and I journeyed to Cologne to visit the Felten and Guilleaume Carlswerk, a major German manufacturer of cables of all kinds, including telecommunications cables. I was to take part in initial discussions of a possible co-operation between Canadian Marconi and the Germans on a major cable project in Canada. Herr Von Koenen was the director of international business for his company. Over the years, we continued to meet and even reached friendship on a first-name basis, quite unusual in the rather formal world of German business of that era.

Herr Von Koenen was not only an important businessman, but he also was recognized in his world as a considerable gourmet and connoisseur. During our first visit to Germany, we were most fortunate that he entertained us on several of the evenings of our visit.

On one occasion, he took us to a famous old German tavern, Der Whälfisch ("the whale"). It was a big, old-fashioned, crowded restaurant. Herr Von Koenen was greeted as a good patron and as a recognized expert on food and drink, as was certainly his due. We were ushered to one of the better tables with more than the usual ceremony.

When the menus came, they turned out to be about the size of a page of a newspaper, and closely written in old German script, which made them completely illegible to us. But Herr Von Koenen patiently discussed the menu with us. He may have had some difficulty, since we, by then, were in awe of his knowledge and weren't about to argue with anything he suggested. However, we finally agreed that he would discuss two different dishes with the waiter and would then choose between them.

The waiter came, and there was an extremely deferential (on the part of the waiter) discussion, which, however, seemed to me to continue for an inordinately long time. We subsequently discovered that, on the basis of this discussion, we were to eat something else entirely, something that had never been mentioned in the preliminary discussions. Nevertheless, our faith in Herr Von Koenen never wavered, and his choice proved eminently satisfactory.

Next came the process of choosing the wine, a matter that is given careful attention and much study by all good Germans, particularly in the Rhineland, where many of the best German wines originate. The wine list proved to be roughly the size of a telephone directory, with the items listed quite closely on the pages. Our host studied the book for some minutes, making no pretense of consulting us, since he had long since determined that our knowledge of wines was minimal.

Finally, he called over the *sommelier* (in this case not a simple wine waiter, but a substantial personage carrying his badge of office, or tasting spoon, with some pride). The two men began by referring to items on several pages of the wine book (it really was too large and heavy to be called a mere "list"). Then they gradually confined their attention to just two items, on two separate pages, and the discussion took on all the aspects of a heated argument. At one stage Herr Von Koenen actually rose to his feet, thumped emphatically on one page of the book, and seemed only barely to restrain himself from shouting. However, this extraordinary clash, which even attracted some attention from the surrounding tables, soon died down, and the *sommelier* departed to bring the wine to our table.

"Herr Von Koenen," I asked, "What was that all about?"

"Oh," he replied, "we were discussing the merits of two 1949 wines." And he went on to explain that in winemaking, the quality of the wine is very dependent on the amount of sunshine the grapevines get, particularly in the last month before the grapes are harvested. Accordingly, the best wines, particularly in Germany, which is relatively far north for a winemaking country, usually come from vineyards which face to the south, and thus get the best exposure to the sun, particularly in the autumn. Most of the best German wines come from the Rhineland, where the Rhine River twists and turns, exposing first one steep bank and then the other to the southern sun of late autumn. And a knowledgeable wine aficionado makes it his business to know the aspect of each vineyard. But, he went on to explain, the year 1949 had had a particularly rainy autumn, so that the vines had less than the normal amount of sun. And what sun there was usually occurred in the evening, since many of the rainstorms cleared up towards the end of the day. That meant that vineyards facing the setting sun in the west would receive more of the available sunshine than other vineyards. Accordingly, he was trying to convince the *sommelier* that a wine from a particular west-facing vineyard would be superior, in that particular year, to a wine from a south-facing vineyard just around the bend of the river, even though the latter was generally accepted to be a superior vineyard. That was the one the *sommelier* favoured.

We were much impressed with the very detailed knowledge and understanding of the interrelated factors that he displayed. Imagine knowing all that just in order to choose a wine with confidence! "Did you win?" I inquired.

"Of course," he replied, as if anything else would have been unthinkable.

"Then we're going to drink the wine from the west-facing vineyard," I said, secure in my newfound knowledge.

He looked at me almost in horror. "You don't think I'd actually drink a 1949, do you? We're having a 1951, a much better year."

Oh well, maybe it helped in the continuing education of the *sommelier*. It certainly gave me reason to doubt I'd ever become an expert in wines.

PUB CRAWLS, HOWEVER INNOCUOUS, CAN CAUSE TROUBLE

As I've previously described, my buddy Bill and I spent considerable time in the mid-sixties, travelling around the capitals of Europe, promoting the sale of the Canadian Marconi tactical radio relay system.

We both worked for the Canadian Marconi Company, which was a subsidiary of Marconi's Wireless Telegraph Company (MWT) of England. But we weren't a wholly owned subsidiary. MWT owned only fifty-one percent of our shares and appeared to live in fear and trembling that the other forty-nine percent would somehow take charge.

In our travels, we frequently passed through England. Indeed, London was one of our favourite cities. We often met with our friends in MWT headquarters in Chelmsford. Nonetheless, mindful, I guess, of the supposed dangers of allowing two colonials to run loose all over England, actually talking to customers and possibly engaging in other potentially more dangerous activities, MWT insisted that we report to their London office whenever we stopped in England. This applied even if we had no business planned in the UK. I must say that wasn't too severe a stricture, as the manager of the London office was George Kelsey, who seemed to believe that his sole role in this scenario was to entertain us at any and all opportunities.

I liked George. He was my idea of a dapper little man, always perfectly dressed, clothes immaculate, never a hair out of place, and always with a carnation in his buttonhole. You'd never guess that he was a wartime hero, having parachuted into France on espionage missions on a number of occasions, helping to establish clandestine radio communications. His main duties as London manager were to maintain smooth relations with the British government offices in London. This was important, of course, as they represented major customers of MWT. I thought he was the ideal person for that activity. His role as a Canadian-minder was only one of his minor functions.

There came the occasion when, at the end of a week, Bill and I had nearly completed a tour through the European capitals, but we still had some business to conclude with MWT in the UK. We both liked London, so we decided to spend the weekend there. And we also decided to stretch the rules and not tell George of our presence until Monday.

Otherwise, we knew he'd feel obliged to leave his home in the country to come into London on Saturday night to entertain us, and we thought that quite unnecessary.

On Saturday morning, we sallied forth from our hotel at pub-opening time, intending an extensive pub-crawl. Well, it couldn't be all that extensive, given the restricted pub-opening hours of those days. After a few stops for sustenance along the way, we ended up at the Audley, our favourite pub for Saturday lunch. It was a beautiful, early-twentieth-century pub with polished woodwork and a rather elegant appearance. Best of all, it had an excellent cold table and you could have a magnificent plate of salads and cold cuts at a very reasonable price. When we were finally sitting at the food bar, equipped with food and drink, I remarked to the barmaid that we liked her pub very much.

"Oh," she said, "this isn't a pub at all. You need to visit a real country pub to see what a good pub is like."

I was somewhat taken aback, not least by the fact that it might prove somewhat difficult for visitors like us to arrange a country pub-crawl, and I said as much. However, I did ask her if she had any particular country pub in mind. She recommended the Jolly Farmer near Chalfont St. Peter in Buckinghamshire (pronounced, in typical English fashion, with little reference to the spelling, "Bucknamshur"). I took note of the name, but with little hope I'd ever have any use for it. Closing time approaching, we left and returned to our hotel.

But when we reached our hotel, there was a message waiting for Bill that he should return to Canada immediately, to deal with some emergency. It was decided he'd catch the night plane, and I would stay and complete the meetings with MWT the following week.

And so it was that I found myself with a whole Sunday to myself in London. What to do? Well, I "remembered me of that fair young maid," as the song goes, and of the pub she recommended. And my *Green Bus Guide* indicated that there were indeed buses going to Chalfont St. Peter. I would have been extremely surprised if there hadn't been. You could go almost anywhere on a bus in England in those days. And when I climbed aboard the bus, the driver said he did indeed know the Jolly Farmer. The bus ran right past it, and he'd be sure to point it out.

An hour later, I stepped off the bus at the laneway leading to my objective. The Jolly Farmer proved to be a large, low-slung, white building on a bit of a hill. It had probably sat there for several centuries, and looked most attractive. However, once inside, I found that it had been modernized, or "tarted up," as they say. Its chief claim to fame now was that it served five hundred and one different sandwiches. It didn't seem quite what I was looking for, but it was crowded and seemed popular, and

I was to find that the patrons were very friendly. I bought my pint and ordered one of the sandwiches, then turned my attention to getting into conversation with the locals. I was soon part of a group who, when I explained my objective to visit good country pubs, told me I was in the wrong place. "You want The Greyhound," they said. "It's an old coaching inn, and is very quaint. Hanging Judge Jeffries stayed there when he was holding court in this district." (I wonder, sometimes, that the most unpleasant and even gruesome events often later become the reason for fame and fortune for a house or a district.) They said The Greyhound was "just the other side of the village green."

Thus it was that, after managing to buy a "round" for my newfound friends, I started to move towards the door, intending to find this paragon of a country inn, "just across the green." But my new friends stopped me, saying they were leaving anyway and they'd take me there. We all squeezed into their small car and set off. It was lucky they took me, because "just the other side of the village green" proved to be several miles away. However, I was duly deposited in the courtyard of a magnificent old coaching inn. When I invited my new friends to join me, they demurred. "We don't belong to this pub. We belong to the Jolly Farmer." Their logic escapes me even to this day.

When I entered The Greyhound, I found that it was divided up into a number of quite small rooms, with low ceilings, blackened wooden beams, and lots of polished brass around. Each of the rooms, reeking of age and long use, was a separate barroom. It was just as you would expect such an ancient inn to be. I was very pleased at my good fortune in finding it.

Again I purchased my pint and again I set about getting into conversation with the locals. I noticed one group of late-middle-aged men all standing together, and by listening in to their conversation, I determined that this was a gathering of local men who had grown up together. They were holding a reunion with one of their old group who had emigrated to South Africa years before. He was now retired, and had returned to visit his old neighbourhood. His friends were teasing him unmercifully for being a "colonial." Well, there's only one side of that argument I could get into, and I dug in with some enthusiasm to support the returning emigrant. We had a very good time, and I must have acquitted myself satisfactorily, because when the publican called, "Time, gentlemen, please" (the signal for closing time), I was seized by both arms and marched through each of the barrooms of the pub. I was introduced to each barman in turn: "Bill, this is Mr. Hamilton, and the next time he comes in, he's a local." Surely that was a considerable achievement for a single visit. I was extremely pleased.

The next morning, in London, I called George Kelsey in his office, in accordance with instructions, and, as expected, he promptly said, "Come on over and we'll have some lunch."

In those days, Marconi had a "club" for its more senior employees on the top story of their office building on the Strand. And in the lounge that day, there were a number of people I'd met before.

"When did you arrive?" they asked. "You were alone all weekend in London? What did you do?"

So I told them the story of my country pub-crawl and my achievement of being declared a local at The Greyhound. My story was received with its due ration of chuckles and smiles all round, with the exception of George. It seemed to me that all the time I was describing my adventures at The Greyhound, he was becoming more and more upset and displeased. When I'd finished my story, I asked him, "George, is something the matter?"

"Do you mean to tell me you were at The Greyhound yesterday at noon?" he spluttered.

"Yes. What's the problem?"

"Well, the Greyhound's my local, and I was just up the street working away in my garden, and it was hot and dry, and I was just wishing for an excuse to visit the pub."

I believe there are over one hundred thousand pubs in England. I had to choose George's local pub to visit without either of us knowing it. You never know the ways you can get into trouble. However, I must say that George wasn't one to hold a grudge for long. Our relationship quickly recovered, and we remained good friends for the rest of his life and shared many a glass together.

Some years later, I visited the same area of England with my wife, Jean. She'd heard the story of The Greyhound many times and insisted we go and visit it. When we drove into the courtyard, I found it had lost none if its charm. And, as we walked through the door into the nearest bar, the barman looked up and said, "Good afternoon, Mr. Hamilton. You haven't visited us for some time."

A STROKE OF MARKETING GENIUS

The first thing you think of when you consider a restaurant is the food. A good restaurant must have excellent food. It may be food in a particular style, or representing a specific country or area. But it must be consistently good. The foundation of any restaurant lies in its kitchen, and in the expertise of the chef and his assistants. Many of the great restaurants of the world carry the name of the master chef. Indeed, there have been a few master chefs, Père Bocuse, for example, who have revolutionized the restaurant business by inventing new styles of food, and in the process have themselves been almost immortalized. A visit to one of those great restaurants takes on aspects of a pilgrimage. You will see patrons entering almost reverently, as if into a shrine, or at least a place where they may treat their stomachs to an experience that may well approach ecstasy, religious or otherwise.

There are, of course, other elements necessary for a good restaurant: ambiance, location, quality of service, expert staff, an outstanding *maître d'* or headwaiter. They all contribute to a satisfying culinary experience. And an important element of the food is its presentation. A major factor of Père Bocuse's *nouvelle cuisine* is the manner in which the food is presented. No longer is the food to be served in large quantities, scooped onto a plate. It must be served in modest quantities, and carefully arranged on the plate to delight the eye, long before the taste buds or the olfactory senses are engaged. The meal becomes a visual work of art, as well as a treat of taste and aroma. And it must be presented at the table with the care and respect appropriate to such a work.

I'm not sure whether M. Barrier, whose restaurant we visited in Tours, was the master chef who'd given the restaurant his name. It is certain that someone there was a master of presentation and also of marketing.

It was 1969. Jean and I were on one of our periodic peregrinations through Europe, taking a car and driving through a section of a country, with little or no planning. We relied heavily on guidebooks and local information bureaus for advice of all kinds, and in particular, to find rooms each night in whatever town or city we happened to find ourselves. In this instance we were exploring the Loire valley, that beautiful area of France to the south and west of Paris where the nobility of the pre-Napoleonic era built their chateaux. Many of those chateaux exist to this day and represent some of the most beautiful architecture in the world. These are not militarily defensible castles. Rather, they are elegant country residences of the very rich nobles. We were greatly enjoying the opportunity to explore these grand buildings, even though many of them were disappointingly devoid of furniture. It seems the nobility of the time spent much of their time in Paris as guests of the king, in one of his grand palaces. However, the king's bounty did not extend to the kind of furnishings the nobility would like to display to their rivals. Accordingly, when they left their chateaux, they normally took all the furnishings with them. One had to use one's imagination to visualize what those magnificent rooms might have looked like when inhabited.

Another irritant was the habit the caretakers of the castles had of closing them for large portions of the day. You might find one in the morning, explore it, and then try to rush over to another, before lunch. You were likely to find it closed for an extended lunch hour. It was difficult to be efficient in your sightseeing. Nevertheless, the whole aspect of the district was very enjoyable.

We arrived in Tours, a good-sized town, and found a room right in the centre. The hotel was small, clean, and neat, and met another criterion that I often adhered to: it did not have a restaurant of its own. That meant it was easier and less embarrassing to discuss restaurants with the hotel staff and to obtain reliable advice.

In this case, when I asked the two girls who were on the front desk to recommend a restaurant, they asked if this was our first visit to Tours. When I said it was, they insisted that we must go to Barrier's. They explained it was one of only six five-star restaurants in all of France, and we shouldn't miss the opportunity. I was concerned, firstly, that this could prove to be an extremely expensive adventure, and secondly, that any restaurant of that class was usually fully booked weeks in advance. To the first concern, I decided, "What the heck, we only live once!" (And I've since learned an important truth: The difference in cost between a very good restaurant and a more ordinary one, particularly if the ordinary one has any pretensions, is usually relatively small.) To the second, my helpful young ladies called the restaurant and promptly obtained a reservation for that very evening.

We drove to the restaurant, which is near one end of the main street of Tours. We were shown into a room brightly lit with crystal chandeliers (the French believe you should be able to see what you're eating), and perhaps fifteen tables with white linen tablecloths, good china, and gleaming silverware. Barrier's certainly passed the test for ambiance.

We were ushered to a table that could have accommodated four quite easily, and in due course were brought the menus, which were large and printed in very legible type. (There is nothing more frustrating than being in a restaurant that should be very good, if you could only read the menu, which has been printed, very artistically, in fine print on a coloured page, making it extremely difficult to decipher.) And of course, mine was the only one with prices listed; one certainly wouldn't want one's guests to know the cost, would one? (Well maybe one would if one were trying to influence an impressionable young lady, but that place would impress anyone without advertising the cost.) In any event, the cost wasn't exorbitant—about twenty-five dollars for a five-course gourmet meal. That was some years ago, and would equate today to perhaps a hundred and fifty dollars. It was certainly far less than I had anticipated.

The menu offered several choices in each segment of the meal, starting with appetizers and working its way through to cheese and dessert. We ordered our meals, each of us taking care to order different items in each category, in order to experience the greatest variety.

Then we came to the presentation portion of the entertainment. There were perhaps eight or ten staff in the room, ranging from the maître d' through waiters and assistants down to lowly busboys. The kitchen was in an adjoining room and each new dish issued separately through a serving hatch in the wall of the dining room. When a dish appeared in the hatchway, each member of the serving staff immediately took up an assigned task. A junior waiter would approach the table with a silver tray carrying the necessary cutlery, and an assistant transferred the cutlery to its allotted place on the table. The dish itself was carried on another tray by a more senior waiter, and was carefully and lovingly transferred as befitted a work of art, from the tray to its place in front of the diner by the senior waiter. If there was a sauce or condiment required, it was carried by yet another junior waiter, and served by a senior waiter. The delivery of every dish involved nearly every one of the waiters. Each dish became the occasion of a theatrical presentation. You felt you were being treated royally, or at least with all the respect the excellent food deserved. And the food was superb, worth all that respect.

You will imagine that the serving of a bottle of wine also became a very considerable ceremony, as befits good wine in such a setting in France.

The meal progressed majestically through all its stages. We enjoyed ourselves immensely, and when we were finally relaxing after this great experience, the maître d' approached, expressed the hope we had enjoyed the meal, which must have been obvious, and offered us an after-dinner drink, "a *poire*, perhaps?" (*Poire* is a local liquor, prepared, I believe, by the distillation of fermented pear juice.) I declined, explaining that we had dined extremely well and wouldn't want to overdo matters and spoil the effect of such a meal. "But," I said, "bearing in mind that tomorrow is Friday night, and presumably one of your busy days, could it be possible for us to come back to dinner tomorrow night?"

"But of course, *M'sieu*; you will have the same table," he said with a flourish.

So it was arranged. We stayed over a second day, a flexibility that is nearly always possible under the rules of peregrination, and the following evening found us entering Barrier's for the second time. This time, the little lobby was crowded with people trying to persuade the maître d' to give them a table in his already crowded restaurant. He saw us come through the door into the crowd, swept the crush out of the way, and ushered us, like royalty, into the restaurant, past all those people, some of whom must have been, or thought they were, quite important. We were ushered to the same table, just as promised, except that on this occasion, the table had a large of bouquet of red roses in a big silver bowl. We made ourselves comfortable and awaited the "entertainment" with anticipation.

When it came time to present the menus, the maître d' (I've always wondered if perhaps he was M. Barrier himself) announced that tonight he would order for us. He then proceeded to arrange a superb meal, which, wherever appropriate, included samples of all the delicacies on offer on the menu. The spectacular service continued as it had the previous evening. We enjoyed ourselves even more. And at the conclusion of the meal, we decided that on this occasion we would indeed indulge in an after-dinner drink. Searching my memory, I remembered that the maître d' had recommended *poire*, and I proceeded to order it from the young waiter whom I'd identified as being responsible for the dispensation of such libations. As he went away to fill our order, I saw the maître d' whisper to him, and I said to Jean that I suspected the maître d' had remembered his offer of a drink on the previous evening, and that we would probably find it was on the house. And indeed it was; the *poire*, all of the several servings we enjoyed, did not appear on our bill. However, we did find we had become part of a marketing ploy, a ploy that may have started with the bowl of roses on our table, clearly intended to attract attention.

Our order for *poire* took a few minutes to fill, but in due course, the hatchway opened, and a silver tray emerged, carrying a large stone crock, dripping with sweat, and with the date 1946 in raised lettering on the side. I don't know whether there are good and bad years for *poire*, much less whether 1946 was a good year for this liquor. But 1946 was certainly an auspicious year for anything else in Europe in those days, marking, as it did the end of the war and the liberation of France and other countries from their invaders.

The tray was claimed by a middle-level waiter. He approached our table followed by a considerable retinue. There was a boy carrying a large bowl of ice, another with a tray with two largish brandy snifters, and several others, including the maître d', all of whom had a part to play in this particular presentation. The two brandy snifters were seized by a waiter and held out while another waiter lifted cubes of ice into them with silver tongs. The glasses were then swirled vigorously until they were heavily misted, and chilled to the swirling expert's satisfaction. The ice was then dumped into a second waiting silver bowl held by yet another helper. The maître d' then seized the glasses, and the senior wine steward took charge of the stone crock. He poured out a good measure into each glass. Finally, as if presenting a religious offering, the maître d' placed the glasses in front of us. The entire entourage stayed there, watching and waiting, until we finally took a sip. When we smiled and indicated our approval, there wasn't quite a sigh of collective relief, but there was certainly a relaxation of the "team," as with a job well done.

We realized afterwards that while all this was going on, every one of the other patrons was watching the show. Virtually everyone in the room decided they had to have some of that, whatever that was. Everyone ordered "the same." So that while the maître d' in his generosity presented us with several servings of *poire*, the result was to sell *poire* to nearly all the rest of his patrons. .

I've always thought that was a stroke of marketing genius.

THE WAY TO A MAN'S HEART

I am a very lucky person. One must take care to be a person these days and not a man or a woman, both of which I always thought were honourable estates, but apparently they are not any more. I am very lucky in that I have always been successful in associating myself whether as a son, a grandson, a nephew, or a husband, with superb cooks. As a result I have achieved a state that I prefer to refer to as pleasingly plump, and have even gained an entirely undeserved reputation as a minor gourmet. But I will eat most things—at least once.

In the circumstances, you'll understand that food for me is a serious business, not to be treated in any frivolous or irreverent manner. However, the following few anecdotes may serve to indicate some of the vicissitudes one may encounter in pursuit of culinary excellence.

GRANDMAS' BUNS

My grandmother died when I was a small boy. Amongst her many fine attributes, I remember her as a great cook. Perhaps that's because whenever we visited her, there was always an ample supply of cookies, cakes, pies, and especially of Grandma's bread buns. Grandma certainly knew the way to a man's heart, or at least to the heart of a small boy. I particularly liked her buns. They were light and soft, with a special "fresh bread" taste, and sometimes had a slight glaze on top. I remember they tasted particularly good with honey from Uncle Cliff's farm.

Grandma lived in a big old Victorian house in Fenelon Falls, a small, old-fashioned village in the Kawartha Lakes area in Ontario. Her house had extremely high-ceilinged rooms and enormous windows. I remember my father helping to install the storm windows one autumn. The windows were about five feet wide by seven feet high, and it took two men to slide them up two ladders placed side by side, and put them in place. There was a big kitchen with an enormous cast-iron cookstove—a twelve-holer, I believe—in one corner. So far as I know, that stove was never allowed to go out. I subsequently came to believe that stove played a great part in Grandma's magic with those buns.

My mother also was a very excellent cook, as you would expect coming from my grandmother's family. She made many different kinds of cookies and was a particularly dab hand at chocolate cakes. Hers were a rich, dark chocolate, and were lighter in texture than any others I've ever sampled. But, for some reason, she never made any bread or buns. I considered that a major oversight, likely to blight my entire young life, and I wasn't behindhand in saying so.

Finally, my pleadings had their effect and Mother wrote to Grandma for the recipe. The great day came. Mother assembled the ingredients and set to work. Soon the dough was ready to set out to rise. But it just sat there on a corner of the kitchen table and sullenly refused to do anything. Mother wasn't long on patience, so she soon concluded the dough needed more kneading. Again the dough was set out and importuned to rise. And again it simply sat there, if anything more sullenly than before. Finally, after several hours of this unequal contest, Mother threw in the towel. To my dismay, she dumped the whole stubborn mass of dough into the garbage can on the back porch.

And that might very well have been the end of buns in our house, if that garbage can hadn't been standing in the sun. For when I came by a couple of hours later, the lid of the garbage can was perched a good two feet above the rim, on top of a great mound of dough, that was swelling perceptibly, even as I watched.

There was, of course, considerable discussion about this misguided dough that refused to rise when treated nicely, and then tried belatedly to recover when thrown into the garbage pail sitting in the hot sun. It was concluded that the culprit was Grandma's old-fashioned cookstove. You see, when she set out her dough to rise, she just set it on the most convenient surface: a back corner of her cookstove where it was nice and cozy and warm. She'd done that for years, and, like many good cooks, she never thought to include that in her instructions. Now, our kitchen was much more modern (it was, after all, the 1930s) and we had a gas range. The poor dough, expecting a warm spot in which to do its stuff, was clearly dismayed when it was expected to rise in the chilly (to it) centrally heated comfort of our modern kitchen.

Mother was a determined lady, and she tried again, this time wrapping the dough in a comfortable blanket, and setting it on the warm radiator to rise. Those buns were a great success, and we often had buns after that. In the winter, when the central heating was on, the dough was set on a nice warm radiator to rise. But on a summer day, Mother would occasionally, a bit surreptitiously, set out the dough, carefully wrapped in towels, to rise in the sun, the way it seemed to like.

A good cook must always be ready to compromise, or so it seems.

MRS. TREMBLAY'S BOEUF BOURGIGNON

Mrs. Tremblay lived across the street. Although the Tremblays, like most of our neighbours, were French-speaking, she herself was of English-speaking origin. That could have influenced the strong friendship that grew up between our families.

I would like to be able to say our children played together, but I well remember watching, one winter day, when Cathy, our eldest daughter (then about three years of age), was sent out to play in the snow with her friend Janet. The Tremblays' door opened, and their son Marc, stuffed into one of those snowsuits that made it difficult to move, was thrust out, obviously under instructions to "go and play with Cathy." Marc trundled across the road with a cheerful grin. The two girls spotted his approach and went over to meet him in what I thought was a very friendly spirit. I was a bit taken aback when they immediately sought to establish feminine superiority by giving him a couple of good belts about the ears. Marc, in astonishment, made a tentative swing in retaliation, at which the two girls promptly set up a loud complaint that Marc had hit them. Fortunately for neighbourhood peace, the two mothers applied common sense and castigated all participants equally.

But no, I can't say our children played together.

Dr. Tremblay was a medical doctor, so naturally Mrs. Tremblay became the local authority on all things medical, being called into our house for advice at health crises, major and minor.

But it was in matters culinary that her authority reached its pinnacle. She was an excellent cook, and her access to the supposed secrets of French-Canadian cuisine gave her that added *je ne sais quoi*. My wife, Jean, would consult with her whenever a culinary crisis threatened. What more natural than, when Jean decided to serve Boeuf Bourgignon at a party, and found that her many cookbooks were unaccountably silent on the subject of this delectable stew, for her to call Mrs. Tremblay and ask for her recipe. Mrs. Tremblay promptly obliged, dictating the recipe then and there over the telephone.

The dish was a great success, and it immediately became a reliable standby in Jean's roster of party dishes. And Jean always made a point of generously crediting Mrs. Tremblay with this recipe.

Some years later, after both families had moved away from that location, I met Mrs. Tremblay, and we fell to reminiscing. I commented that her Bouef Bourgignon had always been a favorite in our house and was famous among our guests. She smiled and said she remembered that and had always been embarrassed about it because, she explained, she'd never made Bouef Bourgignon in her life. When Jean had called asking her assistance, she'd wanted to help, so she'd told her how she imagined Boeuf Bourgignon should be made. The resulting dish was such a success that she'd never had the courage to confess.

I guess a good cook, particularly one with an established reputation, must be ready to "wing it" when the situation calls for it.

GOOD OLD-FASHIONED COUNTRY WISDOM

My father was originally a country boy and, I suspect, was secretly convinced this gave him an advantage over city folk, particularly when it came to purchasing any sort of farm produce. Certainly he loved to do the marketing, and especially liked to go to the farmer's market near his office. Such an excursion was not to be taken lightly. He would first do a complete survey of all the produce stands to identify the best offerings with the freshest fruits and vegetables, and to establish the going prices. In this way, he tried to establish a good base from which to start his bargaining. And he had a lot of little tactics to ensure nobody tricked him or passed off inferior goods on him.

For example, in blueberry season, the people with berries to sell would display their baskets of fruit on their stalls, often in the sun. Blueberries, in those conditions, will tend to settle and become soggy. To disguise this, the sellers would often keep a basket of fresh berries in the shade under the stand, and would periodically sprinkle a few fresh berries on top of the baskets on show, to give the illusion of freshness.

Father was well aware of this technique, and had established a counter-strategy. When he intended to buy blueberries, he brought his own basket with him, and required the vendor to pour his berries into this new basket. If the berries were not fresh and had been the subject of the sprinkled-berries technique, they would betray themselves by not pouring freely. Dad would then look disappointed, return them to the vendor, and pass on to another stand.

I witnessed this strategy in action one day when I went with Dad to the market. He walked up to one of his regular blueberry suppliers and asked if he had good blueberries that day. "Oh, yes," he answered with a smile, but then, glancing at Dad's basket, he added, "but not for you!" He obviously wasn't about to waste his time on a losing effort.

I came to realize Dad saved a lot of time and trouble with his "country wisdom."

However, my father was not averse to adopting good advice or ideas from others into his collection of country wisdom.

In the west end of Montreal, there were a number of fruit and vegetable stores, all operated by various members of a Chinese family named Young. There were not very many Chinese in our neighbourhood in those days, but the Youngs' stores all had produce of superior quality. We often went to them.

One day, I went with my father to do the shopping. We were in Young's store, and my father was looking through a bin of Swede turnips. The Chinese proprietor came up to us and asked if he could help us. My father replied that he wanted a nice sweet turnip. The Chinaman immediately searched through the bin, and selected a turnip, saying it would be very sweet. My father took one look at it, and said, "But I don't want that turnip. It's all worm-eaten!"

The groceryman insisted that we buy it, repeating that it would be very sweet, and explaining, "You know, you can't fool the worms when it comes to selecting a sweet turnip."

We bore our purchases home, including that ugly looking turnip. When Mother was unpacking the groceries, and came across the turnip, she exclaimed, "Bruce, whyever did you buy this turnip? Look, it's all worm-eaten!"

My father just looked wise, and said, "But My Dear, if you want a really sweet turnip, you should always look for a worm-eaten one. You can't fool the worms, you know."

The turnip was, indeed, very sweet, and that bit of "country lore" became a permanent addition to my father's collection. An expert must always be ready to enlarge his store of knowledge.

I had reason to remember and adapt the worm-eaten-turnip theory some years later, when we lived in Zurich. Our Swiss garden contained a number of fruit trees, planted many years before by some wise gardener. Included were two plum trees and an apricot tree. During our first year first in the house, I was standing near one of the plum trees one day, when a wasp flew by me, almost hitting me in its haste, and landed directly on a plum, which he immediately started to eat. I wondered if there was a connection between that wasp and the worms and the turnip. Could you fool a wasp about sweet fruit, I wondered? I chased him off his meal, picked the plum, and tried it. It was the best plum I'd ever tasted. I realized the wasps were better judges of the ripeness of fruit than I would ever be.

From then on, I always waited until the wasps attacked the fruit on any of our trees before picking the fruit. I found the wasps always waited until the fruit was absolutely dead ripe. The results were fruit of a flavour and sweetness far superior to that of fruit you could buy in any store.

A DIFFERENT METHOD FOR MENU SELECTION

My wife Jean came from a family where her mother was all-powerful in her kitchen and certainly wasn't about to let her daughter muck about with any cooking. And after we were married, she came home to a house where the kitchen was dominated by Aunt Eva. So there was little opportunity for her to hone her culinary skills. Thus, when Aunt Eva retired, she suddenly found herself with little knowledge of cooking, in a family used to eating well.

But Jean was, by trade, a manufacturing chemist. And she treated cooking as just another chemical experiment. She followed recipe books with exactness in the confident expectation the recipes would actually work. Now I, exposed as I'd been to all that talk of the "art" of cooking, would never have believed that. But it worked perfectly, and she rapidly became an excellent cook.

However, she didn't make the same mistake as her mother. She encouraged all her daughters to learn to cook. They used to collectively embarrass me in fine restaurants by analyzing the tastes and probable contents of the various dishes, often arguing audibly amongst themselves.

All the girls became good cooks. Indeed, as teenagers, Cathy and Marg would often decide, on a Sunday afternoon, to make dessert for the evening dinner. Now that in itself wasn't a bad idea, but they usually only made this decision on Sunday afternoon, which meant they were limited to the ingredients already available in the house. In those days, the stores were closed on Sundays. Their technique was to empty the cupboards of anything they thought might prove useful, and then go through all the cookbooks for a recipe that could be satisfied with the available materials. Sometimes it took quite a search, but the results that were brought to the table, while sometimes new and different, were, on balance, pretty good. (Although I'm told that on one occasion when Jean and I were away, this technique resulted in a chicken dish that featured copious quantities of horseradish and ginger, and was pronounced by all as "probably pretty good but let's not eat it.")

Anyway, having written this, I have a glimmering of the reasons why so many of our cookbooks became so battered and dog-eared.

DO COOKBOOKS MULTIPLY?

With all the good cooks in our family I have never found it necessary to intervene in the kitchen. Of course I get called in for such important tasks as stove-moving and garbage-removal, but I generally don't get involved in the cooking end of things. (I do refute the rumour that I can't boil water. I can even boil eggs if pushed to it.)

Maybe that's the reason the astonishing proliferation of cookbooks somehow passed me by. When Barbara and I were married, she arrived in Japan with what I thought was a large collection of cookbooks (this in spite of the fact she's an excellent cook and no more needs any help from a cookbook than I need plans for the things I build. On the other hand, thinking of the embarrassing mistakes I occasionally make in that activity, maybe there is some method in her cookbook madness.)

Our kitchen in Japan was pretty small and was quickly overrun with the cookbooks. So I measured up the length of the cookbooks (or the height when stacked up if you wish), selected a piece of vacant wall, and built her a bookshelf with several feet of excess space. It was hardly finished when more books magically appeared to fill up all that reserve space. And in spite of my best efforts, cookbooks began again to spill out over the kitchen.

When we moved back to Mississauga, and to a much bigger kitchen, I immediately selected a convenient nook and installed a whole series of shelves, more than adequate for the cookbook collection. But do you know, new and unfamiliar cookbooks began to appear almost immediately, and are now again overflowing onto the counters? Do you suppose it's because of the confined quarters they live in on those shelves, or is it all those TV cooking experts who are responsible? I mean, how many recipes can there be, anyway?

I am certain that if I break down and build more shelves, the time-honoured Hamilton tradition that all horizontal surfaces must instantly be covered will come immediately into play, and the cookbooks will continue to overflow.

THE MARTINI, KING OF COCKTAILS

Mankind must have invented thousands of alcoholic liquids by now. And he has experimented with many, many combinations of those liquids, sometimes in combination with non-alcoholic additions, to make cocktails. Of those concoctions, only a few have gained general acceptance, and fewer still are popular. I believe the noblest of all is the martini: in its best form, a simple mixture of gin and dry vermouth.

It has been said there is no bad beer, only good beer and better beer. The same cannot be said of martinis. It's quite possible to make a bad martini. I have only to think of a poor, misguided stewardess on a British Airways aircraft vainly trying to explain to me that her martini was extremely dry. "After all, it's over half vermouth." I explained to her, as an indication of the amount of vermouth I expected her to use, that I had in my briefcase a miniature bottle of vermouth that I carried to enable me to make martinis in aircraft where they did not have pre-mixed cocktails. I'd been carrying it for at least six months and it was still three-quarters full! She gave up and brought me the bottles to do my own construction work.

The proper construction of a martini requires careful attention, not only to the ingredients, but also to the process. Surely, the finest example of the art of a master bartender is the construction of an extra-dry martini. I had a masterful demonstration on a warm summer noontime, while sitting in the cool of the Aviation Club in Brussels. The maître d' had an order for three martini cocktails, all extra dry, two straight up (that is, without ice, in a cocktail glass), and one on the rocks (that is, over ice, in a short tumbler).

He first set out his cocktail shaker, a bottle of gin, and a bottle of vermouth. The gin would have been already chilled, in his refrigerator. Then he set out two cocktail glasses and one short tumbler. He filled them each with ice to chill them thoroughly. He also half-filled his cocktail shaker with ice. He swirled it around to ensure it was thoroughly chilled. He then tipped it up to pour out any water that had been accumulated during that process. One mustn't dilute the gin, you see. He then poured a measure of vermouth into the cocktail container and stirred it around. After a brief stay in the container, the vermouth was also poured out into the sink, with a flourish, of course. He then poured a quantity of gin into the container, over the ice, which had been so carefully exposed to vermouth. A couple of careful stirs, not too vigorous in order not to "bruise" the gin (translation: "in order not to dilute it with water from ice melted from too vigorous a stirring"), and the martini was ready. So far, I was fully in agreement with his procedures, which were calculated to deliver the minimal amount of vermouth demanded by any serious martini drinker, in circumstances where any possible dilution of the gin was minimized.

It was his next action that marked him as a real expert. He disdainfully dumped out the ice from all the glasses. I'd expected him to retain the ice in the glass intended for the martini on the rocks. But no, that ice clearly wasn't good enough, and was summarily discarded with the rest. The martini in the container was carefully poured in equal amounts into the three waiting glasses. I needn't say his measure exactly filled the two cocktail glasses. To complete the martini on the rocks, he carefully spooned ice from the cocktail container into the short tumbler. That ice was clearly superior, as it had already been soaked in martini.

I thought that was the move of a master.

The martinis were then each garnished with a decorative twist of lemon peel, as I prefer them. The slim strip of lemon peel naturally curls itself into an elegant spiral. Some bar-tenders prefer to give the lip of the glass a gentle wipe with the lemon peel, others give the peel a swift little twist in order to deposit a minute drop of lemon oil into the cocktail, before depositing the peel itself into the glass. I believe the lemon has a much more subtle effect on the flavour of the martini than the more robust olive, used by some martini aficionados.

GREAT MEN AT PLAY

In the course of my career, I met a number of very impressive men, some presidents, chairmen, and managing directors, and some in lesser roles. I found they had many characteristics in common, notably, a commitment to hard work, and the ability to lead others to success. But, surprisingly, another characteristic they all had in common was the ability to relax and enjoy themselves. They all seemed to recognize the necessity of relaxation. In their total commitment to their work, they needed some "down time," some opportunity to relax and recoup their energies. This capacity for fun and relaxation displayed itself in many forms. In some there was a commitment to exercise and physical recreation, in others it found expression in their wit and willingness to play simple games and carry out simple—or even complex—pranks.

This chapter is not intended to list all the exceptional men I met. Rather, I plan to review examples of some of those memorable people at play.

A HANDSOME APOLOGY

In the fifties and early sixties, the Marconi empire, headed by the Marconi Wireless Telegraph Company (MWT) in Chelmsford, England, stretched to many parts of the world. And, in the tradition of an organization that had been in the forefront of the development of radio communication, all the Marconi companies around the world engaged in research and development to design their own products. Canadian Marconi was as active as the best of them. And that, inevitably, led to considerable duplication of effort amongst the various companies of the group. Even within the central laboratories of MWT, the largest laboratories in the group, there was considerable duplication, and yes, jealousy between the various product groups and individual laboratories. I once pointed out to their Director of Development that he had six different groups all trying to develop a specific type of power supply, something only I, as a visitor, was ever likely to find out.

I always felt Marconi wasted a major opportunity in not attempting to rationalize the development programs throughout the group.

But then I became the victim of just such a policy.

Mr. Sutherland was the epitome of a businessman of the fifties and sixties. In appearance, he was always meticulously groomed, with suits very well tailored, in the English manner. He was slightly portly, but he always gave the impression of energy, authority, and being completely in control. He was the managing director of MWT, and in that position, his influence throughout the group was almost absolute. He undertook to do exactly as I would have recommended: rationalize those development programs.

However, unfortunately, he chose to rationalize my major program out of existence.

At that time, I was responsible for a major laboratory at Canadian Marconi, which was developing wide-band, long-haul, microwave radio equipment. Such equipment was used to "relay" television and telephone signals across long distances, and was among the most difficult challenges to electronics engineers at the time. There was a similar program within the laboratories of MWT. They, in keeping with their history of advanced research and development, of course were pursuing the "ultimate" design, whereas we, subject to the competition of the North American market, attempted to design a product that was a compromise between cost, capability of manufacture, and performance.

There came a day when I was informed I should present myself at a series of meetings in London, called by Mr. Sutherland, and where I would meet with my immediate superior and our overall division manager from Canadian Marconi. And I was strictly enjoined that I should keep my mouth shut. Surely an alarming instruction, and one I was unlikely to succeed in following, given my nature. When I arrived in London, the meetings had already been in progress for a day, and it had already been agreed that the responsibility for wide-band radio should lie with the laboratories of MWT, and that the Canadian laboratories would henceforth confine themselves to the development of narrow-band equipment. It wasn't nearly as exciting a problem from the engineering point of view, but, as I knew, a much more difficult problem from the point of view of competition, and marketing. I wasn't asked.

I managed to largely follow my instructions for silence, until the final day.

After the conclusion of the meetings, Mr. Sutherland, in the glow of the success he had achieved in this matter of rationalization, invited all the participants to a grand luncheon the following day. We all duly presented ourselves to a grand dining room in a major London hotel, where we were entertained with a magnificent, five-course luncheon.

At the conclusion of the luncheon, all of the MWT engineers, who had come from Chelmsford, about an hour away by train, left to return home (and probably to benefit from the rest of the afternoon off). The Canadian Marconi contingent remained with Mr. Sutherland to enjoy an extra brandy or whatever. Mr. Sutherland waxed loquacious about the wisdom of the Canadian management in recognizing that the knowledge and experience resident in the MWT laboratories made them so much more suited to tackle the more difficult problems, and that the "colonial" laboratories should confine themselves to the simpler problems. Such sentiments were quite common among the English leaders in all disciplines in those days. But I was well aware of the development programs in the MWT labs at the time; I had been maintaining a close liaison with their microwave laboratories for a number of years. I considered their program to be pursuing an impossible standard, unlikely to result in a practical and competitive product. And I could stand the patronizing attitude no longer (and possibly was emboldened by that extra brandy).

"Sir, I wonder if you realize that your engineers are designing you a gold brick?" I said. "It will be far too expensive, and you'll never be able to sell a nickel's worth."

Talk about fouling the doorstep. "Who is this young man? I was told he was relatively intelligent."

The frost set in. I was ostracized by everyone in England, and even my own superiors wouldn't speak to me for some time. And after I returned from England, it was made quite clear that I should not ever return there.

It was perhaps five years later before this matter was considered to have blown over, and seven or eight years before I was sent again to England, again to visit MWT, but in an entirely different role. By that time, MWT had retired from the broadband radio field, their product having proven to be too expensive. Mr. Sutherland had retired, and only visited Marconi headquarters about once a week, presumably to ensure his successors were following the good practices he'd laid down so painstakingly. Certainly there was ample reason for Marconi's in England to regard him as a sound executive who had contributed to their success as a business.

I was walking across the parking lot when a limousine rolled up to the door. (English limousines always roll, they don't just come or drive up.) And I observed, at some distance, that a somewhat portly, but very well-groomed gentleman was alighting. He turned and looked at me, apparently trying to determine who I was. And then Mr. Sutherland walked across the parking lot and stopped right in front of me. He looked me up and down as if to satisfy himself that I was indeed Hugh Hamilton. And then he spoke just three words. "You were right," he said, and he turned and walked away.

Somehow, I always felt I'd received a most handsome apology.

Addendum:

Mr. Sutherland had a well-earned reputation for brief and pointed remarks.

Bernard Johnson was in charge of one of Marconi's major laboratories in the Baddow Research Laboratories. On a day when the laboratory had a group of important visitors, requiring Bernard's attention to show them around his laboratory, Mr. Sutherland telephoned, asking to speak to Mr. Johnson. The engineer who answered the phone explained, "Mr. Johnson is entertaining." There was the briefest of pauses, after which Mr. Sutherland commented tersely, "Strange, I never found him so."

A SURPRISING AURA

I had some interesting experiences early in my career at Northern Electric (soon to be renamed Northern Telecom). I first arrived in the early seventies, in what became known as the Lobb years.

For some years, Northern had been a wholly owned subsidiary of the Bell Telephone Company of Canada. Its chief role in life was to supply the needs of the parent company for telephone equipment, in the Canadian market. For designs, they had relied primarily upon Bell Labs, the design laboratories of the mighty AT&T (American Telephone and Telegraph Company, the largest and most powerful telephone company in the world, which originally had owned a major portion of Bell Canada, and also owned a significant portion of Northern Electric). But the winds of change were already blowing in the late sixties. In a landmark decision, at the behest of the U.S. Monopolies Commission, the U.S. Courts had instructed AT&T to divest itself of all its overseas holdings. While they were doing that, they also divested themselves of their interests in the Canadian telephone companies, and they sold whatever interest they had in Northern to Bell Canada. That meant Northern could no longer survive as a somewhat sleepy adjunct of Bell Canada, which had also suddenly become independent. Northern Electric had to become much more competitive, and quickly.

The chosen solution was to undertake a complete reorganization to reform and revitalize this sleepy company, and make it into an aggressive, market-oriented, highly competitive organization, capable of competing not only in Canada, but in the vast U.S. market. In a situation like this, it is imperative that the man in charge be completely ruthless. It is usually necessary for him to come in from outside the company. The man chosen for this role was John Lobb, an experienced American telecommunications executive with a reputation for ruthlessness in any and all problems he might encounter. He had been with Northern for over a year when I first arrived, and had certainly lived up to his reputation. There were tales of his firing managers at all levels from the top to the bottom, and of his eliminating entire divisions and operations that he found unsatisfactory. Nearly everyone in the middle levels of management went in fear and trembling lest Mr. Lobb cast his gimlet eye on them. He had certainly created an aura about himself.

I should note, however, that those who survived those "Lobb years" were, afterwards, unanimous in their belief that he had saved the company and transformed it into the successful, competitive company it continues to be to this day.

I was brought into Northern to manage their microwave radio business, a field where I'd gained extensive experience while working at Canadian Marconi. I was introduced to the great man quite early in my employment; indeed, I was seated at his table at a company dinner. I found him a bit gruff and certainly autocratic, but he hardly seemed the ogre I'd been led to expect. I thought little more about it as I went about the business of becoming familiar with my new colleagues and responsibilities. I didn't expect to see much of Mr. Lobb at my level.

I was sitting at my desk one morning when the phone rang. When I answered, a gruff voice at the other end said, "John here, Hugh." The voice went on, "I see in the papers that both Raytheon and RCA are trying to sell their microwave tube plants. We should buy one of them!"

I was startled, and concentrated on trying to figure out who "John" might be. I gave only fleeting thought to the question. In the atmosphere at that time in the company, most people, knowing it was John Lobb, would have replied, "Yes, Sir, I'll look into it immediately." But I, in my surprise, didn't stop to consider. And, I'd had many microwave tube makers as suppliers in Marconi, and I didn't think their business was very attractive. About the time I'd figured out it was John Lobb speaking, and without thinking too hard about it, I blurted out, "What in hell for?"

Mr. Lobb, apparently unperturbed, replied, "Well, we could use the tubes in our business."

I was on a subject that I knew well, and gave no thought to the deterring effect of Mr. Lobb's formidable reputation. "I have the only business in Northern that uses any microwave tubes and I couldn't keep a tube production line busy for more than two weeks a year."

"Well, we could sell the tubes, then."

"John, the trouble with the microwave tube business is that there are a zillion different kinds of tubes, and no one ever buys more than four of any one kind."

"You're right. When I was with ITT, they had a tube plant and it never made any money. We won't buy one."

And he abruptly hung up. I later wondered what kind of trouble I might be in for my cavalier responses.

I learned later that Mr. Lobb scoured the newspapers every morning before coming into the office. Every day he had a list of new ideas. And he tested them on whoever he considered might be knowledgeable on that particular subject. He knew perfectly well most of ideas were no good, but if he could find even one that was viable, he'd be quite happy. He was just looking for the kind of answer I gave him. He didn't want the much safer-seeming undertaking to "look into it" that most people in Northern in those days would have given him.

I never worked closely with Mr. Lobb. I'm sure it would have been an interesting experience, but from that day onwards, it seemed he trusted me the few times our paths did cross. That certainly made my life easier. And I had learned to rely on my own instincts and not be too concerned with the fears expressed by others. After this experience, I felt Mr. Lobb's aura of single-minded determination had a greater degree of flexibility than most people suspected. I was somewhat surprised at its vagaries.

I also observed later that while it was quite all right to disagree with John in private, you risked serious consequences if you ever had the temerity to challenge him in public. That was guaranteed to run you afoul of his considerable ego.

THE MAINTENANCE OF AN AURA

Northern's style of management always involved a high degree of centralized control. Every division held monthly operations reviews, lasting a full day, and covering all aspects of the business. Such meetings were attended by the group vice-president-in-charge, and often by corporate officers. And when it came to business planning and budgeting, massive meetings, involving the managements of all the divisions together, were held. In the "Lobb Years," the meetings where final budgets were reviewed and received corporate blessing (or otherwise) lasted most of a week.

On one such occasion, the budget meetings were held in the largest meeting room of a big downtown hotel. There were at least two hundred people present, seated around a huge U-shaped table. It was the practice to make presentations using slides projected by powerful overhead projectors onto two huge screens at the front of the room. To improve the viewing, the ambient lighting was turned down, with the result that the person making the presentation in front of the projectors looked out from a bright glare into what appeared to be complete darkness.

I was making the presentation for our division. We had a good story to tell, and I was confident our budget would be accepted. I had selected ten or twelve key slides for my presentation, but, of course, we had more than a hundred backup slides in order to respond to any conceivable question. I was about halfway through my presentation when a voice came out of the darkness. It could only belong to Mr. Lobb. No one else would interrupt at those meetings.

"Hugh, that seems pretty good, but do you have a chart comparing your budget, line by line, with last year?"

Almost before he was finished speaking, my comptroller, who was operating the slide machines, had thrown up a slide giving exactly the information requested. Since I didn't know exactly what he was looking for, I simply stood there and awaited developments. I was confident the comparison showed significant improvement over the previous year.

After a pause, the voice said, "Well, most of that looks pretty good, but what about line seven, where the expense goes from one and a half million last year to four point two million this year? We can't have that!"

I felt some diffidence as I replied, "I had hoped not to discuss that one, Sir. That's the share of corporate overhead assigned to my division!"

(Of course there was a somewhat long and complicated explanation for the difference, but that didn't seem the time to go into it.)

There were a couple of guffaws, hastily smothered, and then, after a pause, the voice said, "Very well. Continue."

And I finished my presentation without further incident.

That all took place on Tuesday morning, the first day of the meetings. The meetings continued through the week, into Friday afternoon, at which time Mr. Lobb gave a fifteen-minute summary of his reactions. He appeared quite pleased and satisfied with the budget plans. He proceeded to congratulate all the divisions on their performance, assuring us that if we met the budget objectives we would have a very good year, and would continue to meet the corporate objectives to show substantial year-on-year improvements. And then, at the very end, he said, ominously, "And Bud Thompson [the vice-president of Corporate Administration], you and your team will meet with me tomorrow morning at eight to explain why the corporate overhead assessment on Hugh Hamilton goes from one and a half million to over four million."

He'd waited through the entire week before condemning the corporate accountants to work through the night preparing a presentation, and to lose their Saturday into the bargain.

I guess if you have a reputation for ruthlessness, and you believe your objectives depend upon that reputation, you sometimes have to deliberately display that characteristic.

"AND THING"

During the late seventies, Walter F. Light was the president and later the chairman of Northern Telecom. He guided the company through one of its greatest periods of expansion and helped lay the foundations for further growth. He was a tall, loose-limbed man, deceptively easygoing in appearance. In fact, he was extremely intelligent and was seldom in any doubt as to the proper decision or course of action. One needed to be very careful about engaging him in argument.

Shortly after I arrived in Zurich, in 1977, I received word that Walter, along with several senior officials of the company, would spend a week in Europe, visiting customers. I was instructed to prepare an agenda and schedule visits in at least two countries a day. They would visit only very senior executives of the telephone administrations or perhaps the Minister of Telecommunications in a country.

In Europe, where the countries are so close together, such a schedule is possible, assuming considerable co-operation from the customers we wanted to visit. We could charter a private executive jet, and hop from country to country quite quickly.

With some misgivings, I had the schedule set up, and, to my surprise, all the appointments were made quite readily. But when we started the meetings, I was somewhat concerned with Walter's style. He had a well-deserved reputation as an expert on all facets of the telecommunications industry, and the upheavals it was undergoing at that time. His discussions were wide-ranging, covering many aspects of the telecommunications world. But his conversations with these senior people, while fascinating and exhilarating, could also have been puzzling and confusing to them. He would start into a subject, follow it for a few sentences, and then his active mind would suggest an even more interesting subject. He would abruptly stop his sentence in mid-stream, and add the words "And thing," which could be translated as meaning, "We've discussed this subject sufficiently for you to realize the conclusion. In the meantime, I've thought of an even more interesting subject." In retrospect, I eventually realized that one could, indeed, keep up with this process if one were paying close attention. In the meantime, he would start an entirely new thought.

I was so concerned that he had confused his listeners that I scheduled another trip several weeks later to visit the same people. I hoped to explain Walters' thoughts and smooth over any problems. I needn't have bothered. Everyone seemed quite satisfied with their "Walter" experience.

Six months later, I was again "granted" a week of Walter's time to visit customers. And he wanted to visit many of the same people again. Again, I was skeptical. I thought they might have been polite the first time, but feel put-upon to be asked to meet with him again in so short a time. Again, I was surprised to find little difficulty in setting up the appointments. And when we actually arrived, everyone made Walter very welcome and gave every indication of being pleased at his visit.

After several meetings, I continued to be puzzled. I finally asked one of the executives of the Swedish Telephone Authority, with whom we had particularly close relations, why they made such a fuss over Walter. He looked at me for a minute, and said, "Do you think I ever get to meet the chairman of Ericsson's?" (L. M. Ericsson's is the largest telecommunications supplier in Sweden, one of the largest in the world, and a close collaborator with the Swedish telephone company. I guess their executives followed the customs of much of the industry and chose to ignore their customers as much as possible.)

The penny dropped. That was Walter's secret. He understood the value of his position and chose to exploit it as much as possible, all while doing something that he genuinely enjoyed. And those he visited were flattered that he would spend time with them and include them in his reviews of the industry and its development. And at the same time, Walter would make good use of the careful briefing I had given him in advance to touch on any problems specific to the company he was visiting. That added to the impression of the attention he was giving to them.

Throughout his tenure as a senior executive, I enjoyed a week of Walter Light's time, twice a year, to visit his friends (my customers), and help develop the kind of relationships that are essential to a successful marketing effort.

I valued those trips, but I never did persuade him to cease saying "and thing."

THE STAMP

Walter Light liked to enjoy himself when he travelled. He often said, "If you can't have a bit of fun along the way, what's the point?" When we were travelling on that private jet together, he often thought up little games and contests to amuse us. For example, we'd hold a pool on the number of landing lights that would pass our plane before it lifted off the ground on take-off. That was quite a variable number, as the lights had different spacings at different airports.

On one trip, Walter proposed, at the beginning of the trip, that we all try to get an immigration stamp in our passports for each country that we visited. (This was in the days before the EU, and you still passed through immigration and customs in every country. However, it was by no means true that your passport was examined carefully and stamped each time you entered a country.) As I was travelling through Europe constantly, I already had a plethora of such stamps, but for the others, it would be a nice souvenir of their trip.

On that trip, we were to visit the Jutland Telephone Company, in Denmark. There were two telephone companies in Denmark. The Copenhagen Telephone Company provided service in and near Copenhagen. All the rest of the country was served by the Jutland Company, based in Aarhus, a smaller town in the northern archipelago of the country. The Jutland Company had displayed their independence from the capital city by adopting some of our equipment for use in their network. We considered them to be good friends and were looking forward to the visit.

Aarhus itself did not have an airport. We were to fly into a small airport, shared with the military, in a small town about twenty kilometers from Aarhus. But when we landed at that little rural airport, we found that the Danes, doubtless forewarned by the telephone company, had carefully arranged for all the formalities. There was even an immigration guard on duty. He had been well briefed, and was very careful to greet these VIP visitors cheerfully and offer us good Danish hospitality. He stood smiling at the door saying, "Welcome to Denmark. Have a good visit!" all the while waving us through the gate and towards our waiting cars. He certainly had no intention of examining the passports of these important people. We quickly found ourselves outside, next to the limousines. "But we never got a stamp in our passports," someone said.

There was a movement to go back inside and collect the missing stamps immediately, but I pointed out that our hosts were supposedly waiting lunch for us, and anyway, we'd be able to collect the missing stamps when we were leaving in the afternoon. We proceeded to our meeting.

Later, when we returned to that little rural airport, it was to find that same affable immigration officer waiting for us at the exit door. We were each holding our passports ready for his ministrations. "I hope you had a good visit. Have a good flight, now!" he said, with a big smile, as he waved us through the door.

"But aren't you going to stamp our passports?" someone asked.

"Oh, no. That isn't necessary," he replied, with a smile.

"But, I'd like to have a stamp," stated Walter

The guard tried again. "No, no, Sir. It really isn't necessary," with the biggest of all possible smiles.

Walter was not to be denied. "Look," he said, in tones none of us would have thought of ignoring, "I'd really like to have a stamp in my passport, as a souvenir of our visit."

The guard recognized a voice of authority, which wasn't about to be denied. His cheerful face collapsed into an expression of anguish and dismay. "But I don't have a stamp!" he almost cried, in tortured tones.

His day had been going so well as he played his role as official Danish greeter. Now his day was ruined and he had to face the possibility that the honour of the Royal Danish Customs and Immigration Service was to be tarnished by these persistent VIP visitors.

AN UNLIKELY IMP

We're all familiar with the idea that the higher one goes in a company the harder one is expected to work. It follows that the presidents and chairmen of major companies must be very serious fellows indeed.

In 1984, I was moved by Northern Telecom to Japan. In those days, Japan was seen as a closed market for most products, and in particular for telecommunications equipment. The telephone company (Nippon Telephone and Telegraph Company-NTT) was the largest telephone company in the world, and therefore represented a huge potential market. However, it was generally regarded as a hopeless task to sell any non-Japanese products to them. The company was wholly owned by the government, and all its purchases were made from Japanese suppliers. My assignment was to somehow penetrate that market.

I should note that this situation of "tied" markets had been very common throughout the world, with the governments of most countries owning their national telephone companies, and reserving those lucrative markets to suppliers from their own country. However, the advent of new technologies had made it increasingly difficult to maintain the monopolies of the national telephone companies, and the process of deregulation, breaking down those monopolies and consequently opening the markets, had started in many countries. During my years in the European market, I had participated in a number of markets hitherto totally closed. Northern's management, and particularly the chairman, Ed Fitzgerald, believed that a similar opening up of the Japanese market was about to occur.

The plan we established called for our newly opened Tokyo office to develop close and friendly relationships with the management of the telephone company, and with influential members of government ministries, and thus to be in a position to take advantage of any opportunities that might arise. It was to be a slow and careful process.

Of course, the most important executive for us in this process was the head of NTT. Dr. Shinto had been appointed as chairman of NTT after having been one of the key figures in the success of the Japanese shipbuilding industry. He was a most progressive and dynamic executive. We believed the government had selected him with an eye to leading NTT into a new, deregulated world. We thought we'd like to help him in that endeavour. I worked hard to develop a relationship with him, visiting his office whenever I could find an excuse. There are many holidays and festival days in Japan when it is appropriate to visit such senior executives, and you may be certain I didn't miss any of those opportunities. I always found him remarkably affable for such an important man.

The US government has for many years been concerned with unbalanced trade with other countries. The government of the day became increasingly concerned with the growing trade deficit with Japan, and perceived that Japanese trade practices were unfair in the extreme. And there's no doubt the Japanese had many regulations and practices that made it very difficult to develop trade with them. As a result, there were increasingly acrimonious trade negotiations between Japan and the USA. In particular, the US government insisted very strongly that the market for telecommunications be opened to US suppliers.

Notwithstanding that we had major factories in the US and could claim to be American suppliers, we tried to distance ourselves from those pressure tactics and the resulting hard feelings. Instead, we tried to maintain a more sympathetic stance toward our potential customers. Inevitably, this led to some difficult situations.

On one occasion, at a major seminar, a pair of Canadian government scientists, doubtless briefed by overenthusiastic members of the Canadian embassy staff, interjected into their presentation on a quite different subject, a proposal that the Japanese should purchase some Northern Telecom switching equipment. In view of our policies, I reluctantly decided I must introduce myself to the audience. In what I hoped was a humorous manner, I thanked the gentlemen for their efforts on our behalf. I then went on to state that we felt we were receiving co-operation from Japanese authorities, that our products were receiving fair consideration, and that I was confident we would eventually achieve significant sales. All these statements were true, if somewhat unpopular with the US negotiators.

I knew my actions would annoy the Canadian scientists involved and the embassy staffers. I consoled myself by reminding myself none of them would ever buy anything from me. I was much more interested in the reactions of the Japanese audience. Although I didn't know it, the legendary Dr. Kobayashi was present in the audience that day. He was the chairman emeritus of NEC (Nippon Electric Corporation, the largest supplier of telecommunications and electronics equipment in Japan) and the acknowledged dean of the telecommunications managers in Japan. After the meeting, he sent one of his assistants to ask me to meet with him so that he could thank me for my comments. I was very pleased.

I was even more pleased when Dr. Kobayashi followed up a few weeks later at another major seminar. A speaker from AT&T, the enormous

US supplier, and owner of the Bell telephone network, had given a very brash speech. (They were also the main recipients of US government support in the acrimonious trade negotiations.) He had described AT&T as by far the world's leader in innovation in telecommunications, and the inventor of digital technology. He asserted boastfully that his company should be the one the Japanese would feel pleased and even fortunate to become associated with in their future planning.

Dr. Kobayashi, speaking next, commented that there were three companies represented on that platform who were in the happy position that they had escaped from AT&T (Northern Telecom, ITT and NEC had all been part of the AT&T international empire before it was broken up). He went on the say that, to his knowledge, Northern Telecom and not AT&T had been the originators of modern digital technology. His dislike for AT&T was apparent

I always felt these two incidents were closely related and that Dr. Kobayashi was signalling his acquiescence to Northern Telecom having a position in the Japanese market. I also felt this was evidence that our subtle efforts were succeeding in Japan.

Our continuing effort to be friendly and sympathetic placed us in the position of being the players in the white hats, surrounded by all those bad fellows in the black hats. We hoped that when NTT inevitably did decide to choose a supplier from outside the country, they'd think first of those nice fellows in the white hats.

There came the day when, at a time when pressure from the American trade negotiators was particularly intense, we felt strong enough to make a proposal to NTT. Mr. Fitzgerald and I went to Dr. Shinto's office, as we did every time our chairman visited Tokyo. But this time, we gave him a short letter offering to sell, at a very good price, a large quantity of our small telephone switches. We knew they were particularly suited to the Japanese telephone system, as we had already made our equipment compatible with the Japanese network—no small achievement. And, they would be widely applicable to their rural switching requirements, making them economically advantageous to NTT. Further, no Japanese supplier had a similar product to offer. We made the point that we were submitting this letter privately in the hope it would provide a solution to the problems US pressures were creating. If he did not find our proposal interesting, he could destroy the letter. We promised we would never make any public announcement about our proposal.

Mr. Fitzgerald went home to North America, and there was a period of several weeks when nothing happened. Then, I went to visit Dr. Shinto, ostensibly on another matter. When our discussion was complete, and just as we were leaving, I asked him whether he'd given any consideration to our letter. I'm sure he knew from the beginning of our meeting that this was the real purpose of my visit.

"Oh yes," he said, with a bit of a smile, "I would like to discuss that with Mr. Fitzgerald the next time he comes to Tokyo. "

Ed Fitzgerald found it convenient to visit Tokyo the very next week.

When we informed Dr. Shinto that our chairman would be in Tokyo, he promptly invited us to lunch. Mr. Fitzgerald, taking my senior Japanese advisor and myself with him, went to meet with Dr. Shinto and two of his senior executives in a private dining room in a major hotel. As we were served cocktails and hors d'oeuvres, Dr. Shinto began to talk about his experiences in the shipbuilding industry. As Dr. Shinto knew, Mr. Fitzgerald's family had been major shipowners in the Great Lakes, so he, too, had tales to tell about ships. They discussed ships all through the cocktail hour. The rest of us didn't say much of anything.

We moved to the dining table. Still Dr. Shinto talked about ships with Mr. Fitzgerald. They talked ships through the soup course, the main course, the dessert course, and through coffee. The rest of us continued to say little.

Finally, after nearly three hours, Dr. Shinto and his party stood up to leave. We thanked them for a truly sumptuous lunch. And they walked out the door. Not one word had been said about our proposal. We were dismayed. But, at the doorway, Dr. Shinto turned, and with a twinkle in his eye, and a mischievous little grin, said, "Oh, by the way, that proposal you gave me. We intend to pursue that!" And he reached over and shook Mr. Fitzgerald's hand. Then he turned, without another word, and left.

I'm sure Dr. Shinto thoroughly enjoyed himself on that occasion. Ed Fitzgerald told me afterwards that the hardest thing he'd done in some time was to resist asking about our proposal, and to continue to discuss ships. And I thought Dr. Shinto displayed a surprising, hidden talent for impish behaviour. Who would ever expect such a trick from such an important person, and on such an important subject?

As for me, I knew the Japanese did most business on the basis of a handshake. They considered that signified their word had been given. And while it took us a further nine months to arrive at a contract, I always believed I had a contract from that moment. The contract proved to be the biggest contract NTT ever awarded to a foreign supplier in that era.

A REMARKABLE PUT-DOWN

In my international career, I always felt that being a Canadian gave me an advantage. Canada was seen by many of our international customers as a relatively small country, with no political or military ambitions. We seemed far less threatening than some larger and more aggressive countries. In many cases, we seemed a sympathetic country, struggling against similar problems as our customers. And Canadians, as a race, are much less aggressive, much more easygoing, than many of our competitors. It was a characteristic we took great care to emphasize.

Much of the time, our major competition was AT&T, the American Telephone and Telegraph Company, the largest supplier of telecommunications equipment in the world, with the largest base market in their own telephone companies. Further, their products were designed and developed at Bell Labs, the most prestigious telecommunications laboratory in the world. The telephone network they had designed and built in the United States was the largest and most efficient in the world. Small wonder they firmly believed they had the best products to offer, and that customers would be ill advised to choose any other products.

The representatives of many American firms had much the same beliefs, and reflected them in varying degrees of arrogance when dealing with customers. They all had a tendency to imply to customers, "It works well in the USA, so it must work well for you. Don't question it! Just buy it!"

One example of this American arrogance was the visit of Lee Iacocca, the legendary chairman of Chrysler. When he visited Tokyo, the American Chamber of Commerce arranged for him to address a large breakfast meeting of senior Japanese businessmen and officials. He told them, "We have a great little mini-van that would be ideal for use in Japan. You should be buying them!"

A voice from the crowd called out, "Which side is the steering wheel on?"

"That doesn't matter," replied Mr. Iacocca.

The Japanese drive on the left side of the road, and have horrendous traffic problems. But if he thought about it at all, Mr. Iacocca apparently thought they should ignore the obvious requirements, and buy his vans without question, even though they were designed to be driven on the right-hand side of the road.

The president of AT&T Japan at the time was Mr. Moody. I met him several times; he seemed a nice enough fellow, although he did have one bad habit. He stood well over six feet tall, and was somewhat portly to boot. When talking to you he always stood very close to you, thus forcing shorter people like me to tilt their head back to look up to his face. The Japanese, particularly the older generations, are a very short people. Indeed, I seemed quite tall in comparison. But I suppose Mr. Moody stood just as close to them and thus made them feel even more disadvantaged. Hardly a good way to make an impression of friendliness. And I suppose he had other thoughtless characteristics that might also irritate the Japanese in general. For example, I'm sure he also reflected the overbearing opinions about products so common among his colleagues. I don't know what Mr. Moody did to Dr. Shinto, the Chairman of NTT, but, as you'll see, he must have done something fairly severe.

During the period when we were waiting for NTT to confirm they would offer us a contract to supply small public exchanges, AT&T also submitted a proposal to NTT. However, where we had presented our proposal privately, AT&T chose to make a public announcement of their proposal. That, in itself, would have irritated the management in NTT. Nonetheless, NTT did evaluate both proposals. I suppose the AT&T people couldn't imagine their equipment would not be the winner. Indeed, in mid-December of that year, they received a request to visit Dr. Shinto's office on the following morning. They assumed they were to be awarded the contract, and even held a small celebration, to which one or two of our employees were invited. I imagine they were somewhat chagrined on the morrow when they were told the contract would go to Northern Telecom. It's possible their attitudes at that time managed to irritate Dr. Shinto.

It took a number of months to negotiate the final contract, during which time we worked very hard to satisfy all the NTT requirements. Shortly after the contract was finally signed, the Japanese Electronics Industry Association held a major reception to celebrate their fiftieth anniversary. Dr. Shinto was to be the speaker. Naturally, I led a delegation of Northern staff to attend this event and support Dr. Shinto.

Such major receptions are very common in Tokyo. I believe, if one had the stamina, one could attend such a gathering, attended by up to two thousand people, every day of the week. They're held in the grand ballroom of a major hotel. You are expected to arrive sharp on twelve o'clock, when they open the doors. A magnificent buffet is offered, with all the delicacies of both the Western and Asian worlds, displayed in great abundance on the buffet tables. To a man, all those successful, well-paid, Japanese businessmen would rush to the tables and proceed to eat as if they hadn't eaten in a week. Within fifteen minutes, the magnificent spread of food will be entirely demolished. Then the guests will start to circulate and chat, well supplied with liquid refreshments to fuel their talk. It took me some time to get used to this order of doing things; my inclination was always to chat first, and eat later, but that tactic led to there being little left to eat when I was ready.

As planned, Dr. Shinto gave an excellent speech, or so I was told by my interpreter. He discussed efficiency in Japanese business, and pointed out that, while Japanese factories had a justified reputation for efficiency, Japanese offices were exactly the opposite. He argued that it was imperative for Japanese business offices to become more efficient. I agreed with him on that.

After such a speech, it is the custom to approach the speaker and offer congratulations. A receiving line formed leading to Dr. Shinto, and I duly took my place in line. I should note that two Japanese gentlemen meeting in such circumstances would merely bow to one another, and say a few words. They would never touch one another. But, a Japanese who was used to dealing with Westerners would, when he met you, offer his hand to be shaken. This was a concession to Western habits, and you were careful not to overdo it with any additional contact. However, when it came my turn to speak to Dr. Shinto, and as I extended my hand, he reached over, grasped me by the elbow, pulled me over to him, and threw his arm around my shoulders. I was astonished. This was completely unexpected and out of the ordinary. He stood there talking to me, while I tried to figure out what on earth was going on. Eventually, he must have realized that I was puzzled, for he leaned over and whispered in my ear, "Don't move. Moody is watching us."

As I said, I don't know exactly what Mr. Moody did to annoy Dr. Shinto, but Dr. Shinto certainly planned a very public, and most mischievous, put-down.

A QUIET WEEKEND IN NEW ZEALAND

New Zealand is a relatively small, isolated country occupying a series of islands in the Pacific Ocean, about an hour's flying time to the east of Australia. The islands are quite mountainous, and there are few industries other than sheep farming. There are about three million human inhabitants, and about one hundred and thirty million sheep. Regretfully, from the point of view of the telecommunications business, the sheep have yet to learn to use a telephone. But one would think New Zealand would be ideal for a quiet, restful weekend.

Edmund B. Fitzgerald was the chairman of Northern Telecom throughout the period I worked in the Far East. He presided over a major expansion for Northern Telecom in international markets. He had very wide connections around the world and used them extensively to assist our international activities. In particular, he had used his time as a Marine Corps officer posted in Japan during the Korean War to develop many connections in Japan. He was instrumental in persuading Northern management that the Asian markets, and particularly the Japanese market, would open up. He developed much of the strategy that we employed in addressing those markets.

Ed is a big man, standing well over six feet tall. He always appears a very affable man, which somewhat conceals his great intelligence. He takes great care to be particularly polite to everyone, and not to offend by overpowering anyone with his size and presence. I like and respect him.

Ed spent a good part of his time in Japan and the rest of the Pacific area. There came an occasion when his plans called for him to spend a weekend in Australia or New Zealand. He told us he would like to explore the scenery in New Zealand. Accordingly, our manager in New Zealand was commissioned to plan a weekend trip to the "South Island," reputed to be the most beautiful part of that country. I guess I should have been suspicious when that local manager, who was middle-aged, declined to accompany us on this excursion.

There were five of us on that trip: Ed himself, our area manager, and his assistant, Barbara (my wife, who was also in the area on business and had been kindly invited to come along by Ed), and myself. Early on Saturday morning we presented ourselves at the private aircraft terminal in Wellington, New Zealand. A young man who looked hardly old enough to have graduated from high school introduced himself as our pilot. He led us out to a small twin-engine plane. I should explain that, while Barbara is an experienced traveller, she isn't confident of anyone else's ability to drive any vehicle, and she is particularly nervous about aircraft, even massive 747s. The sight of that teenaged pilot and that tiny aircraft was far from reassuring to her (or for any of us, for that matter). However, Ed maintained the stoic indifference of an imperturbable Marine Corps officer.

We all squeezed ourselves into the tiny cabin, and we took off over the bay at Wellington. There proved to be considerable turbulence, and that little aircraft bucked like a bronco. It seemed to take forever for it to bounce itself up to cruising altitude where we could relax and enjoy the scenery unfolding below us. It was a period of threatened hysteria. A thermos of hot coffee, liberally laced with brandy, uncovered by the area manager, certainly helped reduce the tension and allowed Barbara to maintain her aplomb.

I was concerned that Ed feel satisfied with the arrangements and not be upset by any shortcomings. However, he continued his impression of an unflappable marine officer.

After a flight of about two hours, the latter part of which was quite pleasant, we spiralled down into a deep valley in the middle of the South Island, to the town of Queenstown. It is reputed to be among the most beautiful places in New Zealand. However, we had little time to admire its beauties. We had hardly touched down when a uniformed girl appeared at our door.

"Are you the Northern Telecom group? Your helicopter is waiting to take you to your jet-boat ride."

We were hustled over to a tiny Bell helicopter. Ed, Barbara, and I managed to squeeze ourselves into the tiny cockpit, and we took off. That helicopter pilot proceeded to behave like a pilot in the movies; he demonstrated the most exciting characteristics of his craft. He flew us at full speed straight at a towering cliff, and at the last possible second, pulled us up in a vertical climb. We whipped up over the top of the cliff, leaving our hearts in our boots somewhere below.

We were flown over to the middle of a field, near a small river. Ed continued to maintain his pose as an imperturbable marine officer. He did express interest in what the next "event" might be.

We hadn't long to wait. We were hustled over to a small jetty, where a large powerboat was berthed. I suppose I should have been suspicious when they fitted us with life preservers, and instructed us to leave all loose objects such as cameras and purses on shore. We were then seated in the boat, which we were informed was a jet-boat. That meant it had two powerful, reversible, water jets mounted on either side of the boat, for propulsion. That arrangement meant it drew very little water, and was very maneuverable, making it very suitable for shallow, rocky rivers.

The pilot first took us out to the middle of the river and demonstrated he could make the craft spin on its axis simply by reversing one of the jets. He took delight in demonstrating the agility of his craft and his consequent ability to frighten his passengers. He subsequently gave us an extended tour up and down the river, which passed through a steep, rocky gorge. He took great glee in rushing straight at projecting rocks and brushing extremely close to dangerous outcroppings. It might have been a delightful trip, as the scenery, as much as I managed to glimpse, seemed quite beautiful. However, we spent so much time ducking and whirling that we never had much of a chance to admire the scenery.

Eventually, we found ourselves back on shore and standing in the field again, trying to recover our senses. Ed continued to display the aplomb of an imperturbable marine officer. His question about the next "event" brought the response that we would now ascend to the top of the highest peak around by means of a cable car.

We were soon swaying our way up a mountain. It might have been disturbing and exciting if we hadn't just survived the jet-boat, the helicopter, and the small aircraft. As it was, the major drawback proved to be the lack of gin for pre-lunch drinks at the restaurant on top of the mountain. Apart from that shortcoming, Ed maintained his imperturbable aura.

The afternoon was a bit of an anticlimax. Maybe those New Zealanders thought we should be given some time to recover. They forbore to offer us bungee jumping or hang-gliding, both of which I subsequently discovered were available. Maybe those were only for younger folk, or people less likely to be missed. We spent the afternoon on a pleasure steamer, on a pleasant cruise up the lake to a sheep station. We were treated to the spectacle of those amazing sheep dogs, herding sheep and selecting individual sheep from the herd. A shepherd controlled the dogs with whistles and hand signals, sometimes at a distance of up to a quarter of a mile. It was a quiet but interesting interlude. And the steamer had an adequate supply of gin.

We spent a quiet evening in a hotel in Queenstown. I learned we were scheduled to fly farther south in the morning, to view the deep fjords on the south coast of the South Island. I wasn't at all sure how much we might enjoy being cramped into that tiny plane again. I suspected there might be a repeat of turbulence over those fjords.

However, when we arose in the morning, it was to a dense fog. The weather forecast was for continuing fog. It was quickly decided the fjord trip would be useless and we decided to return to Wellington. However that entailed a further problem. It seemed our aircraft wasn't equipped with instrumentation to allow it to fly above the clouds. It was required to fly low and maintain visual contact with the ground. That would force us to fly out through a narrow gorge, which sounded ominous. However, our young pilot claimed it was quite simple and that he'd done it dozens of times, a claim that, in view of his apparent immaturity, I took with a grain of salt. Ed maintained his imperturbable appearance, but did insist the pilot obtain Barbara's assent to this procedure.

Again we crammed ourselves into that cramped cabin, and we took off. Almost immediately, we entered the mouth of a very narrow valley, with extremely steep walls. It seemed hardly wide enough to accommodate the wingspan of our tiny plane. As the valley twisted and turned, the pilot hugged first one wall of the gorge and then the other, in order to negotiate the tight turns involved. I remember watching a sheep, seemingly standing almost on our wingtip, sticking his tongue out at me. At one point, a loud alarm went off; we were all startled and Barbara asked sharply, "What's that?"

Ed replied, in his best imperturbable manner, "Oh it's just the stall alarm. The pilot has had to stall the plane in order to get it around this bend." Hardly an explanation calculated to calm the nerves.

Nevertheless, we survived that turn, and countless more. Finally, we flew out into the open. Barbara sighed with relief. "It's over!"

"Well, for now," the pilot said, " but there's still the upper gorge to get through!" I guess he didn't want us to become too sanguine.

Eventually, we won our way through yet another gorge, equally as thrilling as the first, and flew into clear air above the rolling landscape.

There remained one more thrill to our quiet weekend. We approached Wellington harbour over the sea, and, again encountered thick fog. We were forced to descend to a very low level, almost touching the waves. For some minutes, it appeared we were close enough to the water for those whitecaps to reach up and slap us out of the air. I, for one, was happy when our wheels touched down on the tarmac.

Those New Zealanders had succeeded in demonstrating to us that their little country was far from dull. I discovered afterwards that they have a reputation for thrilling vacation activities. However, they also demonstrated the quiet side of their natures to us. We had some difficulty in finding a restaurant in Wellington that was open for dinner on a Sunday night.

Ed maintained his imperturbable demeanor throughout. I suspect he started with an inkling that his quiet weekend might not be all that quiet. And I also believe he enjoyed playing hooky from his more dignified role as a CEO. He told me that I needn't tell any members of the board of directors about his quiet weekend. He wasn't so sure they'd approve of their chairman's recreational activities.

MONSIEUR PAGET ACQUIRES MARCONI

Monsieur Paget was by no means a captain of industry. Rather, he was a simple French Canadian farmer, living in Morin Heights, in the Laurentian Mountains, north of Montreal. I include him among my list of great people because he had at least as good a grasp of marketing as anyone I met I my long career.

The early part of my career at Canadian Marconi Company was spent in a laboratory devoted to the development of microwave radio relay equipment. These radio systems are used to relay signals from one station to another across the country. They carry either large numbers of telephone signals simultaneously, or television signals. In those days, they were really the only practical method of achieving large-capacity, long-distance transmission. Their tall towers, topped by huge parabolic antennae, which beamed the radio signals from one station to the next, were to become a familiar sight.

The design of the equipment represented, perhaps, the most difficult challenge of the day for electronic engineers. The problem is that as the signal passes from station to station, it picks up minute quantities of noise and distortion, no matter how well designed the equipment. If the noise and distortion rises beyond a very low threshold in any one station, then a signal passing through a series of relays will accumulate sufficient distortion as to become unsatisfactory. It's nearly impossible to measure with sufficient accuracy the performance of any single circuit, or indeed of one complete radio, when you're looking for such minute errors. One of the solutions to that problem is to build a test system of two or more stations, and to actually operate a microwave system for test purposes.

In our case, we started out in 1956 by locating our laboratory outside the main Marconi building, in a building partway up the side of Mount Royal, in Montreal. We then planned to have a microwave station about thirty miles to the north, on the crest of the first of the Laurentian Mountains. That would give us the necessary "line of sight" to enable the signals to beam from one parabolic antenna to the other.

In those days, there was great concern that Soviet aircraft might spy on North America, and even attack us, by flying over the North Pole. Hence there was considerable activity in the Canadian Arctic, building radar systems to detect such intruders. (I believe they actually detected countless migrating geese.) Canadian Marconi had a large division devoted to the construction and maintenance of such systems.

The construction of our test link seemed to be a suitable task for the "experts" of that division. Who better to select the site, purchase the land, and have the building erected that would house the equipment? In due course, we heard they had located a suitable site on the crest of the hills, and had purchased a plot of land from the local farmer, a Monsieur Paget. And a few weeks later, we heard that a building had been erected on the site and we could move in.

We later learned that the Marconi construction experts involved had asked M. Paget, who seemed a simple French Canadian farmer, to recommend someone who could build a small chalet for them. Monsieur Paget volunteered that he could do that himself, and that he would do it for fifteen hundred dollars. But our experts had a very good idea what it should cost to build such a building. Monsieur Paget's bid was so far below their best estimate that they disregarded his offer for fear they'd have endless trouble getting the building finished by someone who obviously didn't know what he was doing. Accordingly, they went to the nearest good-sized village, and found a local contractor who bid three thousand dollars for the job. (Remember, this was in the fifties, when you could still purchase a respectable car for about $1000.) That was much closer to their estimate. Our experts gave the contractor the job, and left. I gather they didn't go near the site until the job was finished.

Suffice to say that when we, from the laboratory, went to see our new building, we found a very nice four-room chalet, with running water, and rudimentary cooking facilities. We were very satisfied.

However, one day during that first winter, when I visited the site, I found that the water supply was frozen up. And since M. Paget had followed the custom of the countryside and looked after us in an almost proprietary manner, we asked him if he could fix our water supply. He readily undertook the task. To my astonishment, he went into the field across the road, dug a hole in the snow, and easily located the well supplying our water. Why it was over there rather than on our own property, I don't know. But M. Paget soon had our water running again.

I observed that he was pretty smart to know the location of the well. "I ought to," he said. "After all, I built this house."

"Oh, no," I said, "it was built by a contractor in St. Jerome."

But M. Paget laughed, and explained that the contractor really didn't want to do such a small job himself and had come looking for someone to do it for him. Monsieur Paget, who lived right next door, was given the job.

"How much were you paid?" I asked.

"The same as I asked Marconi; fifteen hundred dollars."

I suppose our experts slept more soundly at night knowing they'd put this construction job in the hands of a reliable contractor.

Monsieur Paget continued to look after us, and was always ready to help in any task that arose. He seemed fascinated by the "scientists" and their work, and would sit watching us for hours. I got the impression he wouldn't have welcomed anyone else from the surrounding countryside getting too friendly with us.

When we were ready to install the first cabinets of equipment, we anticipated some problems. Each cabinet weighed something over six hundred pounds, and we could only drive to a spot on the road some fifty feet down the hill from the cabin. We told ourselves that we'd get M. Paget and his team of horses to accomplish the move.

When we arrived with our two cabinets laid in the back of a big station wagon, M. Paget appeared promptly to see what interesting things we were going to do this time. We explained our problem and asked him to bring his wagon and team of horses. To our mystification, he said, "I'll get my sons" And he soon returned with two young men who towered over him in height and bulk. Monsieur Paget instructed them tersely to move the cabinets into the chalet. Whereupon, they each picked up one end of a cabinet as if it were a modest stick of wood and walked off up the hill. Inside the hut, they stood patiently, waiting for instructions, before setting the cabinet down. So much for our anticipated problems.

We spent the rest of that day setting up the cabinets and putting them into operation. Monsieur Paget and his sons sat in a corner and watched in apparent fascination. When we were finished for the day, I went out to the kitchen for some beer. I brought back three extra bottles for M. Paget and his sons. But when I went to give the beer to his sons, M. Paget reached out and took their bottles. "They're too young," he commented. For drinking beer, I assumed, not for moving heavy loads. But I also noticed no inclination on his part to return the beer to me.

As I explained, M. Paget treated us in a very proprietary manner. We, and Marconi, were his, and his alone. Any little jobs that arose he happily did.

One day in the spring, he approached me with the question, "Marconi, that's a big company, no?"

"Yes," I answered, wondering what had brought this on.

"Well, don't you think a big company like that should have a nice, gravelled road up to its building? I could do that for you. I have some gravel in my yard and I could make a nice road with my team and a plow."

"But how much would that cost?"

"Not very much—fifteen dollars." This was a long time ago, but that was still very cheap. I remembered that he'd built the building for only fifteen hundred dollars. And he'd accurately gauged the amount I could authorize without any reference to headquarters.

And so it came pass that on our next trip to the field station, there was a neat gravelled roadway leading up to the building.

Before we left that day, M. Paget again approached me with the question that was to become very familiar: "Marconi, that's a big company, no?"

I started to recognize a pattern. This time he convinced me that a big company like Marconi should have nice gateposts of squared timber, painted white. This time the cost was ten dollars.

And in that manner, M. Paget gradually brought our establishment up to the standard he felt was suitable for "Marconi, that's a big company." We acquired gates, flower gardens, a fence, rocks to border our driveway, and all manner of trimmings, all offered one at a time, and each at a very modest price. And in each case, M. Paget prefaced his presentation of his new proposal with, "Marconi, that's a big company, no?"

Monsieur Paget knew a lot more about how to deal with "a big company" and to capitalize on his opportunities than most sophisticated people. I've often wished I had him on my marketing staff.

IDIOSYNCRASIES IN BUSINESS

"My goodness," exclaimed the observer, as he watched two railway trains rush towards each other, at breakneck speed, on a single rail line. "What a funny way to run a railway!"

There are all sorts of idiosyncrasies as catastrophic as that way of running a railway company. There are all sorts of idiosyncrasies in business; some are subtle, some obvious, some merely comical, and some reflect the inherent characteristics of the business. Some are the result of actions of individuals. Some reflect the general conditions of that kind of company.

It is these idiosyncrasies that give a company personality and character. Certainly, they provide amusement for the bystander observing the foibles from a safe distance. I have always been amused by these distinctions in businesses and frequently enjoyed dissecting business operations for their idiosyncrasies. I have collected a few examples in this chapter to illustrate some interesting situations and characteristics. In some cases, the company involved progresses through a process of change, whereas in others the very characteristics of the business provide the interest. I hope you will be equally intrigued by these stories.

LEVEL PLAYING FIELDS

Throughout my career in international trade, I worked in an atmosphere of closed and protected markets. In the telecommunications field in particular, most markets were heavily protected. A characteristic of telecommunications is that the capital investments tend to be very large. And in most cases outside North America, the telephone company was a government monopoly. Thus it was fairly easy for the government to protect its perceived interests by controlling the purchases of the telephone authority, and insisting they be from local suppliers.

Other governments, notably the US government, which had large imbalances in international trade, took note of these limitations in trade and routinely demanded that trade become more open. The buzzword for their demands became "a level playing field," meaning that conditions for trade should be equal for all suppliers regardless of country of origin. The US government pursued their demands for level playing fields very aggressively, to the point where I believed they were harming their own interests. And, because the market for telecommunications was always so large, that market became on of the major battlegrounds for "a level playing field."

In those early days, there was little knowledge of or sympathy for global trade, and little appreciation of the benefits that might accrue to anyone practising open trade policies.

While I would have welcomed any easing of the barriers to sales, I recognized that individual countries had the right to protect their markets if they so wished. However, in so doing, they might suffer the drawbacks of not having immediate access to new technologies and techniques. I felt we had superior products, and it was our job to persuade clients of the advantages of purchasing our products. And I certainly thought it would be unwise to unnecessarily irritate our clients by making demands on them, particularly before we made any sales.

I believed the so-called playing fields belonged to the country in question, and they should have some say in the operation of the "game" within their own territory. I felt we should learn the rules of the local "game," and learn to compete in that "game." I felt that we could and should demonstrate that our products offered sufficient advantages to our customers to overcome any perceived advantage from protected markets.

The cynical might observe that, in the absence of any power to change the situation, that attitude was at least realistic.

The mechanisms used to protect markets were many and varied. The first line of defence was inevitably import tariffs and quotas. Countries like Australia, which was relatively isolated in international trade, imposed very high tariffs in order to protect their local suppliers, and that served them well for a while until it became apparent that their local industries were falling seriously behind in new technologies. For most countries, tariffs were reduced almost to zero, although the US negotiators sometimes failed to recognize the fact. Many countries used quotas for many types of goods. The Japanese made extensive use of quotas, for a wide variety of items, and still do to this day.

The most common ploy in telecommunications was to demand that products meet rigid specifications in areas that might affect the operation of the whole telephone network. In this, there was a legitimate concern that the operation of the entire network could be compromised by a single piece of non-conforming equipment. However, this factor was often greatly exaggerated. Much of this specification activity was unwarranted. The lists of specifications went from the trivial to the extremely complicated. As an example of the trivial, there was the German standard for telephone handsets, which required that the mouthpiece be two centimetres further from the ear-piece than the normal measurement elsewhere. To meet this requirement, a potential supplier would have to completely redesign all the moulds for his handsets. (I often suggested, jokingly, in private, that this confirmed that Germans were blockheads.)

At the other end of the scale were the French, who habitually responded to any request to qualify a product with the one word answer, "Non." Simple, straightforward, and clear, but not very helpful.

In most cases, the authorities would respond with a complex specification that your equipment would be required to meet in the event they decided to employ it. It usually entailed extensive modification and testing work, usually without any guarantee of successful sales.

As an example of the way the system worked, and the methods we used to overcome some closed markets, let me describe our experiences with the Deutsches Bundespost, the post and telephone company in Germany. They were one of the strongest monopolies in Europe at the time. We had been quite unsuccessful in finding any niche where we could introduce our products.

But the winds of change were blowing. New techniques and technologies were becoming available, which made it possible to provide greatly expanded service to clients, particularly business clients. In addition, the new technologies were much less dependent on access to the main network. Major national telephone companies were facing intense criticism from business for not providing the latest in technology and features for business users, who found themselves disadvantaged in competition with companies using more modern systems. In many cases, this was leading to the breakup of the established national monopolies, as new technologies could be introduced by independent service suppliers. The Bundespost response to this threat was to offer any and all new technologies themselves, thus maintaining their monopoly.

Thus it was, when a new technique emerged for data transmission called packet switching, the Bundespost undertook to provide a packet switching network. They were horrified to discover that there was no German firm that had a suitable product. However, Northern Telecom did, and we were invited to open discussions on the subject.

I must admit that although our salesmen were very enthusiastic, I was quite skeptical that the mighty Bundespost would agree to make such a major purchase from a foreign company. I attended the first meeting with the German authorities and questioned them closely. In particular, during the course of the morning, I asked, not once, but several times, whether we would be subject to German electrical standards. Each time, the senior German present, a vice-president of the Bundespost, assured me there would be no problem. However, he must have realized I had legitimate concerns. As we broke for lunch, he asked me to come with him, and he took me to a fairly large room, perhaps fifteen feet square. It was filled with stacks of paper, piled as high as you could comfortably reach. There were easily tens of thousands of pages of documents in that room.

He said to me, "Dr. Hamilton, this is where we keep all the records of our standards. There is no one person who knows all the standards in this room. But I can assure you, if we find a supplier that we don't want, we can always find a standard he doesn't meet." And then he smiled: "But in your case, we need you and your product, so we won't come near this room."

We'd found a way to play on his playing field and win. We subsequently installed in Germany one of the largest packet switching networks of the time, representing many tens of millions of dollars of business.

In the case of our Japanese marketing efforts, we found that a major impediment was the inbred assumption of all Japanese that any Japanese product is superior to any foreign product. That barrier is, of course, not subject to governmental management and control. I'll take an example from an entirely different field. In the mid-eighties, the US government was much exercised about the quota that the Japanese imposed on the import of American beef. One weekend, I noticed that the meat department of our local market was offering, side by side, steaks of Japanese Kobe beef and American beef. Now Kobe beef was the product of a careful process that involved each cow having a "cow-maid" who massaged it each day to force the fat into the beef. And each day, the cow received a large measure of beer to fatten it up. This produced exceptional beef, with outstanding flavour, and so tender you could cut it with a fork. But, of course, that Kobe beef was about three times as expensive as the American, and that American beef was very good as well. I marked the top steak on the pile of American beef. Three weeks later, I looked again and that same steak was still sitting there. The problem wasn't the quota; it was the disinclination of the Japanese housewife to purchase non-Japanese products. The Americans would have been far better advised to mount a campaign to persuade the Japanese consumers of the benefits of their product.

In later years, when explaining my beliefs in this matter, I would often refer to the experiences of Frank Filchock.

Frank was a professional football player. He was very good; indeed, for a time, he was the quarterback of the New York Giants, one of the premier teams in the National Football League in the USA. However, he and some of his teammates were accused of betting on games, and they'd been banned from the league. Frank came to Montreal, where he became the quarterback of the Montreal team in the Canadian league.

I never heard that Frank complained about having to play in an inferior league, nor that he had to play a game where the rules were considerably different from the game he knew. The Canadian game had only three downs instead of four, each team had an extra player on the field, the field itself was ten yards longer and thirteen yards wider, many of the rules differed, and even the scoring was different. But Frank was playing football, however strange the conditions, and apparently happy to have the opportunity.

Frank didn't even complain about the field the team used. They played at an old baseball stadium. It wasn't quite big enough to accommodate a full-sized football field, so the field was shortened by twenty yards. And since it was a baseball stadium, it had a pitcher's mound in one part of the field, which the stadium owners declined to remove just because someone wanted to play a bit of football. Frank took all that in stride; indeed, he even designed a series of plays where he would run over to that pitcher's mound, stand up on top of it, and throw passes from his advantageous perch, while his linemen down below fended off the opposition trying to get at him.

Rather than complain about the problems, Frank and his team went on, one year, to win the championship and the Grey Cup.

I always felt that was a good illustration of my belief that the best way to deal with an uneven playing field, in business or in life, is to learn the rules of the game as the locals would play it, and then to figure out how to win.

THE IMMUTABLE LAWS OF WAX AND WANE

It seems to be the rule for all organizations to wax and wane over time, and often, when waning, to be gathered up by a new entity that is in its "waxing" period. This seems to apply to large and small entities, from complete civilizations and great empires to companies, corporations, clubs, and even the local church. So it was with Marconi's Wireless Telegraph Company (MWT). There came a time, in the late fifties, when it was considered too small to survive in a world where electronics companies were becoming larger and more powerful every year. Even the pioneering history and technical reputation of MWT wasn't proof against their growing rivals. So it was decided to merge with the English Electric Company, a very large conglomerate that had grown rapidly in England during the war years, chiefly as a major manufacturer of warplanes. That they had little or no activity in the electronics field was not seen as a drawback. Indeed, quite the contrary. In those days of conglomeration, it was thought Marconi's would give English Electric additional strength by adding an electronics capability.

The chairman of English Electric was Lord Nelson, a self-made industrialist with a reputation for getting things done. By the time he became associated with Marconi's, he was in late middle age, and his son, who of course was known throughout the group as "Half Nelson," would take over the reins before too many years. But that's another story. I should, however, make it clear that I respected Lord Nelson very much, admired his capabilities, and liked him as a man.

Shortly after the merger took place, Lord Nelson was brought, in a cavalcade of limousines, to the London offices of MWT to view the visible evidence of his new possession. Marconi House was an imposing, seven-storey office building on the Strand. While it was not actually the headquarters of the company, it functioned as its very imposing London presence, and often appeared to be the headquarters. To add to its panache, the building was once the site of the first regularly scheduled radio broadcasting station in the world, Marconi 2LO.

It was also the site of Short's Wine Bar, a venerable institution in that section of the Strand. Short's had existed since before the memory of living man, so to speak. The English have long since put their priorities in proper order, and as a result, take a dim view of any plan that would result in the demise or even the moving of any well-established drinking establishment or watering hole. Thus, older pubs are deemed to have freehold rights over the land on which they stand. But those rights seem to apply only to the space actually occupied by the establishment. There seems to be an understanding that the air above the actual pub building is "fair game" and may be utilized in developing the whole area around the pub. Thus, when they came to build this new, modern, imposing office building on the site, Short's declined to move. And that was all there was to it. They had to build the new, modern, imposing office building around Short's, leaving it in its original location, and with its original, somewhat worn, but comfortable decor, but now as a part of a much bigger building, of quite a different style.

So it was that, as Lord Nelson stepped out of his limousine in front of the magnificent building that had so recently become a part of his empire, his eye fell on Short's, its ancient front occupying a prominent portion of the façade of the otherwise modern building.

"*What* is that?" he asked incredulously.

"Why, that's Short's, Sir."

"Well, what's it doing *there*?"

"Well, Sir, it's *always* been there."

"Well, get *rid* of it!"

And so, it was assumed, the fate of Short's was sealed. The great man had spoken.

In due course a letter, on the impressive engraved stationery of the chairman of the English Electric Company, was prepared by the company secretary, and dispatched to the "Chairman" of Short's Wine House, Inc. It read something like this:

> Dear Sir:
> I have the honour to address you on behalf of the Chairman of the English Electric Company. It has come to our attention that your enterprise occupies a portion of the property otherwise occupied by Marconi house. We do not believe such an arrangement is appropriate. Therefore, we wish to acquire your business, and to that end we would be obliged if you would advise us of your price for Short's Wine House.
> Yours, etc. etc.

There was a long delay, several weeks, in fact. But eventually, an envelope of impressive, expensive-looking paper, addressed to the Chairman of The English Electric Company, was received. And the letter inside was on the equally impressively engraved stationery of the chairman of Short's Wine House, Inc. Of course, it's possible the long delay in replying was the result of the time it took to acquire the stationery. The letter is reputed to have read something like this:

> Dear Sir:
> "We have the honour to be in receipt of yours of the 16th of last month. We regret to advise you that Short's is not for sale. However, we would be interested in your price for The English Electric Company.
> Yours, etc. etc.

Lord Nelson's reaction to this reply is not recorded.

Lord Nelson's wishes with respect to Short's were eventually carried out, but only after protracted negotiations. It was necessary to purchase a new location across the Strand from the original. The ancient wine house was dismantled, piece by piece, and reassembled at its new location, looking just the same as it always had, with all its woodwork displaying the patina of age and comfortable use. This was at a very considerable cost, of course.

I regret that Lord Nelson is now long gone. English Electric was subsequently deemed to have entered its waning period, and was, in its turn, amalgamated into an even larger waxing entity, the General Electric Company of England. And Marconi House passed into other hands, was demolished, and was replaced by an even more impressive building. But Short's is still there, apparently in blissful ignorance of the laws of wax and wane.

ETIQUETTE IN ELEVATORS

Stanislaus was the concierge at Marconi House in the Strand. He was of Polish origin and brought to this position an unusual air of old-world dignity and courtesy. As well, he had a remarkable ability to recognize everyone who entered the building even occasionally. I remember being quite surprised and pleased when, on the second occasion that I entered the building, some months after the first, he addressed me by name and title as I approached his desk.

Of course, Lord Nelson, the chairman of English Electric, who kept an office in the building from the start of Marconi's association with this conglomerate, was entitled to respect. But Stanislaus made certain that his treatment within the ground floor reception area under his command was impeccable.

There were three elevators in the lobby, serving all floors, and they were usually quite busy in the morning hours. But Stanislaus kept a sharp eye open for the arrival of Lord Nelson's limousine. He would then go promptly to the nearest elevator loading in the lobby and ask everyone to vacate that car, as "Lord Nelson required the use of it." And such was his influence that everyone would duly file out of the elevator and stand respectfully in the lobby.

When Lord Nelson came briskly into the lobby, he would thus find an empty elevator awaiting him. He would bid all those standing there a good morning and step into the car. He would then look around him in some apparent surprise, and remark, "But there's plenty of room in here. Why don't all of you come in?"

And all those who had just vacated the car would file back in, the doors would close, and the car would disappear on its upward journey.

I understand that Stanislaus never varied his routine, presuming, I guess, that it was not for him to decide who should ride with the great man. And I believe Lord Nelson would have enjoyed these brief opportunities to meet some of his myriad employees. I don't suppose he ever wondered why there was always a vacant elevator each morning when he arrived, nor realized that all those people who, each morning, he found waiting for an elevator, had just vacated a car for his private use.

PLUS ÇA CHANGE

A store—or shop, as our British cousins call them—usually has a very definite personality. The modern department store is often a model of gleaming, impersonal efficiency, but try and find a clerk in the shoe department, or someone who knows where your size of hat is kept. A big supermarket is run with great organization but without anyone to answer your questions, and seems to have every possible item except the particular one you need. A smaller corner grocery takes on the personality of its owner and often offers friendly and personalized service, but the owners' tastes had better coincide with yours. In today's world, you can choose the type and style of store you prefer.

Henry Birks and Sons is a specialty shop, catering so successfully to the public in the field of jewellery, silverware, fine china, and crystal that it became almost a tradition in Canada. For over a century, it was one of the flagships of the Canadian retail trade.

The first Birks store stood on the corner of Phillips square in Montreal, in the heart of the downtown shopping district. It was a fine Victorian structure; everything about it reflected solidity and reliability. The window displays were discreet understatements of the wonders to be found within. Everything in the store was beautifully displayed, each item carefully placed, to be seen at best advantage. Everything was immaculate, the silver was polished, and the crystal was gleaming. I always felt I was walking through a private treasure house.

The staff of the store somehow created a very special atmosphere, whether by training or simply by learning from their predecessors. They somehow conveyed the impression that they were privileged and perhaps slightly superior people. There was just that faint hint that they knew things you did not. You felt ever so slightly inferior. But somehow, you had a feeling of superiority over anyone who didn't shop there. I always felt that making a purchase at Birks was a special experience.

Even the robin's egg blue boxes from Birks were of a somewhat better quality than those of other stores. Their boxes became a symbol; the contents were a superior item of the best quality in its class. Brides looked for the blue boxes among their gifts, as giving assurance of welcome surprises within. Birks became a tradition of all things that were good and valuable in Canada.

In later years, Birks branched out and opened stores right across Canada. And somehow they managed to transplant that special atmosphere to each of their many stores. Each was immaculate, with beautifully chosen and arranged merchandise. And somehow that faint air of superiority was also transmitted throughout the chain of stores.

But gradually there came hints that all was not well in this paragon of retailing enterprise. Profits were dropping, year by year. Then, horror of horrors, there were hints of losses. Public reports of shareholders' meetings were discreetly noncommittal. But to me, and to many others, it was unthinkable that a fine institution like Birks shouldn't prosper and endure.

Shortly before Christmas that year, I dropped in to the Birks store in a nearby shopping mall to purchase a necklace that my wife wished to give to a friend. I knew exactly what she wanted. It was a necklace of Austrian crystal, available in several colours, a very pretty piece of upscale costume jewellery.

When I entered the Birks store I was surprised to find it empty of shoppers. It was a few days before Christmas, at a time when all of the surrounding stores were full of customers. But there, right on the nearest counter, was a rack of the necklaces I wanted, so I didn't stop to ponder the phenomenon. Well, perhaps I had the thought that maybe those newspaper reports of Birks's troubles had some substance.

I selected the necklace I wanted and looked around, expecting a clerk to come over to me. But while there were a number of clerks, none seemed to notice me. It was Christmas, so why get annoyed? Instead, I tried to remove the necklace from the rack in order to take it to a clerk. But the necklaces were cleverly tied to the rack, probably to prevent anyone from making off with one of them. At the point where I had succeeded in getting everything thoroughly tangled, a somewhat imperious and displeased clerk approached, and said, a bit sharply, "Sir, you can't do that. I need to do it for you!" She proceeded to disentangle the necklace from the rack.

I explained that I had been waiting for several minutes and no one had come to serve me, so I was trying to help by taking my choice over to a clerk. Having already established her superiority, she became more chatty, and commented that things had deteriorated so much in the stores. "Why, with all the cuts and staff reductions, we don't have enough staff to serve all the customers these days."

I felt that explanation didn't quite satisfy me. I asked her to humour me by turning around and facing towards the back of the store. "How many customers do you see?" I asked.

"Why, you're the only one, Sir."

"And how many clerks can you count?" I continued.

"Nine, Sir."

"Well don't you think one of them might have seen fit to come and attend to me?"

"Oh, but Sir, they're all busy, you see."

And on examination, so they were. Some were dusting the merchandise, some were adjusting the displays, one was tidying the office, and several were filling out what may have been sales reports or inventory lists. This left no one free to carry on the business and attend to customers.

A few weeks later, Birks announced its bankruptcy, citing bad economic conditions and changes in public buying habits as the reasons for their failure. I thought I might just know another reason.

That was a number of years ago. Birks still operates, having been sold to another retailing chain. And one supposed that the new owners would institute certain reforms to improve the business. However, they did retain the outward appearance of the standard Birks store.

Several years later, I had occasion to go into the same Birks store to purchase a gold chain to support a pendant I had purchased for my wife during my travels. Birks, even in its reduced, more parlous state, seemed to me to be the correct place to make that purchase. With me, old habits and inclinations die hard.

The store looked much the same. There were the same beautiful displays of elegant merchandise, although perhaps not quite the same quantities of goods. Everything was still immaculate. And I regret to say there was still a marked absence of customers. But the greatest change appeared to be that the number of staff had been drastically reduced. Indeed, apart from one lady who was serving the only other customer, I could see no one.

I wandered down the aisle and spotted one girl sitting on a stool below the level of the counter, almost crouched down. When I stood in front of her, she somewhat reluctantly asked if she could help me. When I explained my mission to purchase a gold chain, her Birks background came to life, and she tried to assert her superiority by asking, "Yes, Sir. Ten or fourteen carat, Sir?"

That wasn't a subject I'd given any thought to. When you come to think of it, it doesn't seem that the number of carats in the gold in a fine chain is a very safe subject to investigate. After all, it's extremely difficult to determine the difference with the naked eye at any distance. And when worn by the lady owner, the chain is usually displayed on an expanse of attractive female flesh, exposed by a low-cut dress with more than a hint of cleavage. If you got your nose close enough to determine the gold content, you'd be likely to get your face slapped, or worse. I fell back on my usual defense; "Let's see what you have."

Having established the traditional Birks-to-customer relationship to her satisfaction, my young lady became quite helpful and led me across the store to the displays of chains. We quickly picked out a suitable chain, which I purchased. She even complimented me on my decisiveness. And she went away to write the bill and find a suitable Birks box.

But I had noticed as we approached the display of chains, that there was another girl nearby, also sitting on a stool, and hunched down below the level of the counter. When my clerk went away to complete my transaction, this girl looked up, smiled, and said, "Hello". We started to chat. To make conversation, and perhaps expecting to hear of all the changes that had been made in the store, I told her the story about the difficulties I'd had getting service under the old regime. I was gratified when she said, "Yes, isn't it terrible the way we sometimes lose track of the customer?" But then she went on to explain that she wasn't really hiding under the counter; she was taking inventory. "And," she said, somewhat indignantly, "you've no idea the number of times today I've been interrupted by customers!"

The title of this article is the first line of that well-known French saying:

"*Plus ça change, plus ça rèste le même*," which translates as, "The more things change, the more they stay the same."

This seems especially apt for this idiosyncrasy of Birks.

THE GOOD OL' DAYS

I was fortunate to have a career that spanned at least the vestiges of what has been called the good old days of business, a time when senior managers expected and received extraordinary treatment and perks. As an example, when I first started to travel around the world, in the fifties and sixties, most big companies, particularly in Europe, had management lunchrooms of varying degrees of elegance and opulence. They represented one aspect of those expected perks. All served excellent food and drink. Most of them operated as a sort of private club, whose membership consisted of the managers above a certain level in the company. The better ones had a most convivial atmosphere, and I enjoyed visiting them, the more so since Canadian Marconi, for whom I worked at the time, in line with the somewhat more strait-laced traditions in Canada of those days, had no such amenities for its managers.

One of the best of the lunchrooms I was privileged to visit was that of The Marconi International Marine Company, or MIMCO as it was known throughout the group.

I should digress to explain that the early history of radio was largely bound up with communications with ships at sea. This was the first practical application of the new radio technology, starting about the turn of the century. It was the only way of communicating with a ship on the high seas, and was thus considered vital to the safe and profitable operation of a ship. The Marconi group had pioneered in this technology and, for many years, marine radio constituted the major portion of the company's business. Up until the end of the Second World War, Marconi maintained what amounted to a worldwide monopoly on this business. They had two very simple tactics. First, they insisted on renting the radio to the shipping company at very lucrative rates, rather than selling the equipment. In addition, the ship's radio operator was an employee of Marconi rather than of the shipping company. Thus they maintained control of all wireless applications at sea. Second, they also operated a complete network of marine depots around the world that serviced the radios, and, later, the other electronic equipment on the vessel. Since the radios and other electronics were notoriously unreliable, requiring constant care and attention to maintain operation, these service depots represented a critical element of the entire operation. Against that network of service centres, it was well-nigh impossible for any other company to break into that business. Finally, after the Second World War, other giants emerged in the electronic field. In addition, the equipment became much more reliable, reducing the problems of maintenance to more manageable levels. Thus, competitors appeared on the scene. However, Marconi remained a major name in the marine field throughout my time there. It continued to maintain a network of active and profitable marine depots around the world. It was this whole marine business that was entrusted to MIMCO.

As you might expect, nearly all the managers of MIMCO were old ships' operators, accustomed to all the privileges of officers on large seagoing ships. Accordingly, their lunchroom was most elegant, in keeping with the expectations of men accustomed to dining at the captain's table. It was furnished in Chippendale, offered excellent food, usually accompanied by a selection of wines, and always preceded by a more than adequate supply of pre-luncheon drinks. For a while, I was responsible for the operation of the marine depots in Canadian Marconi territory, and thus had good reason for occasional visits to the MIMCO headquarters, which were also located in Chelmsford. I always looked forward to my visits, but was careful not to schedule any difficult work to follow a MIMCO lunch.

My normal contact in MIMCO was Iain Dick, the second in command. He was a Scot, as many of the managers were, and had served as a radio officer and, subsequently, as manager of an overseas marine depot. It was on one of my periodic visits to MIMCO, when I was sitting in Iain's office going over some business, when he remarked that we mustn't be late for lunch. "Mac" Maguire, the rugged managing director, and the epitome of a retired sailor, had apparently decreed that we turn up sharply at 12:30. Iain could give no reason, but nothing loath, we entered the lunchroom exactly on time.

Mac was standing at the door, but instead of his usual warm welcome, he presented me with a tumbler full of Scotch, with the stern admonition, "Drink that!" Which I did, only to be told to get another drink right away. Which I also did. Only when I was well into my second drink did Mac explain that a new chairman of MIMCO had been appointed, and he was making his first visit that day for lunch. However, the new chairman, while no teetotaler, had formed the opinion there was far too much drinking in the lunchrooms of the Marconi group (I couldn't think how he might have reached that conclusion), and had issued an instruction that pre-luncheon tipples should be limited to a single drink. Mac was torn between supporting his new chairman and his customary open-handed hospitality, and had devised a plan to get most of the drinking over before the chairman arrived.

In due course, a lookout, who had been posted at a window overlooking the front entrance announced that the chairman's car had just arrived. All the glasses and bottles were spirited away, so that when the great man entered the room, he found a group of serious and sober-looking managers patiently waiting to greet him. He looked around, and smilingly said, "Gentlemen, I'm very pleased to meet you all. Shall we all have a drink before lunch?"

I always wondered whether he found any of the conversations that day suspiciously peculiar.

I WAS GODFATHER TO A BOAT

I have known of many small start-up companies, started by individuals or small groups of people. Generally, they're based upon a specific idea or invention, sometimes brilliant, and many with the potential to grow into successful businesses. But while the idea may be excellent, the trick is to bring it to market efficiently, to persuade the customer to buy the product, and to manage the little company so that it grows and prospers.

I have observed that one of the idiosyncrasies of these start-up companies is that the owners become too protective of their property, possibly in the fear that someone will steal their idea from them, or perhaps in order to keep all the benefits for the originator of the idea. But few individuals have all the knowledge or experience necessary to bring a company to final success. Nearly everyone needs the help of outsiders, and in many cases they would be better off to give a portion of their precious company to others in order to gain that necessary expertise. All too often, the result of this particular idiosyncrasy is that the originators lose control or that the company fails.

In the early seventies, I undertook to establish a small factory in Montreal, to manufacture a number of ground-based aerial navigation aids under a major export contract for an American company. I located a suitable space, which was already under lease to a company named Performance Sailcraft Limited, which had invented a new type of sailboat, the Laser. They had recently moved to larger premises and were agreeable to sub-leasing the space to me.

The Laser was no ordinary pleasure craft intended for a quiet Sunday sail around the bay; it was a fast and agile, one-man sailboat, requiring considerable skill and athletic nimbleness to sail. It was intended to become a new class of competitive boat. It rapidly became very popular with competitive and active sailors, and indeed, today, has achieved its goal of becoming a separate class of competitive boat. In those early days of its history, I found that the space I'd leased contained almost an entire year's production. I stored over a hundred boats for some time while I arranged for my own factory to be set up.

Because it was a sub-lease, I suppose, I was required to visit the new offices of Performance Sailcraft at the beginning of every month to deliver the rent cheque. I discovered that the Laser had been invented or designed by four people, all of whom had been part of the Canadian

Olympic sailing team. They'd apparently decided to pool their sailing skills and knowledge of boats to design and market this remarkable boat.

The first time I visited their new offices, about the first of August, I believe, I found that the owners were very pleased with themselves; and indeed, they had good reason to be happy. They'd just been awarded orders for Lasers totalling 5,500 boats, all for delivery for the sailing season of the following year. I congratulated them and went on my way.

The next month, when I visited them, the office was in deep gloom. Everyone was very downcast. They explained to me that while they had orders for 5,500 boats, they could only make three boats a day, and they'd realized they'd never make all those boats in time. I suppose I should have realized that if it took them all that time to recognize this problem, there was a much more serious shortfall of experience around. These folks may have been excellent sailors and brilliant designers, but experts on production or business they apparently weren't. I asked, helpfully, how they actually made the boats.

The boats were a very clever design, requiring a minimum of parts. The hulls and the decks, including the cockpit, were each laid up in fibreglass as one piece, each on a separate wooden mould. The two pieces were then glued together and presto, there appeared a marvellous little boat, easy to assemble, with a beautiful aerodynamic shape. Their problem lay in the fact it took them eight hours to lay up one set of pieces.

I asked helpfully, "How many shifts are you working?"

"Shifts, what's that?" (Oh, dear!)

"Well you can have people work shifts through the night, so you can work three eight-hour shifts a day."

For a moment, they all brightened up, but only for long enough for them to apply their newfound knowledge of production rates and realize that nine boats a day still wasn't nearly enough. The gloom returned.

I asked them why they simply didn't get additional moulds.

"Oh, they cost too much, and we don't have any money."

"Well, how much do they cost?"

"About $2,500 a set."

In the circumstances, that didn't seem an insurmountable barrier to me.

"Well, how about borrowing the money from a bank?"

"The bank's told us they won't lend us any more money."

"That seems strange," I said. "When did the bank tell you that?"

"Last spring, when we were setting up our factory."

"You mean, before you had all these orders? I suggest you take your big fat order book to show your friendly banker and see how long it takes for him to lend you $25,000 now."

They were extremely skeptical about my assurances that the bankers were human, and even intelligent. Somewhat reluctantly, they agreed to do as I suggested.

But, the next month, when I visited them, everyone was all smiles again. They had ten pairs of new moulds working around the clock in the factory, and were on track to meet their commitments for 5,500 boats in the spring.

The next month, when I visited, the gloom had returned. I anxiously asked what had happened this time? They explained that the Laser was designed to be packed in a single carton, and the cartons could be stacked six or eight high for shipping. Or that had been their plan, when they quoted on the supply of all those boats, most of which they had to deliver, freight paid, to northern Minnesota. But now, the railway companies were all refusing to stack the cartons more than one deep. That would send their shipping costs sky-high, and destroy their profits on the project.

I asked about road transport, but they insisted the truckers were equally as uncooperative.

"There must be another way," I said, but my pessimistic friends insisted there was no solution.

"You know, if I were going to ship a number of boats shaped like the Laser, I'd be inclined to use the system used by rowing clubs to transport their shells," I suggested.

"What do you mean?"

"Well, you'd start with a flatbed truck, build a set of Christmas trees down the centre, and stack the boats on the branches of the Christmas trees."

I was describing the transports I'd seen, many times on the highway, on their way to regattas.

"But where'd we get something like that?"

"Well, there's a truck-trailer manufacturer just at the other end of the street. When I came by there just now, there were two flatbeds sitting in their yard. I'd bet they'd make you up a trailer very quickly!"

I left them with that suggestion. Our sub-lease expired, and I never had to visit them again. But the next time I passed their factory, there were two, newly painted, flatbed trailers with Christmas trees down the centre, parked in their yard. I heard they made a great success of their sale in Minnesota.

And that's how I became a godfather to a boat

The Laser went on to become extremely popular, both locally and internationally, in competitive circles and among the more active sailors. Indeed, when I moved to Zurich, a few years later, I used to say you could walk across the lake on the decks of the Lasers sailing on a Sunday afternoon.

However, in subsequent years, while the Laser was very popular, something happened to that founding group. I don't know what happened but I surmise they went into debt, or somehow lost control of their brainchild. Somehow, the curse of the start-up business struck. Certainly, the Laser went out of production in Canada for quite a while. At the time, I never thought about it, being engaged on other problems. In subsequent years I thought they might have been wise to recruit me to assist them in their planning. Maybe some outside help might have overcome that idiosyncrasy of small start-up businesses.

MANAGEMENT TRAINING

The idea that the performance of managers could be improved by sending them to management courses or seminars has been popular with company managements for some time. I'm not certain, but it seems to me that idea first reached popularity in the early sixties. All of a sudden, it became the fashion for companies to employ consultants to run courses alleged to improve various aspects of the work of their employees. Certainly, one aspect that was significantly improved was the bank balances of the consultants.

When I was in school, I was a serious student. And, when I first ventured outside the sheltered life of a university into the real world, all of life seemed very serious. Business was serious, and to be a success in business, it seemed I should be serious, too. There seemed to be all sorts of possible problems and troubles, and innumerable potential disasters to worry about. It took me a while to learn that nothing was really that threatening, and that there was lots of room for me to enjoy myself without risk of upsetting the ordered progress of the business universe. I believe my early realization that the world isn't really terminally serious contributed a great deal to my enjoyment of my work and my career.

THE MANAGEMENT GRID

Over the years, I attended many management courses. I won't deny that at most of them I learned something that was subsequently applicable to my work and responsibilities. Some of these courses taught very useful things about company structure and management. Others gave detailed analyses of actual company situations. But I do believe the most important thing I learned was at the very first such course I attended, and I'm reasonably certain it wasn't exactly what I was intended to learn.

The course was known as the Management Grid, so called because it was based on the idea that an individual's characteristics and performance could be plotted on a chart, or grid. The course assigned interest in profit to one axis and interest in people to the other axis. Thus, someone who was graded as nine-six would be more inclined to favour profit motives over consideration for his staff, while someone graded six-nine would be more interested in the welfare of his staff than in the profit outcome. Someone who scored ten-ten in his associates' assessment was considered an ideal manager. However, the main thrust of the course was to demonstrate to managers the advantages of team action, and to develop a team approach to the resolution of problems. The program was also designed to subject participants to heavy stress and thus, perhaps, enable them to learn to deal with the stresses of everyday management.

Canadian Marconi decided to send all their managers to this course. Sessions were held outside the company at a small resort hotel. We soon started to hear stories about how stressful the course was; we heard tales of people working all night on some of the assignments, and of acrimonious sessions where individuals became extremely upset. We even heard rumours that, in another company, two participants in the course had committed suicide. It didn't sound like a lot of fun.

There were to be four or five separate, week-long sessions, with groups of about thirty in each session. I was scheduled for the second session, but managed to be too busy to go. For the third session, I discovered some urgent commitments that couldn't be postponed. But, for the fourth session, the president himself called me and told me I had to go. Under the circumstances, I went, but with considerable misgivings.

The course started on Sunday afternoon, with a pre-dinner, get-acquainted cocktail party. While everyone there was a Marconi employee, the company was so diversified that there were only a few with whom I was even acquainted. There was no one else from my department. However, I did meet one engineering manager from a different department whom I knew slightly. While we were talking, we noticed our nametags were both orange. Others around us had green, red or blue tags. Our razor-sharp engineering minds promptly deduced that these different colours represented different teams for the coming week, and that we were to be on the same team.

While we were chatting, I commented that I'd heard horrendous tales of people working all night on assignments, and returning home from the course absolutely exhausted. "I have no intention of doing that," I stated. "Neither have I," said my friend. And so we made a pact that, while we'd work hard at the course, we'd refuse to become involved in any excessive, late-night, work sessions. In the long run, that proved to be a critical decision.

After dinner, we were all assembled in a large conference room, and sure enough, were divided into teams as determined by the colours of our nametags. Each team was assigned a team room, and we were sent away to become acquainted with the other members of our team. Our group proved to be made up of people from all over the company, with a wide variety of duties and responsibilities, ranging from a broadcasting engineer through research, sales, and accounting. I commented that Bill and I had met at the cocktail party, and we had decided that, no matter what the pressure, we wouldn't work beyond ten o'clock any night. In light of the rumours we'd all heard, the others agreed wholeheartedly.

We'd hardly completed the introductions when there was a knock at the door, and one of the course directors came in with a questionnaire, several pages long. He told us that we were to answer as a team as many of the questions as we could, and that he would return in exactly one hour to collect our results. Perhaps fortuitously, he handed the papers to me.

I took one look at the questionnaire, and saw that there were 120 true or false questions. For some reason, I focused on the fact that we'd have thirty seconds per question. Almost without any thought or discussion, I appointed one of our members, the accountant I think, as timekeeper. I instructed him to allow us just thirty seconds for each question. He would read out the question, allow twenty-five seconds for discussion, and then take a vote on the answer. He was to allow no extra time or discussion on any question, no matter how interesting, or whether there was any disagreement about the answer. No one argued. That proved to be the second key decision we made at that course.

The questions varied in their difficulty, but our timekeeper, with the inbred commitment of the accounting profession to the rules, allowed us no deviation from that plan. The result was that when we returned to the conference room, we had an answer, good, bad, or indifferent, for each of the 120 questions. We turned out to be the only team that had even come close to completing the list. And we soon found that while we earned points for every correct answer, we suffered no penalty for the inevitable wrong answers. The result was that we had much the highest score. The other teams, who had not managed to answer anything approaching all the questions, all scored less than half our points.

The director reviewed the program, and suggested that, obviously, there should be ways of improving the performance of our team. He instructed us all to return to our team rooms, there to examine our methods and approaches to determine a better system. We dutifully returned to our team room and sat down around the table. We looked at each other, and someone asked, "What are we doing here? We won, didn't we? I don't think we could improve too much on that!"

With that, we left the room, went to the bar for a nightcap, and went off to bed, well pleased with ourselves.

When we reassembled in the conference room the next morning, it developed that the other three teams had worked into the small hours of the morning, arguing, with varying degrees of disagreement, about better methods of approach to the assignment. One of the teams hadn't gotten to bed at all. The result was that we were the only team that was really awake and rested that morning. When the director distributed another assignment, requiring us to answer a new set of questions, this time a bit more difficult, we had a clear advantage over all the other tired, sleepy, and somewhat ill-tempered competitors. Again we won, by a wide margin, and again we saw little potential in returning to our room, and further examining our navels, or other portions of our team's anatomy. We repaired to the bar for a drink before lunch.

The late afternoon found us again faced with a question-and-answer contest, and again the fact that we were rested, and that we had developed into a smoothly working team, led to another victory. Indeed, all the other teams had fallen into various degrees of acrimony, which probably didn't help them very much.

And so it continued throughout the course. We were rested; we were confident; we were winning consistently. We always felt completely justified in ignoring the repeated instructions to return to our room and discuss our supposed shortcomings. We found a number of opportunities to go to the bar and relax.

The consultants running the course became very suspicious. I later learned we were making scores far higher than they had ever experienced. At the end of the third day, they came to us and asked how we were doing it; it transpired they thought we'd obtained a book with all the answers to their quizzes. We denied this, of course, but agreed on the last day to reveal our secret formula.

As I said, the course was designed to create a lot of stress. The last part of the course required the teams to evaluate their individual members' characteristics and qualities. A series of prescribed procedures were set out based on the Management Grid theories. Without going too deeply into the specifics, you may realize that being evaluated by your peers in such a stressful environment can be a devastating experience if not managed carefully. And on those teams where there had been disagreements and acrimony, there was scope for a lot of hard feeling. I believe there were some violent outbursts, and some members left feeling very upset. However, on our team, where we had all enjoyed our success so much, and had developed respect for each other, no such problems arose. I believe we did an excellent job of evaluating our members; indeed, the consultant who sat in on part of the day congratulated us on our evaluation methods and results.

On the last day, for the afternoon wrap-up session, we were true to our word. We prepared a presentation to reveal our methods. For the first time we worked through lunchtime to prepare. We presented a series of flip charts, each representing one letter of the alphabet, as in A is for ambition, B is for business, C is for commitment, D is for determination, and so on. Each one was followed on the page by our key objective, which was, as you'll have guessed by now, TO GET TO THE BAR.

Our presentation was well received; even the consultants seemed to enjoy it. But I noticed that afterwards the director confiscated the flip charts. I don't think he wanted our formula published any more widely. Perhaps he wanted people to take the course, and his world, more seriously. But I always felt that one of the key principles I learned at that course was to work hard but not to take anything too seriously.

After that course, everyone in the company was constantly forming teams and working on team decisions and team management systems. A lot of time was lost, as it was difficult to get a decision on even the simplest things without convening a lengthy team meeting. However, any teams where I was involved tended to work much more efficiently. You see, I had also learned that a team works best when it is given clear instructions and a minimum of time to debate them. I'm not sure the course directors would have been too pleased with that interpretation of their teaching, either.

SOME TAKE THEMSELVES TOO SERIOUSLY

I suppose if you are a director of a business course or seminar, you really should at least appear to take it all quite seriously. In my career, I experienced a wide variety of courses, one or two of which were less than deserving of any such consideration. I can think of one where the leader was too impressed with himself by far.

Someone in Northern Telecom decided to preface a meeting of about twenty of the most senior managers with a brief inspirational presentation, designed, so it was claimed, to convince us we could accomplish anything we really set our minds to. The speaker was a young man who introduced himself as a former professional tennis player. He freely admitted he'd been less than successful on the professional circuit. He told us he'd become a teaching professional, and in the course of teaching tennis—often to awkward clients who were not very athletic—he'd become convinced one could achieve any goal simply by concentration. (One therefore presumes he didn't concentrate hard enough on becoming a successful competitor on the tour, but we'll ignore that.) He challenged us to state how long it should take someone to learn to play tennis. He went on to say he could teach anyone to play in just fifteen minutes. And he had a videotape to prove it.

The tape showed him leading a young lady onto a tennis court. She appeared to be a solidly built, even overweight girl, although it was difficult to tell, as she was enveloped in a colourful mu-mu or caftan, which fell from her shoulders to her ankles. Certainly, there were to be none of those cute, athletic blondes in brief white tennis shorts here to divert our interest. We were assured she'd never been on a court before. Her subsequent actions gave us no reason to doubt this. He handed her a tennis racket, and instructed her to swing it back and forth in her right hand. She stood there, looking a bit foolish, swinging the racket back and forth. After she'd achieved a relatively smooth, rhythmic swing, he started to bounce tennis balls past her. He instructed her not to try to hit them, but just to keep swinging rhythmically. But, with his advertised skill as a tennis pro, it was no problem for him to hit her racket with the ball. Soon she reached the point where she could stroke most balls back across the net. Towards the end, he even had her move a few steps to make her shots, although the entire session was limited to straightforward forehand shots. There was no suggestion that anything called a backhand existed in the game of tennis.

When the tape was finished he stated triumphantly that we had seen this girl, totally new to the game of tennis, learn to play in just fifteen minutes. "Wasn't that amazing?" he asked. He seemed to believe all this, but it should have been clear to him that his audience was far from impressed.

"Come," he insisted, "when you saw her hitting the balls over the net, what did you think?"

Most of our razor-sharp management minds had long since transferred attention to other fields. In later discussions, I found that any of those still engaged by this charade were addressed to whether this obviously buxom girl was wearing a bra under that mu-mu, the consensus being that she wasn't. We didn't think that was the answer he was so earnestly seeking. Mercifully, it was time for us to start the serious meetings of the day, and his presentation was cut short.

I do believe that to be treated seriously, one should have something to be serious about. I wonder if he even realized that teaching people to play in fifteen minutes could be counterproductive. I imagine most teaching pros aim to drag out the learning process as long as possible. It helps the cash flow.

THE CARE AND FEEDING OF CUSTOMS OFFICERS

If you're a world traveller, you may be certain of a number of things. Inevitably, there will be delays and frustrations in your travels; sometimes there will be pleasant surprises; and, always, with great regularity, there will be customs inspectors. Even in this modern age of the EEC, with its minimal border procedures, one still encounters customs officers all too often. When I was travelling frequently, customs officers were an even more regular occurrence.

I must say the job of a customs officer leaves much to be desired. They must feel that most of their "clients" have something to hide, and nearly everyone is trying to put something over on them. It would be a small wonder if they didn't develop an attitude of suspicion and confrontation with those clients. But they have a universal reputation of lacking courtesy and consideration, which may not be entirely fair to them. Remember, their clients normally encounter them at the end of a journey, tired, irritable, and above all, anxious to get out of there to somewhere more amenable. Thus, the normal perception of the customs officer might be a bit biased.

Be that as it may, I usually had little or no difficulty with customs wherever I went. Perhaps, they believed my father's saying, "You can always trust a fat man, for he'll never stoop to anything low." If, indeed, that was a factor, that's probably the only benefit I've ever obtained from my somewhat portly appearance.

I did have one other tactic: I habitually left all the carry-on tags on my briefcase. Sometimes it gave me the somewhat scruffy appearance of carrying a bunch of ragged paper, but I theorized that any customs man seeing my bag with all its tags would recognize I was a regular traveller. As such, he might think I would be unlikely to jeopardize my position by engaging in any smuggling—well not too much, anyway. Or perhaps his logic would run, "If he's got anything, he's so experienced it will be a lot of trouble to find it."

Or perhaps I just have an honest face.

In any event, I was rarely questioned by an inspector when passing through customs. However, there were occasional exceptions.

HONEST, I'LL NEVER DO THAT AGAIN

Harry and I had spent three hard days in Washington, romancing various military officers and government officials we hoped would purchase some of our products for the US military. It was a forlorn hope in those days, in the mid-sixties, as we were clearly not American, and thus, were not seen in the USA as desirable suppliers for military goods. (These were the same Americans who were so exercised about level playing fields when it came to foreign markets!) We were tired and discouraged when we boarded our flight for Montreal, a flight that, in those days, made a whole series of stops as it followed its meandering route north. We stopped at a lot of places we didn't particularly want to see, such as Baltimore, Newark, and Albany, that I can remember, and probably several other places we'd just as soon have missed. The whole process took six or seven hours for what is today, at most, a two-hour flight. When we finally reached Montreal, late at night, we were in no mood to be jolly.

We each collected our luggage and headed for the customs benches. In those days, everyone passed a customs inspection, usually meaning a customs officer asked you a few questions, and unless he was being difficult, allowed you to pass. In this case, I struck an officer who was in no better mood than I was.

"Where have you been?"

"To Washington."

"How long were you there?"

"Three days."

Aha, reason for suspicion! Surely, anyone in his right mind would buy something expensive for his wife having been away three whole days.

"Did you acquire anything while you were away?"

"No, nothing at all."

But then I looked down and saw, protruding from the top of my briefcase, the box of a jigsaw puzzle I'd purchased during one of the interminable stops along the way. It had cost all of two dollars. "Oh, I did purchase a jigsaw puzzle for my children."

"Lemme see it!" And he opened my briefcase to look. But he paid no attention to the puzzle, and instead reached in and pulled out the 35mm camera I usually carried. In those days, cameras were one of the main objects of suspicion for customs officers.

"And what is this?" in triumphant tones, holding up the camera by its strap, somewhat as if he expected it to disintegrate at any moment into something quite disgusting.

I was becoming irritated, so I paused for a moment to examine his prize. After all I should be given time to identify anything so obviously suspicious, now shouldn't I?

"Oh," I said, trying to look surprised, "that's a camera."

The customs man in his turn paused. At this stage, he could have resolved the whole issue by one simple question. Instead, he proceeded doggedly with his "investigation."

"Where did you acquire this camera?"

The camera had travelled many miles in my briefcase, and he should have recognized by its scruffy appearance that it wasn't newly acquired.

"I purchased the camera about five years ago, in Germany."

He thought about that for a while. I was beginning to enjoy myself.

"And did you declare the camera when you brought it back from Germany?" in tones expressing his deep suspicion I was a nefarious smuggler of cameras, in bulk.

"Yes, I did."

"Have you the receipt for when you purchased the camera?"

"After five years?" in tones of astonishment.

You'll note that, thus far, this discussion had been carried out strictly by the rules of the Marquis of Queensbury, as they apply to customs inspectors. Everything was polite; there were no raised voices, much less bad words.

The customs man thought about my latest reply for a while, and just as his lips were starting to quiver with his next searching question, I decided this had gone on long enough. I answered the question he should have asked.

"But I do have a customs card identifying the camera, and stating I declared it, when I brought it in."

Left jab, right cross, slam dunk. His face fell and he showed his frustration as he realized he'd lost his victim. His plans for one final small triumph for the day lay in ruins.

While all this had been going on, Harry had collected his baggage and had been cleared through another customs agent. He looked across and saw that my customs man and I appeared to be in a staring match, and concluded I might need some assistance. He came over and stood quietly at the end of our customs bench.

Harry was an aggressive, bantam rooster of a man. He relied upon his quick wits and facile tongue, together with the occasional outrageous action, to get him through most situations. The customs officer saw him standing there, just at the point when his frustration at losing me as a victim had reached its highest. He turned and said, "Here, what are you doing here? You can't stay here."

And he gave Harry a little shove.

That shove, slight as it may have been, was in contradiction of the Marquis of Queensbury rules as they apply to customs men. They mustn't touch their "clients."

Drawing himself up to his full five feet two, Harry exclaimed with considerable dignity and affront, "Take your hands off me!"

"Oh, all right, but you'll have to leave."

Harry didn't budge, looked him straight in the eye, and said, "Say you're sorry."

Not exactly the thing to soothe the jangled nerves of a disgruntled customs man. He turned several shades of deep red, and seemed to mumble a bit. Then, very grudgingly, he muttered, "Oh, all right, I'm sorry." And then, recovering slightly, and with a bit more authority, "But you'll have to leave."

Harry stayed put. "Say please," he demanded.

The customs man turned almost purple with rage. You could almost see steam coming out of his ears. But finally, realizing he was in a corner, he muttered, "Oh all right, I'm sorry. Now will you please leave."

"Certainly," said Harry, and he turned smartly and walked off through the exit door.

The customs man wheeled around, and pointing his finger at me, almost shouted, "Don't you ever do that again!"

Who me, Sir? Certainly not, Sir. Do what again, Sir?

IT HELPS TO BE WELL KNOWN

Lord Michael Killanin, the Irish lord who became world famous as the president of the International Olympics Committee, also served for some time as the chairman of Northern Telecom Ireland. Thus I came to know him quite well. I enjoyed his anecdotes about his life while he worked so hard to preserve the Olympic games. His term of office came during a very stormy period when the games, supposedly designed to enhance peace, understanding, and brotherhood between nations, became, instead, the subject of political rivalries, boycotts, and general pig-headed disruptiveness. I think very few men could have succeeded in that situation as Lord Killanin did. With his Gaelic wit, his persistent goodwill, and his gentle diplomacy, he succeeded in preserving the games for future generations.

During the period when Lord Killanin headed the international Olympic organization, he continued to live in Dublin, even though the headquarters of the Olympic movement were in Geneva. When it was necessary for him to be in Geneva, he would simply fly over for the day. He could catch the first flight out of Dublin for London, change there to a flight for Geneva, and arrive in time to start business at about nine o'clock. And, having worked all day, he could reverse the whole process, taking an evening flight from Geneva to London, and catching the last flight of the day to Dublin.

This would have been quite normal in Europe in those days. However, any traveller will recognize that it does involve a number of brief encounters with immigration authorities. The first would be on leaving Dublin, where Lord Killanin would be required to show his passport to a polite Irish official. Then, in London, in those pre-EEC days, he would show his passport to separate English officials, on arrival, and again on departure for Geneva. Finally, on arrival in Geneva, he would show it one final time, to an extremely polite Swiss officer. The same process would be required, in reverse, on his return journey.

Lord Killanin told me of one occasion when he travelled all the way to Geneva, as I've described, completed his day's work, and presented himself at the outgoing immigration wicket in the Geneva airport. The officer looked at his passport, looked at Lord Killanin, then back at the passport again. Finally, he cleared his throat, and said, "Lord Killanin, everything is quite all right, you can proceed with your journey. But you do realize this is your wife's passport you're carrying?" He'd travelled all that way without anyone noticing he had the wrong passport.

Lord Killanin spent the trip to London worrying what would happen if he happened to run into an immigration officer in London who wasn't a sports fan. He told me he finally decided his last resort would be to show his warrant card entitling him to sit in the English House of Lords. This is a privilege given to Irish hereditary lords. Their titles in Ireland became purely honorary with the formation of the Irish Republic, but those titles are still recognized in England for those who were alive at the time the Republic of Ireland was formed.

However, he wasn't forced to this tactic, as his immigration officer in Heathrow airport turned out to be an avid sports fan and hardly looked at his passport in his eagerness to shake his hand and obtain the autograph of someone so famous for his son.

It pays to be well known.

BILL BUYS A CAMERA

Bill and I travelled together around Europe on many occasions, attempting to sell Canadian Marconi's tactical military radio relay equipment to the various military organizations in Europe. There were very few capitals in Western Europe we did not visit regularly. At every city, we met with officials and senior officers of the military organization. But that usually left ample time for exploring these cities, and I, in particular, became quite a sightseer. I carried a 35mm camera and took many pictures. Bill was a few years older than I, and sometimes gave the impression he wasn't too keen on being seen with this fellow with apparent juvenile tendencies who acted like a tourist much of the time. In particular, he would have nothing to do with taking photographs. Nothing, that is, until his wife Kay saw some of my pictures and decreed that Bill should do that, too. That transformed me into an instant expert.

We discussed what kind of a camera he should buy and where in the world he could get the best price. After all, we had a wide choice. Eventually, we decided the best source would be Yves, our agent in Paris, who, through his business and social contacts, had access to the PX stores for servicemen on US bases in Germany. It was well known that those PXs had unbelievable prices. So it was arranged. On our next trip through Paris, Yves was deputed to purchase a good 35mm camera when next he visited a US base.

We were back in Paris about six weeks later, and Yves, true to his undertaking, produced a magnificent camera at an exceptional price. Bill was delighted, and started his career as a photographer almost immediately.

That night, in the bar at the hotel, he asked me if he'd have any difficulty getting the camera through customs on his return to Canada. I told him he could probably hang it over his shoulder, and simply walk past the customs man. However, I also pointed out that, at any time in the future, he might be asked to prove he'd declared the camera when he first brought it in. We discussed the pros and cons of the situation and we tried to estimate the duty he might have to pay if he declared the camera. It was a long discussion, requiring considerable liquid input to support it.

The next night, we found ourselves in a hotel in Switzerland, and Bill started off the evening with a renewed discussion on the pros and cons of declaring the camera. We travelled on the next day to Italy, and again, that evening, we discussed whether to declare the camera or not. We discussed that camera in half the cities in Europe, each with suitable liquid lubrication for the discussion. I became heartily sick of the subject.

We ended that trip in London, and on the last evening, in a pub, Bill announced he had made a decision; he was going to declare the camera and pay the duty. Several times during the evening, he reiterated his determination to declare the camera. The next morning, as we got into a taxi for the airport, he repeated, "I'm going to declare the camera." And again, as we boarded the plane.

Finally, we reached Montreal, and as we disembarked from the plane, Bill repeated, for one last time, "I'm going to declare the camera."

I would be glad to hear the last of that camera.

When we collected our baggage, my bag came out of the shute first. I grabbed it and headed for the nearest customs officer. Cheerfully, he asked, "Who do you work for?" (A common starting point for customs men when greeting a business traveller.)

"I work for Canadian Marconi."

"Is that right? I have a brother-in-law who works for Canadian Marconi, and he keeps saying he can get me a cheap TV set." (Marconi made TV sets in those days.) "Do you think you could help him to get me a cheap TV set?"

It was all good-humoured fun. I fell into his chatter, and noting that Bill was coming up behind me, I said, "Oh, I don't know about that, but here's Mr. Baillie, a vice-president of Canadian Marconi. Maybe he can help." Bill was standing there with his camera held out in front of him to ensure it got declared.

"Well," responded the good-humoured customs officer, "now we have three people trying to get me a cheap TV set, haven't we? Well, have a good day, gentlemen." And with a clap on the back, we found ourselves walking out the exit door.

Bill stopped in the doorway, looked at the camera, and spluttered, "But, but—" and then, apparently recognizing a decision of the fates, walked on.

Bill carried the camera on all our future trips, secure in the knowledge that the fates had decreed his right to have it.

CONFUSION IN JAPANESE CUSTOMS

Narita Airport, the international airport of Tokyo, always seems very crowded and noisy. Tokyo is a long way from nearly anyplace, and virtually all the aircraft that land at Narita are jumbo jets carrying full loads of passengers. Thus, the place is always full of travellers. In common with much you will find in Japan, the airport is not particularly convenient; it's a long way from Tokyo, and you really don't want to take a taxi, as the fare into town is about two hundred dollars. Of course, there is a somewhat inefficient bus service that you can use, provided you can work out how to do so. It's definitely best if you can arrange to have yourself met at the airport by a friend or employee. In my case, Ishii-san, to whom I've already introduced you, was faithfully there to greet me, much to my satisfaction. However, there are some compensations to Narita. The customs men are generally very polite, and the duty-free allowances are pleasantly high.

The customs men seem to be particularly polite and flexible with foreigners, apparently adopting the same attitude as all Japanese. To them, foreigners, or gaijins, are abysmally unaware of how to act properly in Japan. However, the gaijins are guests of their country, and thus entitled to friendly and lenient treatment. But, there are limits to even their goodwill.

When you pass through customs on entering Japan, in addition to the luggage you bring with you, including any duty-free items, you may also fill in a form for "goods to follow." These may be anything from a few items purchased while you were out of the country, to your complete household goods if you are moving to Japan. This form, signed by a customs officer, represents much the easiest way to legally import things into Japan.

Barbara and I had been courting for some time. It was somewhat of a long-range courtship, as I was working in Tokyo, and she, initially, was working in company headquarters in Toronto. But, with all the travelling our jobs required, we managed to meet sufficiently frequently. Then, one of the periodic reorganizations, to which large companies seem particularly prone, struck our international organization. Barbara's position in headquarters disappeared, and she took up a marketing job, based in Singapore. She moved to Singapore and took a small, furnished apartment. You might think that would improve our situation, but you must remember it takes almost as long to get to Singapore from Tokyo as it does to get to Toronto.

When Barbara moved to Singapore, she closed up her house in Toronto. Much of her household goods she put into storage, as most of us in the international service did. However, she had some items, twenty-seven cartons in fact, that she wanted to have with her wherever she was. But it was clear her apartment arrangements in Singapore were quite temporary. Since we had decided we would marry soon, it seemed simplest for her to ship her twenty-seven cartons to Japan, and to keep them in my garage until they were needed. Thus it was arranged.

My secretary came in one morning to say that Barbara's boxes had arrived, and asked me where the "Goods to Follow" form was. I hadn't thought about that, and, indeed, Barbara hadn't visited Japan in order to have the opportunity to create such a form. There was only one solution; Barbara would have to visit Japan. In the circumstances, I wasn't too disappointed with this requirement.

As it turned out, the visit could be arranged relatively easily, as Barbara had recently undertaken to travel about the Far East, making marketing presentations at each of our several locations. She would stay for several weeks in one country, meeting customers, discussing their problems and needs, and then move on to the next country. Indeed, Japan was already on her list. It merely took a bit of rearranging of her schedule.

When Barbara had commenced her extended marketing travels, she had given up her temporary apartment in Singapore. Therefore, she was carrying her entire wardrobe with her as she travelled. It made an impressive mound of baggage. Thus it was that, when she arrived at Tokyo's Narita airport, she approached one of those polite customs men, pushing a cart loaded with seven suitcases, a briefcase, a bag of duty-free liquor, and, for good measure, a hammock purchased during her recent visit to the Philippines.

The appearance of this apparition clearly surprised even the normally calm customs officer. He gamely started his routine. "Where are you from?"

The answer was, perforce, a bit confusing, since Barbara had no fixed address, and tried to explain her travels. The customs man had only limited English, and had difficulty understanding. Abandoning that approach as too confusing, he proceeded to the next stage.

"How long will you stay?"

Barbara planned to stay only three days. The customs man couldn't seem to understand why she needed all this baggage if she was only going to stay three days. He decided there was something peculiar here, and requested Barbara to open "that bag, there." Things deteriorated, because that particular bag hadn't been opened for some time as she travelled. It happened to contain one extra bottle of duty free liquor, which she'd purchased some weeks before, when passing through some duty-free shop, and had subsequently packed away and forgotten.

Having justified his suspicions, the customs officer now decided to inspect each of the other bags, All seven were opened and the contents studied. I wonder whether that officer was married, since he seemed particularly puzzled by a bag containing about thirty pairs of shoes, many of them brand new. (Barbara had found a good shoe store in Hong Kong, with an owner amenable to extensive bargaining.) He seemed to doubt any woman needed all those shoes. Well, so does any husband, but most of us have long since learned not to question the need of any female for shoes.

Finally, but most reluctantly, the customs officer concluded he could find nothing more to complain about and signalled Barbara to close her bags, pay the modest fine for the single bottle of liquor, and then to leave him alone.

Barbara, however, had one more bridge to cross. She produced her "Goods to Follow" form, showing twenty-seven boxes to follow, and asked the, by now, completely confused customs man to stamp it for her.

He drew himself up to his full height, and sucked noisily on his teeth, a sign of annoyance among Japanese. He considered at length why a woman who only planned to stay three days, but travelled with all this luggage, would also need to clear twenty-seven boxes to follow. He sucked again most mightily, apparently concluded there was no understanding these gaijins, particularly their womenfolk, took out his stamp, and with a mighty blow, stamped the document. There must still be an indentation on the bench below that document.

After that, we were able to get Barbara's boxes processed with little difficulty, except for one small glitch. The inspectors who eventually examined those boxes determined that the box containing her kitchen utensils also contained a very small bag of rice. That caused considerable embarrassment, as the importation of rice into Japan was strictly forbidden. It was one of those rules designed by the bureaucrats to protect the farm community, and whose main result was to create exorbitant prices for rice in Japan. Our office, however, proved equal to the occasion. It turned out we had inadvertently broken so many rules over the years that we had developed a standard "*Gomen nasai*," or "Please Excuse Me" letter. A copy of that letter, duly signed, was sent off to the appropriate authority, and all was finally well.

I suppose that poor customs officer eventually recovered from his experience with the mad *gaijin* lady.

GULLIBILITY, ANYONE?

There's an old story that I believe every customs officer must know. A little old man shows up at a rural customs post one morning, pushing a wheelbarrow full of straw. The customs officers give the straw a cursory look, and wave him through. The next morning, he shows up again with another barrow load of straw. This time, the customs officers are more careful, but they find nothing wrong with his straw, and allow him to pass. On the third morning, when he again shows up with a load of straw, they're beginning to become suspicious. Who'd want all that straw? They examine the straw thoroughly. Again they can find nothing wrong, and allow him to pass. The next morning, their suspicions really active, they force him to unload the straw onto the road for examination. But still, they can find nothing wrong. This goes on, day after day and week after week. They try x-rays, chemical analysis, everything they can think of, but cannot find anything. They finally give up and allow him to pass every day without stopping him.

After more than a year, the little man shows up one morning and announces that he's retiring; today is his last load. The senior customs officer comes over to him and says, "Look here, Sir, you've gone through here every day for more than a year, with your xxxx'd loads of straw. We're all convinced you're smuggling something but we can't find it. You've driven us crazy! I'll give you full immunity if you'll just tell us what it is you're smuggling."

The little man looked smug, and tapping the side of his nose with his finger, he said, "Wheelbarrows!"

I'm not sure anything like that was going on in the episode I'm going to describe now, but I'm sure something strange was happening.

Nowadays, if you go to meet a friend or relative at the airport, and they're arriving from outside the country, you'll find yourself in a crowded waiting room, without any idea whether your friend or relative has arrived. They may be in process of finding their luggage, engaged in debate with a customs man, or simply lost in the bowels of the airport. Usually, there's a door in an otherwise blank wall, which opens from time to time, to disgorge dribbles of travellers. They may be in any stage of exhaustion, anger at the delays they've suffered or the problems they've encountered, elation or dismay at their success or otherwise in getting their precious purchases past the customs man, or just plain relieved to have arrived. The point is, you, the welcoming committee, are quite powerless to offer any assistance until they finally appear; nor have you had any sight of your visitors until that instant.

It wasn't always that way. In "the good old days," there seemed to be less fear that you might see your arriving visitors prematurely, or until they had been fully processed by airline and customs personnel. In Montreal Dorval Airport, in the early sixties, there was a huge plate-glass window through which you could watch everyone arrive, retrieve their baggage, and hold negotiations with a customs agent, before they finally gained their freedom. The glass was soundproof, so you couldn't converse, but at least you had some idea what was going on.

I had gone to the airport to meet a customer who was arriving from Europe. I arrived quite early, and sat down to wait. While I waited, a flight arrived which, judging by the tropical costumes and wide straw hats worn by many of the passengers, had come from some Caribbean island.

I noticed one family: a man, his wife, and their young daughter. They started to collect their luggage on the customs bench closest to the window, so I had an excellent view of the proceedings. They kept going off to the luggage dispensers, and coming back with more and more suitcases, bags, bundles, and boxes. I counted more than thirty pieces of baggage when they finally called over the customs man. I thought that if I were a customs man, I'd be a bit suspicious about all that collection of luggage. I watched expectantly, interpreting the many gestures and the various expressions of the actors, imagining what they were saying, since I couldn't hear them.

The customs man, faced with this mountain of luggage, first of all asked if they'd acquired anything in their travels. "No Sir, nothing at all," with much emphatic shaking of heads by the two adults.

"No liquor, tobacco, perfume?" asked the officer.

Even more emphatic shaking of heads. The customs officer, surveying the mound of luggage, looked dubious.

"Well, please open that bag there," pointing to a large suitcase.

There were mildly annoyed looks, together with shaking of heads and waving of hands. "You want that bag there opened? But we've told you we bought nothing."

"Open the bag!"

A look of resignation. "Oh, all right, but all this is quite unnecessary," while ostensibly feeling in pockets for keys.

"Honey, do you have the keys to the bags?"

The lady waved her hands in denial. "No, George, you must have them."

"I'm sorry, Officer, but we can't seem to find the keys. But I assure you, we have nothing." All this with further sincere expressions and waving of hands.

The customs officer had seen this before, and continued to politely insist that they open the bag. Finally, by some miraculous good fortune, the keys were located in the gentleman's back pocket, and the bag was opened. The customs man patted the top of the contents and almost immediately located a bottle of rum, which sold for astonishingly low prices on the islands. He held it up, apparently questioning how it came to be there if they hadn't purchased any liquor.

"Honey, did you put that in there?"

"Gee, maybe I did. I forget." With sincere expressions of contrition all around.

"But Officer, there's only that one bottle, I assure you. There's nothing more. Can we go now?"

But the officer had gone on probing, and quickly turned up a second bottle.

"Honey, was it two bottles?" Surprised expression, mixed with disbelief.

"Gee, I guess it must have been. But I'm sure that's all. That must have been the last one left over at our party."

The customs man, however, had smelt smoke, and called for a second bag to be opened. It turned out the keys had been misplaced during the earlier hassle. The customs man persisted, and eventually the second bag got opened. It somehow contained three more bottles. The customs man called for his assistant, and they proceeded to open every suitcase. By he time they'd finished, they had twenty-seven bottles of rum lined up on the counter. The protestations of the couple were now wearing a bit thin, and their expressions were increasingly woebegone.

However, the customs officer had decided no one could be that naive. Suddenly, the family was surrounded by customs officials, who were now working on the theory that they were smuggling something other than liquor. They proceeded to empty every bag, bundle, and box, and to examine everything minutely. Cosmetics bottles were opened, and candy boxes unsealed. I even saw them cracking open a bag of walnuts.

Unfortunately, my visitor chose that moment to arrive. I couldn't stay for the denouement of this drama. I'll never know whether I'd witnessed the capture of some big-time smugglers, or whether they were simply the most naive family of travellers imaginable.

Through it all, the customs inspectors remained calm, cool, and collected. And all the participants on both sides gave me excellent entertainment during my enforced wait.

A MOST CONSIDERATE CUSTOMS MAN

It was in the late fifties, and Jean and I had set off for a week's vacation, without much preparation or planning. I simply had a period of relative calm at work, and I wouldn't be missed. We decided to travel by car through the Maritime Provinces. Unfortunately, it was early May, and while the weather was very good for that time of year, the tourist industry in New Brunswick and Nova Scotia had signally failed to recognize our presence. We had difficulty finding suitable accommodation, not to mention the good seafood restaurants we had anticipated. I hasten to add that since that time, there have been great changes in the Maritime Provinces, and I'm sure there'd be no difficulty finding great food and suitable accommodations there today.

We travelled along, admiring the scenery, until we finally arrived at St. Stephen, on the border between New Brunswick and Maine. We planned to spend the night in this town that had a reputation as a tourist centre. But the main hotel was still closed for the winter, as were all the motels in town. We did find an ancient and gloomy mansion where we could rent a room, complete with a four-poster bed with red velvet hangings that looked like they'd been there since the last century. The owner didn't offer breakfast, much less dinner, and the restaurants he recommended didn't seem very inviting. We drove through the town, stopped and did some shopping, and finally came to the end of the main street. It terminated in a bridge across a modest river, which formed the border between Canada and the USA. On the other side was the American town of Calais. On the spur of the moment, we decided to cross over.

I'm sure half the population of both St. Stephen and Calais crossed that bridge every day, for one reason or another. The customs posts at either end of the bridge seemed to ignore most of the cars passing. However, we stuck out like a sore thumb, since we had Quebec license plates, and thus must have come from further afield. We therefore qualified for closer attention.

A customs officer from the US post ambled over to our car. I suspect he was under the eye of his boss back in the office that overlooked the parking area. He politely determined that we were on vacation, hadn't any fixed plans, would probably be in the US for only a couple of days, and seemed satisfied. But then, perhaps feeling the eyes of authority fixed on the back of his head, he decided he'd better make some gesture towards inspecting our car.

"What have you got with you?"

"Oh, the usual things, our bags, golf clubs, lunch box—"

"Lunch box, where's that?"

We carried a carton of food and made a practice of stopping for a picnic lunch every day along the road. The carton was sitting on the back seat, for ease of access if we wanted a snack at any time. Indeed, when shopping in St. Stephen, we'd bought five nice grapefruit, which were on sale in the local store. We'd tossed them on top of the lunch carton, possibly with the thought that if we had to stay in that gloomy mansion, at least we'd have something for breakfast.

The customs man spied the grapefruit. "What're you doing with those three grapefruit? You can't take those three grapefruit in with you."

Citrus fruit has many strange properties, the most surprising of which is the way it can become inadmissible into the United States even after a brief trip outside its borders. As you may know, the Americans take great exception to the fact that the Japanese limit the import of oranges into Japan, but please don't try to carry any citrus fruit into the US. The argument is that there is danger that any citrus fruit may carry with it disease, insects, and all sorts of other unspecified menaces. It would seem this risk increases enormously for fruit entering the USA. Indeed, one state, California, even prohibits fruit from outside the state. Those grapefruit of ours were marked as product of Florida, but in their brief sojourn in Canada, had somehow picked up some property that made them an instant threat to the entire citrus industry of the States.

I was about to discuss the illogical ramifications of this regulation with the customs officer, when I realized he had said, "Those THREE grapefruit." There were five grapefruit lying there in full view. To make certain I understood, he repeated himself. "You'll either have to eat those THREE grapefruit right here or you'll have to throw those THREE grapefruit into the river."

He had arrived at a formula for demonstrating his zeal to the watching boss, while considerately leaving us enough for breakfast.

I hope his boss observed us throwing those THREE grapefruit into the river, and was satisfied with this zealous application of the regulations.

We found an excellent motel a mile or so down the road in Calais, and had a Maine lobster dinner that night. And we had grapefruit for breakfast, courtesy that considerate customs man.

I never observed that our two grapefruit had any detrimental effect on the American citrus industry. You don't suppose there's a threshold level of grapefruit just above two fruit, below which the threat is too weak to matter?

MAINTAINING A REPUTATION

I've always believed that most people will normally treat you fairly and even helpfully. Very few will actually try to cheat you. All my life I've applied that belief, and I've rarely been disappointed. Over the years, that policy certainly saved me a lot of time I might have wasted worrying unnecessarily about what people would do to me. I think this attitude could be more widely applied.

However, you might say, you really can't apply that policy universally. There are some groups of people who won't respond as you hope and you'll certainly suffer some disappointment, not to say some damage, if you apply this theory impartially.

As an example of a group who wouldn't respond to such a positive approach, most people would select taxi drivers, and more particularly, New York taxi drivers. They have an unparalleled reputation for toughness and lack of courtesy. People thinking that might be in for a surprise.

By the very nature if their work, taxi drivers are often subjected to abuse and complaint; they must contend constantly with heavy traffic and bad drivers; they work long hours for poor returns; and are often forced into boring waits and delays. I suppose that might lead to the brusque, impolite, and sometimes downright rude manner in which they have been known to treat their customers. Among taxi drivers, the New York taxi driver has probably the worst reputation, as tough, rude, impatient, uncooperative, and exceptionally unreasonable. I know that I once subscribed to that standard stereotype. However, I now suspect it's all a façade they adopt to shield themselves from the rough world in which they work.

I had the experience of getting lost in New York. We were, for some reason I don't recall, driving through the northern end of the city, way up in the streets numbered in the hundreds. We were quite uncertain where we were or how to find our hotel. I drove up beside an empty taxi at a stoplight and called across to the driver, "How do I get to the Victoria Hotel?"

He replied, "Follow me!"

And we did, for some half an hour, as he led us all the way back downtown, and right to the door of our hotel. When we arrived there, he simply waved to us and drove off, without waiting for the tip I thought I owed him. Now it's quite possible he was going downtown anyway, although I would have thought he'd be looking for a fare. But it's quite unlikely he intended to pass right in front of our door. I certainly appreciated that gesture.

On another occasion, I arrived in New York from Newark, just across the river. Someone had recommended I take the Manhattan ferry, "for the experience, you know." I was also warned that the New York taxis were on strike, and I'd have to use the subway to get to my hotel. Come to think of it, I was probably influenced to travel by that route because I'd have had trouble getting in from the airport, in the absence of taxis.

When I got off the ferry, I walked up a fairly long street, jammed with cars on both sides. While that, in itself, couldn't be considered unusual, I soon realized all those cars were taxicabs, but all with their rooftop signs removed. Each had a driver, waiting patiently. I asked one of them if he was working and would take me to my hotel. He replied, "Nope, I'm on strike. We all are."

"Well, what are you doing here?"

"Well, you see, each of us has a regular fare, to meet every morning at the ferry and take to his office. Now, we couldn't let our customers walk, could we?"

And so, to make things legitimate, all those tough, inconsiderate, taxi drivers, several hundreds of them, had removed the signs identifying their cars as taxis, thus by some magical process transforming themselves from striking taxi drivers into normal civilians. They had gone, thinly disguised as ordinary people, to await their "regulars" and keep them from the inconvenience of having to walk. And sure enough, there was a stream of well-dressed gentlemen with briefcases, who each came along, selected "his own" taxi, climbed in with little ceremony, and was driven away.

I thought that was a remarkable action for a bunch of tough, street-wise cabbies, all of whom would, later in the day, probably transform themselves back into striking taxi drivers, and proceed to demonstrate uptown.

On still another occasion, I arrived in New York by train, which meant I was delivered, along with my two suitcases, into the magnificence of Grand Central Station. I've always thought that Grand Central Station is the epitome of what a really major railway station ought to be. It's a huge place, covering at least four city blocks, and possessing a magnificent main hall with an enormously high ceiling, marble walls, and many, many shops and restaurants of all descriptions (including some top-class eating establishments) within its walls. None of the smoky dinginess you find in so many railway stations. No Sir, this station is appropriate to the centre of commerce of the United States, a suitable place to start or end a major journey. It's an impressive monument to the age of great trains and great railways in North America.

But it is a large building, and somewhat confusing to the visitor, simply because of its size. I'd been in Grand Central several times, but always had difficulty in locating myself. On this occasion, I knew I had a hotel reservation at one of the hotels that are immediately adjacent to the station. I hoped to come out close to that hotel and thus reduce the distance I had to lug those suitcases. (I'd been on the road for about three weeks at the time, and thus had extra luggage.)

Eventually, I found my way out an exit door, and I set my suitcases down on the sidewalk while I found my bearings. There was a taxi rank right outside that door, and the leading taxi driver was leaning on the front fender of his car. "Kin I help ya?" he called, in that brusque manner of New York cabbies.

I looked at him, recognized that he was a taxi driver, and said, "Nope, I don't need a taxi."

Almost instantly, he was right in front of me, with his nose only inches from my own. "That ain' what I as't ya," he snarled. I felt he could hardly resist grabbing me by the lapels and shaking me.

I'm quite good at recognizing impending trouble, and it didn't take me long to respond, "You're right. I'm sorry. I'm just looking for the Hotel Manhattan, which should be close by."

Without a word, he bent down, picked up my suitcases, and marched off towards the corner of the street. When he got there, he set my cases down, pointed to a building half way down the block, and growled, "There it is." And swinging towards me and shaking his finger at me, "Don'cha ever do dat again!" And he marched off, with a bit of a swagger, back to his cab.

He'd managed to squeeze in yet another helpful act, while all the while maintaining his pose as a rough, tough, unreasonable New York cabbie.

My room in that hotel was on the twentieth floor, on a corner, so that I could look down the cavernous lengths of both an avenue and a street. The traffic, far below me, was primarily taxis, all painted brightly in reds, yellows, and greens, and formed an interesting pattern. They would all have been the standard New York taxi of those days, which were manufactured by the Checker Taxicab Company. They had extra-large rear seats, and were a bit higher than normal cars, thus making them much more suitable for use as taxis than the ordinary sedans we get today. They were supposed to be more rugged to withstand the rigours of being a taxi (a characteristic of so many of their drivers too, I'd say). But they were considerably more expensive than a normal private car, and I suspect that modern pressures to reduce initial costs at the expense of durability gradually influenced the situation.

Sadly, those tough, ugly, but convenient taxicabs have faded from existence. I do hope the tough, ugly, but deceptively helpful New York taxi drivers have not similarly disappeared. As I looked down on those streams of brightly coloured cabs, I thought my experiences with New York cabbies had been surprising, in view of their reputation. It was all most satisfactory, bearing in mind my lifelong belief in people.

DUMB ANIMALS, EH?

We commonly refer to all members of the animal world as "dumb animals." Probably, that's because they don't appear to act like humans, and don't appear to communicate as humans do. Why that should win them the label of "dumb" is, of course, questionable. But, we do, casually, make the assumption that they don't reason as humans do. However, most people who have been acquired by a dog or a cat, and thus come more closely under their pet's influence and management, will insist that their particular pet is extremely intelligent, and is "almost human." And they will have stories to tell to support their claims.

You'll note that I imply that one cannot really acquire a cat or a dog, in spite of the fact that money may change hands between humans to seal a transaction. I think the reverse is much closer to the truth. I think it's more appropriate to say our pets "acquire" us and thereafter manage us to meet their own desires as much as possible.

I am thoroughly convinced that animals do indeed reason, communicate, and show remarkable intelligence. The following tales are my contribution to the ongoing discussions about the intelligence of animals.

STUPID HUMANS

Over the years, we have been acquired by a series of blue roan English cocker spaniels, always two at a time. They've tried to manage our lives to their mutual satisfaction over those periods. There were always two to ensure neither dog became lonely in the event we were away for a few hours.

When there are two dogs in a house, one dog invariably assumes the role of senior dog. It's often quite amusing to see a happy-go-lucky being rapidly transformed into the much more dignified being he believes the role of senior dog requires. At the same time the other, junior, dog seems to believe that his role allows considerably more latitude in behaviour. And the senior dog often finds he has to apologize for the behaviour of his more junior partner. In the event the senior dog dies, it's even more amazing to see the hitherto carefree junior dog transform into a dignified and responsible senior dog.

I believe the English cocker spaniel is among the most aristocratic and noble breeds of dogs. I think their long, aristocratic noses, their elegant hanging ears, their long coats, rippling along their underbellies, and the pretty feathers of fur on their paws, make them more outstanding in appearance than others, but I could be prejudiced. They are a loyal and loving breed. They seem to have the knack of continuously expressing their joy and happiness with life, and their satisfaction with the behaviour of the family they happen to be managing at the time. However, I would not say they are particularly noted for intelligence. But, there are notable exceptions to this. Tara was one such exception.

Tara was a blue roan bitch, meaning her coat was a mottled mixture of black and white, which someone in the distant past imagined looked blue. It's a standard colouring for this breed. She was remarkably intelligent. Many dog owners will tell you their dogs consider themselves to be a part of the family, and as a result, the dogs believe they have "human" status. Tara, by contrast, believed she was, by far, the most superior member of the family and thus entitled to all possible perks, some not available to the human members of the family. When we entertained, she habitually tried to sit up at table in what she considered her rightful place. I'm convinced she considered herself to be a superior being, in relation to humans.

With all this, she wasn't a particularly obedient dog. Indeed, if you told her to do something, she was very likely to give you a special look, which meant, "You don't really expect me to do *that*, do you?"

It was early summer. Barbara and I were in the course of moving up to our cottage. Since the cottage is a considerable distance away, we usually plan for an extended stay and take both our cars, each loaded with rather more goods and supplies than its designers really intended. On this occasion, Barbara left first, taking Tara and Rufus, our two dogs, with her. I followed some hours later, as I had some business to attend to first. When I arrived, Barbara had already unloaded the considerable cargo she had transported, including her complete computer set-up. Typically, she claims she cannot live without her computers. On my arrival, I asked her to connect up the computer, as I had a couple of messages to send out by fax. This she proceeded to do. I should note that while I can type with two fingers on a computer keyboard, my knowledge of these mysterious machines is minimal. As long as I can keep it that way, I am able to avoid a lot of work by calling on Barbara's considerable expertise in most things related to computers. In this case, for example, it was Barbara who had to reassemble the computer station.

All of us—people, and dogs who thought they were people—proceeded to the bedroom, with its computer space. The dogs and I sat on the bed while Barbara worked her magic to get the computer reassembled. She seemed to be making excellent progress when she came to an abrupt halt; she couldn't find the cable to connect the display to the computer. She thought she recollected picking it up as she was leaving the office at home, but it couldn't be found in any of the cases and satchels in which she'd packed the various bits and pieces. I asked her to describe it and she showed me a similar cable, but with not quite the right connectors. She looked through all the bags again, and I looked with her. Our search proved fruitless, and we finally decided one of us would have to drive to Ottawa the next morning and procure a replacement cable.

Tara, of course, carefully observed all this activity.

Having abandoned our search, we all returned to the main lounge of the cottage. Tara went over to a shopping bag full of toys for the dogs, which had yet to be emptied of its contents. She whimpered quite insistently. I went over to see what she wanted, reached into the bag and pulled out her favourite frisbee. Nope, she disdained that and continued to insist that I look in the bag. I reached in again and pulled out her favourite piece of rope. Nope, that wasn't it, either. Nor was her teddy bear, nor was a ball. Finally I put my hand in one last time and pulled out the missing computer cable, which had apparently been stuffed into the nearest bag at the last minute. I realized Tara had recognized that we were looking for a cable and had known that the cable had been stuffed into this particular bag during the confusion of departure.

Tara gave a self-satisfied sniff, and then, with a very superior air, stalked away to inspect the contents of her dinner dish for items she deemed suitable to her station. It was quite easy to interpret her body language:

"Stupid humans."

PRICKLY PROBLEMS

I guess the porcupine is one of the animals most often seen in the wild. They're slow moving and easy to spot, and not much afraid of anyone, man or beast. Their prickly armament makes them relatively safe from normal molestation. Cottagers dislike them, in spite of their being somewhat of a curiosity to the children. That's because of their habit of chewing any piece of wood humans may have touched and where even a vestige of the salt in human sweat may remain. After you've repaired a doorpost, or the door itself, where they've chewed through it in pursuit of a tiny vestige of salt, you may harbour some ugly thoughts about these moving pincushions.

When I was a teenager, I worked for a summer at a boy's camp near Peterborough. The camp was supported by a local service club, which had built a large central mess hall, several large cabins, each accommodating eight or ten boys, and a very substantial outdoor toilet or biffy, which for reasons unknown to me, was known as the Kybo. This was a magnificent establishment, as biffies go, having two benches facing each other, each having six holes, with each position provided with a hinged cover over the hole. I'd never seen a twelve-holer before, or have I since, but it suited the purposes of a boy's camp very well.

One night, early in the season, we were all awakened by a disturbance in the Kybo: BANG, Bang, Bang, bang, bang, bang, bang!—BANG, BANG, Bang, Bang, bang, bang, bang, bang! Nearly everyone got out of bed, and stood at a respectful distance around the biffy. There was much speculation about the source of this mysterious banging, which came in series of descending magnitude. Some suggested a bear, others a hostile visitor from the Indian reservation a few miles up the lake, and still others proposed mysterious, supernatural beings, or even beings from another world. A bunch of boys can be quite imaginative in such circumstances, and we were gradually working ourselves towards panic. And the banging went on: BANG, BANG, Bang, Bang, bang, bang, bang!

Finally, two of the bravest counsellors, armed with large sticks and strong flashlights, ventured inside. There was a pause, some shouting and thumping, and we heard something scurry from the far side of the biffy. When the victorious counsellors emerged, they declared the emergency to be over. It turned out that a large porcupine had found his way into the biffy, under the seats. He'd detected a new and exciting source of salt on the edges of the seats where we'd all sat at one time or another. As he proceeded to chew on the seats, his head, bobbing up and down with each bite, bumped the seat cover up and down, thus producing the disturbing—nay, frightening—banging we had heard.

Fortunately, porky hadn't been allowed to persist for too long and the damage to the seats was minimal. Otherwise, we might have had an epidemic of slivers in some very delicate spots.

Most animals in the wild are well aware of the "prickly" disposition of the porcupine, and give them a wide birth. A face-full of quills is no laughing matter for an animal in the wild. He has no way of getting them out, and may die of starvation because the quills prevent him from eating. Surprisingly, the domesticated dog seems to have completely lost any inbred caution about porcupines, and even more surprisingly, it never seems to learn about this prickly danger. I've known dogs that would get themselves a face-full of quills several times in a single season, without ever seeming to recognize the cause of their trouble.

Laddie was a big, half-wild farm collie, a beautiful-looking dog, but definitely not the friendly fellow of the Lassie movies. He lived on a farm near the Wilsons' cottage on Lake MacDonald, in the Laurentians, north of Montreal. The old farmer had largely given up any pretense of farming his very marginal land, and contented himself with running a few cows, which were duly herded by Laddie. I don't suppose Laddie received much attention from the farmer beyond the occasional dish of food. He made a career of avoiding all other visitors in his domain

At home, the Wilsons were our neighbours, and Mr. Wilson and my father were close friends. Dad and I used to travel to their cottage in the Laurentian Mountains, north of Montreal, every spring to help open it up, and again in the fall to help close it down. And we made several less strenuous family visits for weekends in the summer. Thus it was that, on a warm spring morning, we arrived to start the new season, only to find Laddie lying on the verandah with a very large number of quills stuck into his muzzle. Contrary to his usual standoffish ways, he thumped his tail encouragingly, and whimpered a bit to ask for help. But remembering his normal unfriendly ways, we all proceeded to perform the various chores to open the cottage: taking down the winter shutters, getting the water system started, and so on. Halfway through the afternoon, when most of the urgent matters had received attention, we paused, and realized Laddie was still there, looking woebegone. I guess he knew his chances of getting any attention from his master, the farmer, were pretty slim.

I said to Dad, "I guess we'll have to do something about that dog. I'll hold him if you'll pull the quills."

Thus it was that I climbed over Laddie's back to hold him down. I'd read somewhere that if you grabbed a dog's nose and pushed his lips into his mouth over his teeth, he won't bite for fear of biting his lips. And that seemed to work, although I think Laddie was trying to be as co-operative as possible through his ordeal. Certainly he allowed me to sit on him and hold him still when he was powerful enough to throw me off, and wriggle free, if he'd wanted.

Porcupine quills come in a range of sizes, from tiny ones a fraction of an inch long to the large size from the back and tail, nearly six inches long and about an eighth of an inch in diameter. It was this large economy size that Laddie had collected in abundance. Nature designed those quills to be very troublesome by shaping them like a crochet hook, with a barb at the business end, which prevents them falling out once they've been lodged in the target. To ease the problem of pulling them out, it's necessary to cut off their ends, thereby releasing the air trapped inside the quill and rendering it somewhat more flexible, particularly at the end with the barb. Even at that, it's often necessary to push the quill through into the dog's mouth, and pull it out from the inside. This whole exercise was not a lot of fun for anyone, particularly the dog.

Dad worked away with his scissors and pliers for more than an hour, and finally declared the job complete. I jumped off Laddie's back, he stood up, gave us a happy grin, wagged his tail once, and went off about his business. Dad and I basked in that sense of well being you get when you've accomplished a difficult good deed, and, moreover, one for which the thanks seemed minimal.

We didn't see Laddie again that weekend.

About a month later, we returned to the Wilsons' cottage for a weekend. And as we arrived whom should we see, lying in the sun on the verandah, but Laddie. He wagged his tail with great enthusiasm when he saw us. We found he was again fully supplied with a face-full of quills, and had come to the only place he knew where there was someone who might help.

LIVE AND LET LIVE

Most people fear skunks, those sleek little black animals with the distinctive white stripe, and the even more distinctive and unpleasant smell. That unfortunate aroma is the result of the skunk's spraying the contents of a gland located beneath his tail. The result of a spraying can be quite devastating. If it's you who has been sprayed, the only solution is to destroy your clothes. If it's one of your pets, they say a thorough wash in tomato juice is at least partially effective. But if it's your pet and he happens to be one of the larger species of dog, you'd better be purchasing tomato juice at wholesale prices. Even after the tomato juice treatment, you may want him to sleep outdoors for a time. And for quite a long time, you will be reminded of your dog's adventure every time he gets a bit wet. The skunk's calling card is persistent.

Nevertheless, skunks can be excellent neighbours. They don't like the smell much better than you do, and unless startled, will usually stay calm and avoid shooting. I've met many skunks, particularly in the evening (they're night creatures, usually), and never had any problem. They'd often come to the door of the verandah at the cottage, if I was cleaning a catch of fish, in search of their share. They have little fear, since they know everything in the woods will give them a wide berth. Indeed, a skunk that has had its scent gland removed makes an excellent pet, since he has no instinct to bite or scratch. On several occasions, I have lived with a skunk in the backyard, and have had a happy and peaceful relationship with him. Even our dogs seem to be able to cohabit with careful skunks.

I've read that a skunk can only shoot if he is standing on the ground and can brace his hind feet so that he has leverage to expel the contents from his scent gland. Now, if a skunk should turn his back on you and lift his tail, it behooves you to move fast. One thing you can do, according to this theory, is grab him by the tail and lift him off the ground. If this theory proves 100 percent correct (99 percent won't do; we don't want any leaks around the edges in this case, do we?), he won't be able to exert any leverage through his hind feet, and he won't be able to expel his scent. I've never heard of anyone actually trying this, probably because, having carried out this manoeuvre, and even assuming it is successful, there remains another problem. What do you do with the irate skunk, which you are carefully holding up, presumably at arm's length? It doesn't seem to me it'd be a good idea to set him down anytime soon. But do remember it was me who gave you the solution to the initial problem.

Jean's family owned a cottage situated very conveniently on an island in the Lake of Two Mountains, quite close to Montreal. The island, Île Cadieux, is a long, thin spit of rocky land, jutting out into the lake and joined to the mainland by a short, single-span bridge. The island is moderate in size, about two miles long and no more than two hundred yards wide at its widest point.

When I first visited the cottage, Jean warned me to take care, as there was a bear on the island. Now, as I was courting her at the time, it behooved me to display my superior knowledge of woodcraft. I scoffed at the idea and asked what made them think they had a bear on this relatively tiny island. I was told, somewhat firmly, that every night the garbage pails were tipped over and the contents scattered around, and that everyone knew that bears were notorious for attacking the garbage. I suggested that their problem was more likely to be raccoons, who were equally as interested in garbage pails and much more likely to be resident on that island. To prove my point, I drove a large spike into a tree and hung the garbage pail on it. For several nights, there was an absence of tipped-over garbage pails. And then, one night, we heard the lid of the garbage pail go clattering, and we looked out through the gloom, to test the truth of our respective theories. We could see two happy raccoons ensconced in the pail, up on the tree, eating their fill. And my arrangement proved to have considerable advantages, because the raccoons would sit in the pail until they'd eaten everything edible, leaving behind only paper and inedible trash. It was like owning a tidy natural Garburator.

There was a bright "yard light" in the yard. We soon found that the raccoons wouldn't come for the garbage until the yard light was turned off. That apparently was the signal they would have the yard to themselves. Once they had arrived and knocked the lid off the garbage can, they didn't seem to mind if you turned the light back on. We could sit inside the house and watch their antics in comfort, without disturbing them.

Some years later, as we were going to bed, we heard the lid of the garbage pail go clattering. We hadn't watched the raccoons for some time, so we decided to turn on the light. Four startled raccoons, a mother and three babies, put their heads up and looked at us with their comical clown faces, and then returned to their feast. We watched quietly for a few minutes and were just about to retire, when out of the shadows strolled a large skunk. Immediately, the raccoons disappeared up the tree where the skunk couldn't follow them. The skunk stamped around on the ground under the garbage pail for a minute, but since he couldn't get up there, he soon gave up and wandered off into the shadows. He'd hardly disappeared when the raccoons returned. They'd evidently only retreated to the lowest branches of the tree. They'd hardly settled into the garbage pail again when the skunk returned, prompting the raccoons to retreat again up the tree. And so it went for several cycles: The raccoons would descend into the pail and prepare to eat; the skunk would come out of the shadows; the raccoons would retreat. The skunk would accept that he couldn't get at the garbage and wander away again, only to have the cycle repeat. Neither side was getting anywhere.

Finally, when the raccoons returned yet again to the pail, they seemed to hold a conference before they started to eat. And this time when the skunk came wandering out, they stayed put. Instead of retreating, the raccoons dug around in the pail, selected some piece of food, passed it from hand to hand, and apparently decided that, "Yes, that is something a skunk would like." They dropped it over the side, where it was devoured appreciatively by the skunk. When the skunk had consumed this offering, he somehow communicated that it was time for a refill. The raccoons up above selected another tidbit, and threw it over the side. We watched this continue for twenty minutes, so it was no accident. It was still going on when we turned out the light and went to bed.

This seems to me to be solid evidence those raccoons reasoned they'd never get anything done unless they could somehow satisfy that skunk, and they hit upon a very workable solution.

MIND GAMES

Brownie was a "standard" Pekinese, standard meaning he was one of the larger-sized dogs of that breed, weighing close to twenty pounds, not the tiny yappy miniature ones that were bred to be carried around in the voluminous sleeves of Chinese courtiers. Indeed, Brownie wasn't yappy at all; he'd been bred to imitate a miniature lion, and could do "ferocious" extremely well, provided he wasn't expected to actually bite anything. He was quite a friendly dog, although he didn't trust children not to pull his ample hair and would quietly disappear if children came on the scene.

Brownie was a magnificent-looking dog, a beautiful reddish-brown, with shades of gold in his feathers and tail. He knew he was extremely good looking. He was the only dog I ever knew who'd lie for hours, apparently enjoying the ordeal of having his magnificent coat combed. He would then parade around, with his tail up, prancing, to show himself in the best possible light, and expecting to get an ample measure of applause.

I suppose he should have had a Chinese-sounding name like "Fung Chu," but we didn't know any Chinese, and "Brownie" described him very well. He didn't seem to mind.

Brownie acquired us when I was about ten years old and he was about three years old. Astonishingly, he'd been found by some friends of ours wandering along a country road. All efforts to find his owners proved fruitless, and eventually the friends offered him to us.

Brownie's acquisition of us as his family was not easy. It required the patient application of all his tactical knowledge and skillful wiles to make his acquisition. You see, my mother, God rest her soul, was a very house-proud woman who kept her house spotless and in perfect order. She wasn't about to have a hair-shedding, walking dust mop in her house, and said so quite vehemently. It took a lot of persuasion for Dad and me to achieve a very limited trial period: "One week, and if he's any trouble, out he goes." And a rider on that grudging agreement was that the dog would be confined to the kitchen, where the linoleum floor would not collect stray hairs—or if it did, they could easily be picked up.

Brownie quickly grasped the situation and the strictures, and laid his plans accordingly. On his first night, after supper, he sat in the kitchen watching us as we sat in the living room listening to the radio and reading. In particular, he watched Mother, who sat in an easy chair in the corner of the living room where she could see, across a space of hardwood floor, a part of the dining room and into the kitchen. More importantly, she could keep an eye on "the dog" sitting with his paws on the sill of the door into the dining room. Technically, he was still in the permitted space in the kitchen.

Brownie had magnificent brown eyes, whose effect was enhanced by their protuberance from his pudgy face. He never took them from Mother. After about an hour, he ventured to creep an inch or two over the doorsill. Mother said nothing. So after about another fifteen minutes, he crept forward another few inches, all the time fixing Mother with his highest-voltage, soulful stare. By the end of the evening, Brownie had progressed about a foot inside the door, and nothing had been said. Of course, when we went to bed, he was relegated to a bed in the kitchen, where he slept all his life with us.

The next evening, when we moved into the living room, Brownie took up his position on the spot he had achieved the previous evening, about a foot outside the kitchen door. Again he turned his most soulful and appealing stare on Mother; once again, he gradually crept forward, until by the end of the evening, he'd reached halfway to the living room door. Again, my mother made no complaint, perhaps reasoning he was on a hardwood floor, and thus not leaving any hairs, and besides, he was so appealing!

The third evening, Brownie took up his position at the point he'd reached the night before, and having now proved to his satisfaction that he could safely progress, provided the progress wasn't too rapid, he crept forward somewhat more quickly. He reached the threshold of the living room door in about an hour, then progressed until he was right beside Mother's chair. Then he played his trump card; he sat up and begged. Finally, she deigned to notice him and acknowledge his soulful stare. "Oh, all right," she said, patting the chair beside her. Mother was a small lady, and there was ample room for an adoring Pekinese beside her. He was up beside her in an instant, and spent the rest of the evening there. He had achieved his goal and made his acquisition.

From that moment on, he was Mother's constant shadow, following her everywhere for the rest of her life. For her part, she rarely openly acknowledged he was there, but if he happened to disappear, she would immediately search him out.

Brownie had no trouble acquiring the rest of the family. Dad and I walked him, combed him, and played with him, but Mother took charge of his food, as was only right as he was in HER kitchen.

We lived in a two-storey house with a flat "tar and gravel" roof. Somewhere up there, a magnificent black squirrel had his nest. His normal route to the ground was down a large, soft maple that grew close to the house, and thence, across our backyard to his destination of the day. Brownie soon discovered this intruder on his turf, and proceeded to try to run him off. But that squirrel was far too fast for Brownie, and he eventually had to admit defeat. Thereafter, Brownie would lie in the sun at the top of the back steps, and the squirrel had the run of the yard. However, that wasn't a lot of fun for the squirrel; he craved more action in his life. He took to sitting out in the middle of the back lawn and taunting Brownie. But Brownie was wiser than that; he knew he couldn't catch that squirrel, and he determined to ignore him. Brownie would sit there with his eyes closed, basking in the sun, the very picture of a dignified gentleman enjoying his leisure.

The squirrel would redouble his efforts, screaming squirrel-type insults. Brownie would leisurely open one eye to see what was causing all the commotion, and then disdainfully close it again.

The squirrel would move closer, chattering out his insults and his challenge. Brownie would open both eyes and stare at him with utter disdain. He made it perfectly clear he had no intention of undertaking any fruitless chases.

The squirrel would move even closer, and scream even louder. Brownie would give a little warning growl: "Don't go too far, you little imp."

The squirrel knew his objective and understood his target only too well. It might take him as long as half an hour, but finally it would reach a point where Brownie could stand it no longer. With a mighty roar, he'd burst off the steps and charge the spot where he'd last seen the squirrel. (I told you he could do "ferocious" extremely well.) But of course, the squirrel was no longer there. He'd easily dodge Brownie's charge and dash to the other end of the yard. Brownie, his dander now well up, would again charge after him, only to find the squirrel had exchanged ends of the yard again. This uneven war would continue until Brownie was reduced to a quivering, gasping, bundle of dishevelled fur, and he'd return to his position at the top of the stairs to slump down in the sun and recover his breath.

The squirrel, having had his fun for the day, would go on about his business.

If you watched him, you could almost see Brownie make a firm resolution that, on the morrow, he wouldn't chase that squirrel, no matter what the infernal varmint said to him.

So much for good intentions.

HOW I SAVED ROGER'S LIFE

I'm told that when the human body is in the process of formation, its various parts come together by sort of folding around the backbone. In a few instances, this process is not quite perfectly completed, and a tiny fissure is left in the flesh, just on top of the tailbone, or the sacroiliac, as it's known in more elegant circles. And sometimes, if this little fissure is repeatedly irritated, it forms a cyst or a tumour, which can become quite painful to the owner/operator of the body.

I developed one of these cysts, called a pilonoidal cyst. Naturally I developed a somewhat exotic explanation for its occurrence. It was during our first sojourn in England, in the mid-fifties. We'd been exploring an ancient castle in southern England, the kind with lots of walls and towers. While it had been deserted for hundreds of years, one could readily imagine the presence of many knights in armour, fair maidens, possibly even in distress, men at arms, together with plenty of jousting, and many foul and dastardly deeds, all within the precincts of the fortress. But, in climbing to the very top of this imposing place, I slipped on one of the wet, moss-grown steps and fell heavily on my bottom. Shortly thereafter, I noticed this persistent pain in my tailbone (or sacroiliac, if you must). I attributed this to my fall in those romantic surroundings.

However, when I was back in Canada, the doctors quickly disabused me of that notion, telling me my problem was undoubtedly caused by many days of bouncing around England in a very small car. After all, we'd made a determined effort to cover all of England on our weekend explorations, all in tiny Morris Minor cars. I was told this cause of my complaint was so prevalent that my disability had been given the popular name, "Jeep's Disease," honouring all the Jeep-riding soldiers in the war who had developed this problem while bouncing around Europe. That was a much more prosaic and less satisfying explanation, but it didn't alter the fact that my cyst had to be surgically dug out of me.

I woke up in a bed in a ward with four beds. Apart from a very sore tail, I was perfectly healthy and inclined to resent the fact that I'd be spending the next week in this bed while my incision healed. I began to take interest in the goings-on around me. The bed next to me was occupied by a very nice fellow who had suffered a heart attack. He had been prescribed six weeks of bedrest. But, while taking it easy, he, like me, was taking an interest in our surroundings. The third bed, across from me, seemed to be designated as a transient bed. People came and went, but nobody stayed in that bed very long, certainly not long enough for us to get to know any of them.

It was the chap who came to occupy the fourth bed in the far corner of the room who became the focus of this story.

Roger (pronounced Row-Jay), was a French Canadian from a small town near Montreal. He arrived the day after my operation. The only other thing I know of him is that he coached a minor league hockey team in his hometown. He came in very quietly, dressed in his best black suit. The orderly placed screens around his bed, and I presume he got straight into bed. Shortly after, his wife came in, also very quietly, and also all dressed in black. There were whispered conversations, and the occasional muffled sob from behind the curtains. Then his mother appeared, equally as quietly, and similarly all dressed in black. The whispered conversations continued, with, if anything, a higher incidence of muffled sobs.

We were puzzled and intrigued.

Soon the doctors, for whose benefit I presume the screens had been placed, appeared. They came to conduct their initial examination, and to explain to Roger his illness and the treatment planned.

When the doctors had gone and the screens cleared away, we proceeded to introduce ourselves to Roger, and to ask him what he was in for. To our astonishment, he replied, "I've come here to die." Of course we remonstrated with him, but he explained, in all seriousness, that he had a problem with his prostate, and that people with problems with their prostate invariably died.

I told him that, while I was no doctor, it was my understanding that prostate operations were relatively routine and usually successful. Indeed, the chairman of my company had had such an operation, and apart from a diet that seemed to involve the consumption of large quantities of raisins, he seemed perfectly normal to me. (Indeed he lived another twenty years or so). But Roger would have none of that. He informed us that he knew all about prostate problems. His father had been a doctor, and when his patients had prostate problems, they always died. We refrained from pointing out that this could be construed as a rather negative commentary on his father's practice of medicine.

Over the next couple of days, the doctors proceeded with a number of tests on Roger. This only made him more suspicious. He informed us regularly of his impending death. He took to walking up and down the corridors, stopping anyone he met, and telling them he'd come there to die. Of course the doctors and the nurses tried to reassure him, but that only convinced him they were trying to mislead him, and he became even more vehement in his insistence he was going to die.

The doctors decided on an operation, and, in preparation, began doing routine blood tests every four hours. Roger immediately jumped to the conclusion they'd discovered something wrong with his blood. Now he had two probable causes of death to worry about. He redoubled his efforts to inform all and sundry of his impending death.

Finally, to our relief, the nurses came one morning to prepare him for his operation and he was taken, in a sedated state, to the operating room. We looked forward to welcoming him back and, yes, pointing out the error of his ways. But that was not to be just yet. Within a couple of hours he was back, but without the operation. At the last minute, someone noticed an abnormality in one of his blood tests, and it was decided to postpone the operation.

When Roger awoke to discover he hadn't had the operation, he promptly decided the doctors felt he was too far gone to be worth an operation and they had simply decided to let him die. He filled the room with his gloomy predictions and became an absolute scourge for anyone walking in the corridors. No amount of explanation or encouragement from the doctors and nurses had the slightest effect. "They are simply trying to fool me and are lying to me."

Finally, one morning, I asked one of the nurses, quietly, whether there was any truth to Roger's concerns. "Oh, no," she said, "he'll probably be perfectly all right. The last person in that bed had exactly the same operation and he left here feeling perfectly well."

Later that morning, when Roger had completely exasperated me with his dire predictions, I finally said to him, "Look, Roger, I don't know you from Adam. Furthermore, I couldn't care less whether you live or die. You may think the nurses and doctors are lying to you and trying to fool you. But there's no reason why they should try to fool me. I don't care, and they know I don't care. And one of the nurses told me this morning that you're going to be perfectly all right. Indeed the last man in that bed had the same operation and he's fine. I believe her."

He looked at me fixedly. "D'you really think so?"

He turned around, went over to the chair beside his bed and sat there in complete silence, deep in thought, for the next three hours. Then he suddenly jumped to his feet and rushed over to shake my hand. "I want to thank you for saving my life. I don't know what I'd have done without you. You must come and see my hockey team next winter."

He became a changed man. He didn't exactly run around telling people he had come here to survive, but he became quite cheerful and there was no more talk of dying.

And that's how I came to save Roger's life.

I left the hospital before Roger's operation, so I cannot report on any possible further drama. I did hear, some months later, that his operation was a success. As for me, my operation was also declared a success. However, for many years afterwards, my tailbone would occasionally flare up into brief, sharp spasms of pain. Perhaps it was remembering that romantic old English castle.

I BELIEVE IN SEA MONSTERS

I believe in the existence of sea monsters. After all, there's ample evidence that some pretty peculiar things exist in the deepest parts of the oceans. Why shouldn't there be sea monsters, left over from a bygone age, hiding down there in the depths. Maybe there are just one or two, the last survivors of ancient species. We don't know how long creatures, particularly aquatic creatures, lived in the age of the dinosaurs, but surely it's possible they were extremely long-lived, and that one or two have survived to the present day.

Besides, there are a number of places in the world that claim to have a sea monster. Loch Ness, in Scotland, has Nessie, who is probably the most famous. There are many claims to have sighted her, but unfortunately, nearly always at night, in misty conditions. Of course, whether the cause of the mist is atmospheric or alcoholic is sometimes open to question. Some Scotsmen do wander home rather late at night from the local pub. Then there's Ogopogo, in Lake Okanogan, in British Columbia, in Canada, where I'm sure there are occasional mists, too. And there's Caddy, a thirty-metre-long sea serpent who's been sighted in the foggy waters of Cadboro Bay, off Vancouver Island. It's probably worth noting that these same British Columbians also claim the existence of Bigfoot, a prehistoric human, who is reputed to cavort around in the high mountains in the interior of that province. And, I've heard that the natives around Lake Titicata, in the high Andes, in the south of Peru, occasionally speak, in suitably respectful tones, of Tiki, a frightening monster who inhabits that mountain lake. Of course, their perceptive capabilities may be enhanced by the rarefied atmosphere and their habit of chewing on the leaves of the coca bush (for stamina and endurance, you understand).

It would seem these creatures are very shy and try to avoid being seen in clear conditions or at close quarters. They seem to have a genius for disguising or hiding their existence. However, can all those people reporting the sighting of a monster be wrong?

But the real reason I believe in sea monsters is because I've seen one, close up, in very clear sunny weather, when there was no chance of any interference from mists, either atmospheric or alcoholic.

It was a beautiful spring day, warm and sunny, with practically no breeze. Our cottage on Île Cadieux had been closed all winter, and I thought it would be nice to see that everything was in good order. I took two of our daughters with me on the short trip to the island.

Île Cadieux is a long, narrow spit of land, jutting out into the Lake of Two Mountains, near Montreal. Much of the island is low-lying, and some parts are even subject to flooding in the high water of springtime. Our cottage, at the outer end of the island, was on the highest point, and quite safe from flooding. Nevertheless, I wanted to see the state of things.

Sure enough, when we crossed the short bridge from the mainland, the near end of the island was flooded for several hundred yards, but not badly so. The water was only a few inches deep over the road, and, in these clear, calm, conditions I could easily see the road under the clear water. We decided we could still drive in to the cottage provided we proceeded slowly and carefully.

It was quite beautiful, rolling slowly along the road through the trees, with the sun reflecting off the calm water. Then, suddenly, we saw the sea monster. It appeared to be a serpent-like creature, perhaps forty or fifty feet long, swimming in the shallow water across the road. We stopped and watched it for some minutes. It had many individual coils projecting above the water, and had greenish-gold scales and a sharp, spiny fin down the length of its back. The coils undulated and squirmed as it swam along. As we sat and watched the sun reflect from its scales, giving off flashes of a range of colours, we realized the monster must have more than one body. There appeared to be several long, serpent-like bodies, apparently all attached at some point near its head, much like the mythical Medusa. We couldn't see the head, perhaps because the creature had its head under water, searching for food, or perhaps because the head had reached deeper water, and the creature would gradually submerge as it progressed.

None of us had ever seen anything like it, nor had we ever imagined a sea monster quite like this multi-tailed creature. Most of our imaginings had been modelled on the more prosaic dragon pattern. But then, one couldn't be too choosy about the form of one's only sea monster, could one? This one did not seem threatening in any way; indeed, it completely ignored us. We felt quite safe in observing it for some minutes.

However, I should point out there is another possible explanation to what we were seeing, one that skeptics, spoilsports, and scoffers might prefer. Our monster could have been a large school of good-sized carp, who, for some reason known only to themselves, had decided life would be better on the other side of the road. They would all be headed in one direction, as is often the case with a school of fish. And as they crossed the shallow spot near the road, their backs would project out of the water, creating the illusion of a number of very large snake-like beings, about six inches in diameter and as much as fifty feet long. Carp, in the springtime, have quite a bit of colour in their scales, just like our sea serpent. And they do frequent very shallow water at that time of year.

That's the trouble with this modern world. There are too many people prepared, nay even anxious, to abandon all the romance, the mystery, and the excitement of the mysterious world that we know only from legends, and from "unconfirmed sightings," in favour of dry, cold, unexciting logic. And besides, it seems to me that in this case, the supposedly logical explanation relies on conditions that one can argue (conveniently, admittedly) are unlikely. This explanation depends upon the co-operation and discipline of several hundred fish. I've never seen a co-operative fish in my life, and fish, as a group, are not known for their discipline.

No, I much prefer the simple explanation that we saw a huge, multi-tailed sea-monster. Why complicate matters? After all, it was close up, in bright sunshine, with no wisp of atmospheric mist, and far too early in the day for there to be any suspicion of the alcoholic kind. To me, the only thing that remains is to choose a suitable name for him, or her, as the case may be.

I NEVER, EVER, ARGUE WITH A POLICEMAN

WHAT, NEVER?
WELL, HARDLY EVER!

After Gilbert and Sullivan, *H.M.S. Pinafore*

You can't argue with some people. It's a fruitless occupation, sometimes even dangerous. For example, I learned early in life that arguing with my mother was not a promising occupation. Husbands never seem to learn that most wives fall into the same category. Another group that comes immediately to mind is sports referees. By definition, referees are always right, and they hold to that principle in the face of any and all logic and argument.

But policemen are the category "not to argue with" that has always stood out in my mind. Not only are you unlikely to win an argument with these people but the process of losing it is liable to attract unpleasant results. All my life, I have religiously followed the principle of avoiding argument with police officers; well, almost religiously.

ILLUSTRATING THE PRINCIPLE

Jean and I were driving home to Montreal from a wedding in Ottawa. It was late, the road was dark, and the weather was rainy. Because of some (minor) indulgence at the wedding, I was trying to drive particularly carefully, or so I thought. I thought it best if I didn't have cause to breathe on any policeman.

I was travelling along quite peacefully behind another car when, quite suddenly, a car came up behind me and, ignoring the fact that we were rounding a bend, passed me and slipped in between the two cars. I thought his driving more than a bit dangerous.

This intruder car was hardly in position when it blossomed into flashing lights, and revealed itself as an indignant highway patrol car. Its flashing arrows signalled for both us and the car in front to pull over. There was a convenient space at the side of the road with room for all three cars. (Perhaps the existence of that space just at that point was the reason the police rushed to pass us somewhat dangerously?)

I was annoyed; furious, in fact. "I wasn't speeding," I almost shouted. "I'm going to tell that policeman a thing or two! Did you see what he did? He's a terrible driver."

It was sheer good fortune that when the policeman got out of his car, he went first to the car in front. And it was evident that the occupants shared my opinions. They, too, were determined to give that policeman a piece of their minds. I could see them in the light of the police car's headlights, waving clenched fists, and arguing furiously. After a couple of minutes of apparent abuse, the policeman turned away, and walked calmly in our direction. The occupants of the other car, two young men, got out of their car and followed him, continuing to shout, and making angry, threatening gestures. Partway to our car, the policeman stopped, turned around, and said something. Whatever it was he said, the two angry men stopped and stood waiting for him to speak to us before returning to their arguments. While all that had been happening, I'd continued to mumble in annoyance.

But, sometime in the short space of time it took the policeman to walk to our car, I realized that the tactics of the occupants of the car in front didn't seem to be very effective. I had a sudden change of heart. When he reached my window, I asked, as innocently as I could, "Something wrong, Officer?"

"Well," he replied, "you were going a bit fast. But I imagine you were just following the traffic, weren't you?'

"Yes, Officer, I've been following that car for quite a few miles. Perhaps my speed did sneak up a bit."

The officer smiled, and with an admonition to be careful, waved his hand for me to drive on. As I drove out onto the highway, I saw him take out his summons book and turn back towards those impolite, belligerent, and misguided fellows in the lead car.

PATIENCE IS A VIRTUE!

I was on my way to the golf club for an evening round of golf. The club was quite a distance from our laboratory, but I had worked out a route that enabled me to leave the lab at quitting time and still reach the club in time for a quick evening round. The key to my route was that I stayed on back roads for most of the journey, only joining the main highway at a point where much of the rush-hour traffic had already turned off.

But on this particular evening, when I turned into the road leading down to the main highway, I found a long lineup of cars waiting to enter the highway. There was almost half a mile of cars lined up. I'd be an hour late if I had to wait in that lineup. However, they were all lined up in the left-hand lane. The designers had thoughtfully provided two lanes on our side of the road, in order to allow motorists to turn either right or left, and thus, to help ease any bottleneck. Fortunately, my route called for a right turn, and my lane was completely empty.

As I looked down the road, I could see a uniformed figure standing on my side of the road, apparently directing traffic. I therefore thought it wise to proceed carefully. I turned on my right-turn blinkers, and drove carefully, even taking care to stop at a railway level-crossing partway down the road. I thought I had obeyed all the rules. Therefore, I was a bit irritated when, as I approached the policeman, he held up his hand for me to stop.

Up close, he seemed extremely tall, well over six feet, and unusually thin for a policeman. He had a lean face with a neat black mustache. He was impeccably dressed in what appeared to be a dress uniform. I remember noting that his cap had gold braid, perhaps signifying a superior rank (and therefore, I subsequently speculated, not too much experience in this particular duty.)

He regarded me thoughtfully for a minute, and then asked, somewhat menacingly, "And where do you think you're going?"

You'll note in what follows that I followed my principle; I did not argue, or at least, I didn't let him know I was arguing. I was merely discussing!

"Why, I'm going down here to turn right at the corner."

He considered that for a moment. Then, "Why aren't you in line with all these other cars? What do you think they're doing here?"

"Obviously, they all want to turn left, and I want to turn right."

Another pause, a bit longer than the first, while the police mind absorbed that information. "But how do you know they all want to turn left?"

"Because they're all over there in the left-turn lane. If they wanted to turn right, they'd be over here."

There was an even longer pause, while he turned around and studied the intersection and the assembled cars. Then he stared at me for a while. Finally, he drew himself up to his full height, looked down a nose of considerable length at me, and intoned, "Patience is a virtue."

I forbore to say that it certainly was, if one had to deal with many policemen like him.

He considered me for a further minute, perhaps while he tried to think of further homilies to pass on to me. Apparently failing to think of anything appropriate, he motioned me on my way. I arrived just in time for my game of golf.

PUT YOURSELF IN THE POLICEMAN'S SHOES

The Town of Mount Royal lies just north of Montreal, close to the mountain that gives the city its name. It was a "new" town, designed to be a bit superior to other residential suburbs. It allowed no industries within its boundaries, and its residents, most of whom were actually quite nice people, nevertheless gave the impression of being just that little bit superior. Although the town lay across the whole of the back of Mount Royal, it was laid out to discourage any through traffic. Only at its outer borders, on the east and the west edges, were there through north-south streets.

I had taken a visitor to lunch at a restaurant north of the town, and was driving back to our laboratory, which lay to the south of it. Perforce, I was driving along L'Acadie Boulevard, one of those north-south arteries along the edge of the town. It was a four-lane boulevard, with a wide, grassed median down the middle. In keeping with the unspoken desire to limit traffic passing through this "superior" community, the good townspeople had equipped every cross street with a set of traffic lights, which slowed progress to a crawl. This was particularly true at lunchtime, when traffic was quite heavy.

We were stopped at one of those stoplights, and I found myself in the outside lane with one car between me and the intersection. The light turned green. The car in front of me just sat there. After a moment, as a kind of afterthought, he turned on his left-turn blinkers. I suspect he was one of the slightly superior residents, as he paid no attention to those behind him. In particular, he did not pull forward into the intersection between the median, which would have allowed the rest of us to proceed. Instead he just sat there, waiting for a break in the oncoming traffic. Just before the light changed to red, he found an opportunity to make his turn. However, he left the rest of us no possibility to proceed. I was annoyed, so I gave him a loud blast with my horn.

At that point, I looked across the intersection and saw a police car sitting there; the policemen was getting out of the car and motioning me to pull over behind him.

By the time I stepped out of my car, I had my license papers in my hand, and was fully prepared to placate the policeman. "Is there something wrong, Officer?" I asked as innocently as possible.

"We do not use our horn unnecessarily," he replied sternly. Doubtless, the serenity of the townspeople was of primary concern.

"But, c'mon Officer, you saw what he did to me!'

"Yes, but we do not use our horn unnecessarily," he repeated.

"But he could easily have pulled over into the intersection and allowed the traffic to proceed."

"Yes, but we do not use our horns unnecessarily." This fellow seemed to have a deficiency in the variety of his small talk.

"Aw, but Officer, if it had been YOU, you'd have pulled forward into the intersection and allowed the rest of us to proceed."

He looked at me calculatingly, then at the intersection, then back at me. "You're right," he said. He handed me back my license, jumped into his car, turned on his siren, (infinitely louder than my offending horn) and took off with a U-turn to chase the other fellow.

I've thought about that incident a lot. I can only conclude that my comments touched some chord of vanity in that policeman. If he did manage to find the other fellow, I suspect the culprit received a lecture on the "right" way to make a left-hand turn. Maybe the key is to persuade the policeman to get into your shoes.

19 A LEGEND

Strictly speaking, this legend doesn't belong in this book. All of the other stories deal with situations I actually experienced. There's no way I was present for any part of this story, which takes place way back in antiquity. However, I've enjoyed this story ever since I first heard it at boys' camp, when I was a teenager, and I've told it innumerable times when circumstances provided me with an appropriate situation. I hope you'll enjoy it, too.

Have you ever noticed that when a man comes into a room where there's an open fire in a fireplace, or even a nice, warm wood stove, he will almost invariably walk over and stand warming himself? He'll usually stand with his back to the fire, and if his jacket is appropriately equipped, he'll even flip up the tails of the coat, in order that his nether portions may obtain maximum warming effect. There's a reason for this stance, as there is for many phenomena of nature.

You'll remember that way back in the early mists of time, Mr. Noah was called upon to build a huge boat, according to a design detailed by The Heavenly Architect. And, he was instructed to stock it with all the various species of animals. Thus, when the great flood duly arrived, he loaded Mrs. Noah and all the little Noahs on board, together with all those animals, and they set sail over the floodwaters.

Now, Mrs. Noah was a typical housewife, so it wasn't very long before she complained to Mr. Noah, "It seems very damp in here. You'd better have a look around, because there must be a leak in the boat."

But Mr. Noah was a strong-willed man, and would have none of that. Hadn't he built this boat himself, every stick of it? It was unthinkable there should be a leak.

But Mrs. Noah remained unconvinced. She was sure there was a leak somewhere. She just didn't know how to find it in the midst of this huge boat. Then she had a very bright idea. She'd utilize the facilities ready at hand, and send the experts at finding things. She'd send the bloodhounds to look for the leak.

So she called in Mr. and Mrs. Bloodhound and sent them off to sniff and snuffle all over the boat. Sure enough, it wasn't very long before they discovered a place where water was leaking through a hole in the boat.

"Stand out of the way, My Dear," said Mr. Bloodhound. " I'll fix that." And he stuck his nose down into the hole in the boat.

But a bloodhound's nose is kind of pointed, and it didn't fill the hole very well. The water simply continued to squirt in around his nose.

"Hurry up, Dear. Go and get Mrs. Noah," he instructed.

Mrs. Bloodhound took only a few minutes to bring Mrs. Noah, who now had mixed feelings. She'd been proven right. There actually was a leak as she'd said. But against that satisfaction, they'd now have to deal with the leak, and quickly. She said briskly, "Move out of the way, you dogs. I'll fix that right now." And she stuck her elbow down into the hole.

But Mrs. Noah was one of those angular women with bony arms. As a result, her elbow was rather sharp, and it, too, failed to fill the hole. The water just kept squirting in. So she sent the bloodhounds off in search of Mr. Noah.

When he finally came, being pulled along against his will by the two dogs, he took in the situation at a glance. "Out of the way, woman," he said, "I'll fix that." And he promptly sat down on the leak.

Now, Mr. Noah was a man of, shall we say, ample proportions, and his bulk completely covered the hole, and stopped the leak.

Mr. Noah's prompt and effective action saved the day, and they all lived to survive the flood. But that is the reason that, to this day,
- A dog has a cold nose,
- A woman has a cold elbow,
- And a man always stands with his back to the fire.

About the Author

Hugh Hamilton is a retired senior executive and officer of the Northern Telecom Corporation, a major supplier of systems and equipment in the telecommunications field. While he holds a doctorate in physics from McGill University, his career was wider than that of a normal research physicist. It ranged over a broad spectrum, including research, product development, marketing and management. The greater part of his business life was spent as a manager of segments of the business of telecommunications companies. His most interesting assignments took him to Europe and the Far East; he lived for extended periods in Chelmsford, England, Zurich, Switzerland, and Tokyo, Japan, and travelled throughout Europe and the Pacific rim. Many of his tales reflect his observations of the businesses he saw, the individuals he encountered, and the peoples and countries he visited.

Dr. Hamilton has married twice. His first wife, Jean, died of cancer in 1983, and lies buried in Switzerland. He and his second wife, Barbara, live in Mississauga, just west of Toronto, along with their two dogs. Hugh is an active member of Probus, a social club for retired business and professional men. At the same time he pursues his hobbies of gardening, woodworking and writing. Barbara pursues her part-time career as a consultant in information systems, while continuing to be a very active horsewoman. The Hamiltons have four adult daughters, all married. They each had a successful career, and are now concentrating on raising the eight grandchildren they have produced.

To order more copies of

Hugh Hamilton's

As I Remember It
A feast of Anecdotes

Contact:
**GENERAL STORE
PUBLISHING HOUSE**
499 O'Brien Road, Box 415
Renfrew, Ontario Canada K7V 4A6
Telephone: 1-800-465-6072
Fax: (613) 432-7184
www.gsph.com

VISA and MASTERCARD accepted.